Social and Political Study of Modern Hindi Cinema

Social and Political Study of Modern Hindi Cinema

Ram Avtar Agnihotri

Commonwealth

Social and Political Study of Modern Hindi Cinema

ISBN : 81-7169-049-1

Edition : 2019

Published by
COMMONWEALTH PUBLISHERS (P) LTD.
4831/24, Govind Lane,
Ansari Road, Darya Ganj,
New Delhi - 110002
Ph. : 23272541, 23242541
e-mail : commonwealthpublishers2016@gmail.com

Distributed by :
ARJUN PUBLISHING HOUSE
4831/24, Govind Lane,
Ansari Road, Darya Ganj,
New Delhi - 110002
Ph. : 23272541, 23242541
e-mail : arjunbooks2001@gmail.com

Laser Typesetting by :
Dimple Computers
Delhi

Printed at :
Divine Digital Press
Delhi

Dedicated
to
Honourable Daddaji
Pandit Uma Shankar Dixit

Octogerian National Leader,
Ex-Union Home Minister,
Ex-Governor of Karnataka and
West Bengal

Preface

During the preparation on "Social and Political Study of Modern Cinema", I visited Film Archives, Poona and utilised many University Libraries of the country. In respect of this research work, Professor I.N. Tewary, Head, Department of Political Science, Institute of Advanced Studies, Meerut University, Meerut, provided me invaluable cooperation and guidance. I owe high gratitude for him. I am also thankful to Dr. Nafees Ahmad Ansari for his valuable help and advice.

At this solemn occasion, to remember my parents Late Pandit Shiv Nandan Agnihotri and Late Mrs. Shakuntla Agnihotri is my duty. They provided me higher education in spite of severe poverty. I find myself unable to pay a fraction of "parents debt" as prescribed in our religious scriptures, so far. Again, I dedicate my younger brother Late Bhupinder Agnihotri (Bhappu), who left us a day before the Basant Panchami's Saraswati Puja (Worship of Goddess of Knowledge). My true rememberance of my late younger brother is to keep continue the worship of Goddess Saraswati as learning, reading, writing and revealing truth through research.

At the time of publication of this work, I oblige my family members Pandit Jagdish Prasad Agnihotri (elder brother), Mrs. Taravati Dixit, Mrs. Saroj Tiwari (elder sisters), Mrs. Prem Lata Tewari, Mrs. Krishna Sharma (younger sisters), Mrs. Swatantra Bala Agnihotri (wife), Meenakshi Agnihotri (daughter), Lavkush Agnihotri (son), whose motivation made possible to bring this research work in book form.

I am thankful to Hon'ble Mr. Manubhai Shah, Former Union Minister for Commerce and Industry and Hon'ble Mrs. Sheela Dixit, Union Minister of State in the Ministry of Parliamentary Affairs and Prime Minister's office for their blessings for completion of this work.

DR. RAM AWATAR AGNIHOTRI
RESEARCH SCIENTIST (U.G.C.)
Department of Political Science,
Institute of Advanced Studies,
Meerut University.

List of Tables

List of Diagrams

Contents

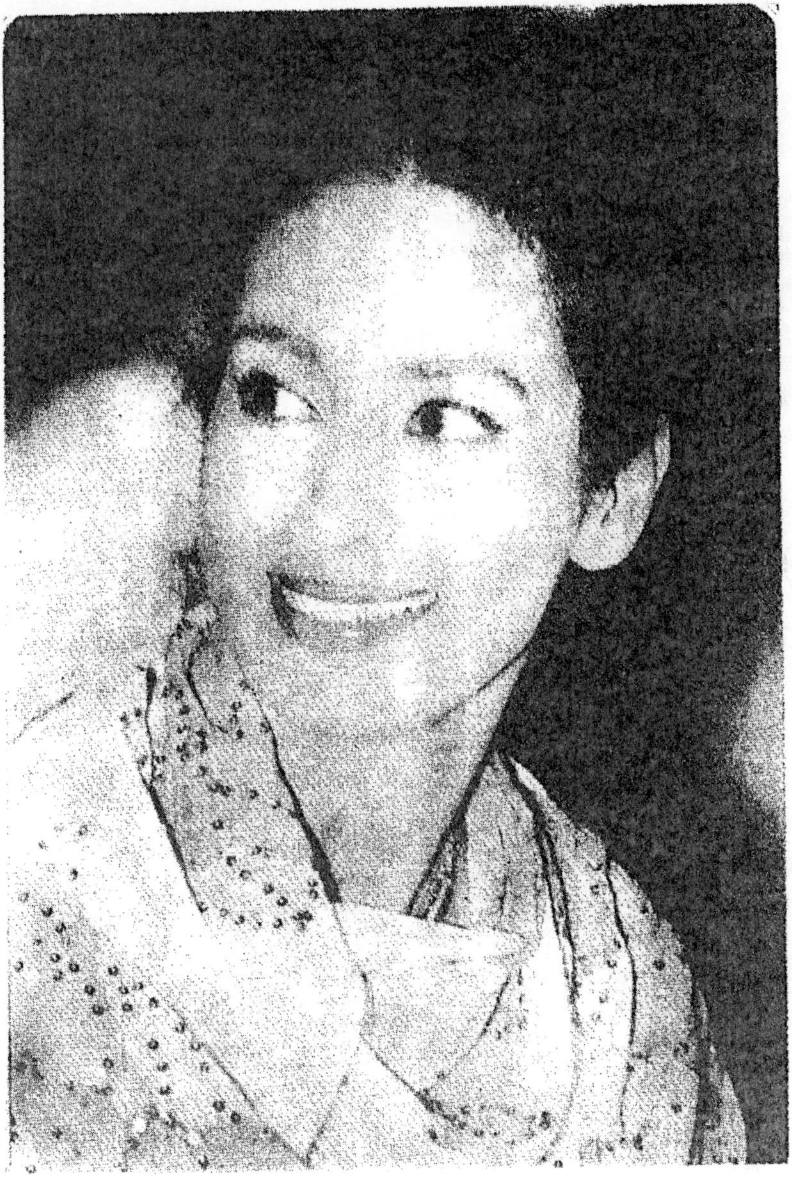

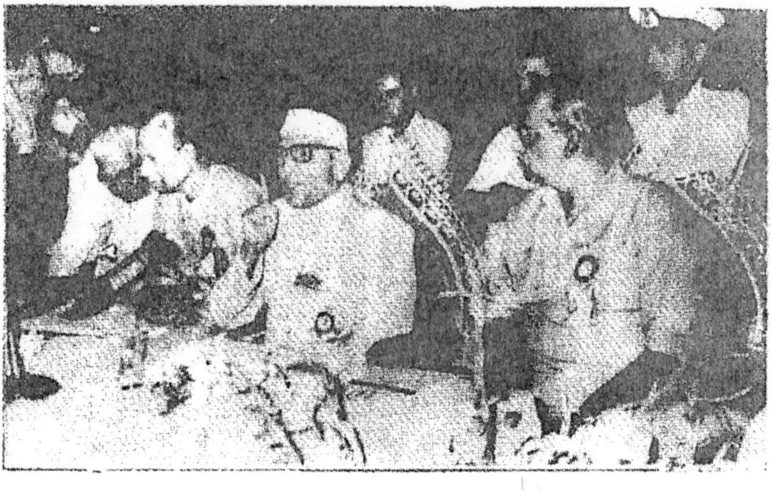

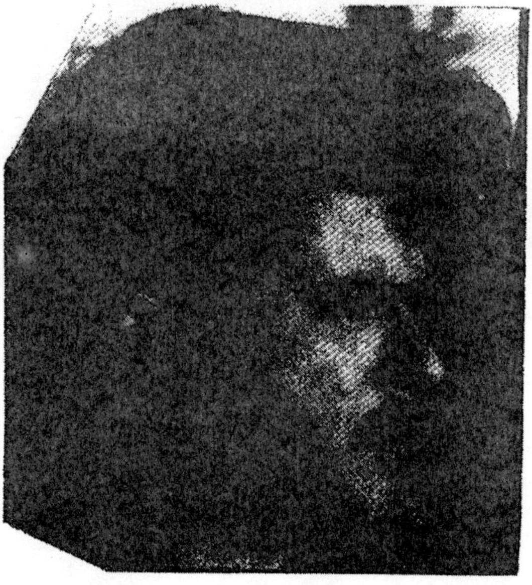

PART I

1

Introduction : Entrance of India in the Cine Era

In contemporary period, cinema is one of the significant part of human life. It plays an important role in entertainment, education and communication. Cinema has been put in the category of arts and it is more effective than other arts. French producer-director Mr. Aastruk defined cinema or films in the following words—"Like written words film is also a language, for whose reading and writing, a new point of view is necessary." According to the ex-president of Motion Pictures Association, United States of America, Mr. Arick Johnston, "Film is the strongest effective medium of communication, as it is a powerful medium to enhance education and international good wishes. If it is said that a picture is more valuable than hundred words, so a film is more qualitative than hundreds of pictures."

The first Prime Minister of India, Pandit Jawahar Lal Nehru said, "In recent times if any art medium has highest effect, no doubt it is films."[1]

---

1. Karuna Shankar, *Bhartiya Filmon ka Itihas*, p. 5.

Birth of Cinema

Well known historian Mr. B.D. Garg expresses his views about the birth of cinema. To him, "About twenty-five thousand years ago, during the first half of the civilization, an unknown artist, at Altamira, in the caves of Spain, made a pig of many feet on the wall, that was the first trial of a human being, in which the speed of the picture got importance."[2] It was the imagination of an artist and this unknown artist would have not imagined about modern cinema.

In the history of cinema the years 1833-1835 are very important. In the words of famous cinema writer Mr. Bachchan Srivastva, "In the invention of cinema, the first important machine was "Jatrop" which was formed in 1835. It was such an instrument, in which many pictures were sticked nearer to each other. Next to it was a revolving wheel. When Jatrop was moved, the viewer felt motion in the pictures."[3]

Before the invention of any cinema instrument, a French scientist Luis Damure invented the camera for photography in 1839.[4] Gradually this camera improved and it motivated to one of the San Francisco photographer for invention of the movie camera. He did an experience in 1877. Dr. Mahendra Mittal writes, "He (Mybridge) put twenty-five cameras in a line and took photos of a running horse. For this experience Mybridge bound the shutters of all cameras with a thread in such a way that when the horse ran before the cameras, one after another thread broke down and the shutters opened and shut up. In this process twenty-five pictures of a running horse were got up. When all these pictures were seen in a serial it looked as if the horse was running."[5] But

---

2. Mahendra Mittal, *Bhartiya Chalchitra*, p. 24.
3. Ibid., and Bachchan Srivastva, *Bhartiya Filmon ki Kahnni*, p. 8.
4. Mahendra Mittal, Ibid., p. 25.
5. Ibid , pp. 25-26.

just for this experiment Mybridge cannot be called the inventor of cinema.

The great scientist Mr. Thomas Alva Addison got the pride of being the inventor of cinema-machine. He also invented 'Effonograph' and 'electric bulb'.[6] He continuously worked for the invention of cinema machine. At last, in 1889 at West Orange, New Jersey (United States of America) situated laboratory, he invented successfully the cinema-machine called "Kenetoscope."[7] On October 3, 1889 he demonstrated his machine successfully.[8] In fact, this instrument was a machine, in which pictures of fifty feet could be watched through a "magnifying lense."[9]

Although 'Kenetoscope' became very popular and there were demands from big cities, yet it had many faults.[10] For this instrument, the pictures were taken at different plates. It used to be taken a lot of time for making such plates and these plates feared to be broken drown.[11] There is a saying that necessity is the mother of invention. An engineer, Mr. George Eastman, invented the film of cellulid, which helped Addison to remove his faults. He made many changes in his machine, and demonstrated the changed "Kinemetoscope" in New York on April 23, 1896.[12] On this occasion, first of all, he used fifty feet cellulid film.[13]

Addison's cinema got popularity in United States of America and Europe. The silence films were made. Addison also established the first film studio called "Black Maria" at

---

6. Ibid., p. 26.
7. Karuna Shankar, Ibid., 14.
8. Mahendra Mittal, Ibid., p. 26.
9. Karuna Shankar, Ibid., p. 14.
10. Ibid., p. 14.
11. Mahendra Mittal, Ibid., p. 26.
12. Ibid., p. 26.
13. Ibid., p. 26.

West Orange, United States of America.[14] The contribution of Lumie Brothers in the history of cinema is significant. They built a cinema hall at "Paris Cafe" and showed small films from the professional viewpoint.[15] However these films were silent yet the people were surprised to look the miracle of science.

Cinema in India

The cinema age started in India in the last years of nineteenth century, just after the invention of it. Late Duhiraj Gobind Phalke[16] (Dada Saheb Phalke) has been accepted as the founder of cinema age in India.[17] Although Phalke has been called "Father of Indian Cinema," as a pride, however there were some efforts of film making and showing excluding him, some of them have rightful evidences.

The First Film Exhibition in India

In this direction the contribution of French Lumie Brothers was very important. Lumie Brothers spread kinemetoscope from business point of view in France. They showed short films. For it, they got one cinema-hall at Paris Cafe, it was fixed only for this purpose. On July 7, 1896, with Lumie Brothers co-operation at Watsons Hotel, Bombay, first of all the films were exhibited.[18] The exhibition of these films in Bombay was not free, there were tickets for Rupees two each. Here it is notable that the price value of that time

---

14. Karuna Shankar, Ibid., p. 15.
15. Mahendra Mittal, Ibid., p. 26.
16. Dada Phalke lived during 1870-1944 period. There is a road named after him at Dadar in Bombay. There are many film studios and institutions at this road. The highest prize in India cinema "Dada Saheb Phalke Prize" has been instituted in his memory.
17. Mahendra Mittal, *Bhartiya Chalchitra*. p. 29.
18. Ibid., p. 27.

Rupees two is equal to hundred rupees of today in 1989. However, in spite of such price, the people were taken over by surprise with the miracle of science.

Early Efforts of Film Making in India

Many persons, and institutions, excluding Dada Saheb Phalke, authorised themselves as the earliest film makers in India. These are following:

1. Late Harish Chandra Sakharam told that before Raja Harish Chandra of Phalke in 1897, he made a short film, which was based on the wrestling of two wrestlers Pandulik Dada and Krishna Nahabi.[19] This film was shown at "Gaeti Theatre."

2. The people of Bengal claimed that Shri Hiralal Sen was the first film maker in India.[20] According to them in 1900 Shri Hiralal Sen made a documentary film based on the scenes of popular dance-drama of that period "Ali Baba."[21] In it, Narendranath Das and Kusum Kumari presented their dances.

   It is also claimed by Bengalis, that in 1911 he also made a film about Delhi Darbar.[22]

3. Some historians think that in 1889 a short film "Panorama of Calcutta" was made up.[23] This film was made up by Warwick Trading Company and showed in London.

---

19. Ibid., p. 30.
20. B.D. Garg, "Fifty Years of Regional Cinema", *Filmfare*, Bombay, March 22, 1963, p. 19.
21. Ibid.
22. R.D. Bansal, "Films of Directors", *Filmfare*, July 8, 1966, p. 47 and Vimal Bose, "Bangla Chitrapat", *Prithiviraj Kapoor Abhinandan Granth* (Hindi), p. 29.
23. Dwarka Prasad Shastri, "Bangla Chitrapat", Ibid., p. 56.

4. The Bengal movement of 1905 is famous in the history. Some people expressed that one patriot of Calcutta Mr. Jyotish Sarkar made a film on this movement.[24]

5. Bombay based Mr. R.G. Torne claimed that in 1909 he made a short film named "Sant Pandulik."[25] In the same year this film was exhibited in Bombay's Coronation Theatre.[26]

6. Some scholars claimed that in 1912 a film called 'Savitri' was made up.[27] About the producers of this film, Dwarka Prasad Shastri comments that in 1911 Anant Ram, Parshuram Karandhar, S.N. Patankar and V.P. Diwakar constituted a film company, and this film was produced by it.[28] The exhibition of it did not get success.[29] Similarly one of the film produced by this company, could not get show performance. This film was made up in 1912, and its story was based on the life character of Narayan Rao Peshwa.[30]

7. In 1899 Mr. P.A. Stuart made a film at Church Gate in Bombay.[31] About its exhibition, it is thought that it was shown at that place where today's "Times of India" publication group is situated.[32]

8. The first Indian 'newsreel' has also been recorded. It was made up in 1901. This film was based on

---

24. Bachchan Srivastva, *Bhartiya Filmon Ki Kahani*, p. 11.
25. Mahendra Mittal, Ibid., p. 30.
26. Ibid.
27. Ibid., p. 31.
28. Dwarka Prasad Shastri, *Prithiviraj Kapoor Abhinandan Granth*, p. 56.
29. Mahendra Mittal, Ibid., p. 31.
30. Bachchan Srivastva, Ibid., p. 11.
31. Karuna Shankar, *A short history of Indian films* (Hindi), pp. 19-20.
32. Ibid., p. 19.

the welcome programme of an Indian doctor returned from England. It was produced by Harish Chandra Sakharam.[33]

A score of claims about the production and exhibition of these films had been presented but none of these have historical evidence. Hence, none of these films could be called "the first film of India." *The First Film in Hindi Language : "Raja Harish Chandra" and Leadership of Dada Saheb Phalke.*

On the basis of evidences, it may be said that the starting of the film production era in India took place by Dada Saheb Phalke and his film "Raja Harish Chandra."[34] This film was exhibited in Bombay's Sandhurst Roat at Coronation Theatre.[35] The cinema-historians have not come on consensus about the date of its exhibition. But it has been made up in 1912.[36] As per the publication of Film Federation of India, Bombay, Indian Talkie 1931-56, this film was shown at Coronation Theatre, Bombay in December 1912.[37] According to Bachhan Srivastva, this film was exhibited in April 1913.[38] Mr. Dwarka Prasad Shastri has also expressed the same opinion.[39]

A little difference in the above mentioned dates presents non-definiteness in history writing. Hence it seems justiceable to present the correct date on the basis of specific and few evidences. From this point of view, this film was exhibited

---

33. Ibid., p. 20.
34. Mahendra Mittal, Ibid., p. 29.
35. Harish S. Buch, "Phalke—Father of Indian Cinema Industry" (Hindi), *Indian Talkie*, 1931-56, p. 20.
36. Mahendra Mittal, Ibid., p. 30.
37. *Indian Talkie*, 1931-56, Film Federation of India, Bombay, p. 75.
38. Bachchan Srivastva, Ibid., p. 13.
39. Dwarka Prasad Shastri, Ibid., p. 13.

on May 17, 1913.[40] Film Archives of India, Poona is also in consensus with the rightfulness about this date.

"Raja Harish Chandra" film may be proudly claimed as the first Hindi film.[41] It can be proved because to show the development of the story of the film, Hindi titles are used and English translation is also provided respectively.[42] Thus, Dada Saheb Phalke recognised the importance of Hindi as national language like Mahatma Gandhi. Though he was a Marathi speaker, yet he accepted Hindi as the medium to communicate with the onlookers of his speechless film. He did not use Marathi or Bengali. Dada Phalke produced this film as per the dance culture of Bharat Muni, and its dramatic features were according to Hindi literary drama-culture, and presented before us.

A complete spool of the making of this film is also available.[43] In it, we can watch Dada Saheb as instructing and directing to the actors. It proves that Dada Sahab knew, what he was doing, was of historical importance.

Hence it is suitable to accept the starting point of Indian cinema history with "Raja Harish Chandra." Upto 1917 Dada Phalke was the only producer in this area. So far he has made twenty-three films, out of these "Bhasmasur Mohini", "Satyavan Savitri" and "Lanka Dehn" got significant popularity.[44]

These all films were based on mythological stories. The dialogue-writing was influenced by Persian Theatrical Companies and acting, scene-change, motions and make-up was like drama culture. The sun light was used for shadows and all the

---

40. B.D. Garg, "Fifty Years of Indian Films", *Filmfare*, March 8, 1963, Bombay, p. 15.
41. Indian Talkie, 1931-56, p. 78.
42. Mahendra Mittal, Ibid., p. 31.
43. Film Archives of India, Poona.
44. Mahendra Mittal, Ibid., p. 32.

units of a film were the responsibility of a single person. In most of the films of Dada Saheb, he was himself the dialogue writer, story writer, director, studio-man, producer, art-director, editor and make up man.

During these days, film production was looked upon with suspicion, on commercial point of view. The contemporary social and political conditions were not appropriate for this industry. However when popularity of Dada Saheb Phalke films increased, the rich people entered into this area to make money. On arrival of big businessmen into this field, the film industry developed and many new cinema halls were opened for showing films.

In 1918, Dada Saheb Phalke went to Nasik and there he established a new organisation, "Hindustan Film Company." The first important film of this institution was "Krishna Janam." Dada Saheb Phalke got inspiration for this film from "The life of Christ", a two spools film. Watching this film, he got the idea that in place of Christ, he can put Krishna and would make a film. In this successful film, the role of Krishna was performed by his daughter "Mandakini".

Earlier Important Film Making Institutions

In 1913, just after establishment of Indian film industry, a score of film making institutions were established in the four corners of the country like Bombay, Madras, Bengal and Punjab. The important of these film making institutions are following:

(1) Bombay Area

Bombay Metropolitan has the pride of being founder city of film industry. The first film was shown here and it was the work-place of Dada Saheb Phalke. Since then, upto today, Bombay has been the "Hollywood" of India. From the technical point of view too, Bombay provided renowned establishments. The highest number of films have been produced in Bombay.

TABLE 1.1

Earlier Important Film Making Institutions of Bombay Area

S. No.	*Film Making Institutions*	*Year of Establishment*
1.	Phalke Film Company	1912
2.	Hindustan Film Company	1918
3.	Maharashtra Film Company	1919
4.	Kohinoor Film Company	1919
5.	Star Film Company	1920
6.	Shri Vishnu Film Company	1923
7.	Sharda Film Company	1925
8.	Imperial Film Company	1926
9.	Laxmi Pictures	1927
10.	Aryan Film Company	1927
11.	Ranjeet Movieton Company	1929
12.	Saroj Film Company	1929
13.	Prabhat Film Company	1929

The above table explicits that in the decade of 1920-1930, Bombay film industry has developed sufficiently.

(2) *Bengal Area*

The Bengalis are famous for their interest in different kinds of art. The Bengalis did remarkable efforts in film making. As earlier stated, some scholars have tried to prove that 'Bengal' got pride in establishing film industry, first of all over India. However, their claims cannot be accepted due to lack of historical evidences. Yet, after some time of the release of "Raja Harish Chandra", many film making companies have been founded in Bengal.

TABLE 1.2

Earlier Film Making Companies of Bengal

S. No.	*Film Institution*	*Year of Establishment*
1.	Madan Theatres	1917
2.	Arora Cinema Company	1919
3.	Indo-British Film Company	1920
4.	Taj Mahal Film Company	1922
5.	Indian Cinema Arts	1926
6.	British Dominion Films Limited	1928
7.	International Films Crafts	1930
8.	New Theatres Limited	1930

(*3*) *Madras Area*

The progress of film industry in Madras area was slow as compared to Bombay and Bengal.

TABLE 1.3

Important Film Making Companies of Madras

S. No.	*Film Institution*	*Year of Establishment*
1.	The East Film Company	1921
2.	Surya Film Company	1929
3.	General Pictures Corporation Limited	1929
4.	Associated Films	1929

(*4*) *Punjab Area*

Before the partition of India, Lahore was an important city of film making industry.

Diagram 1.1 : Number of film companies of Bombay area during 1912-29 in each year

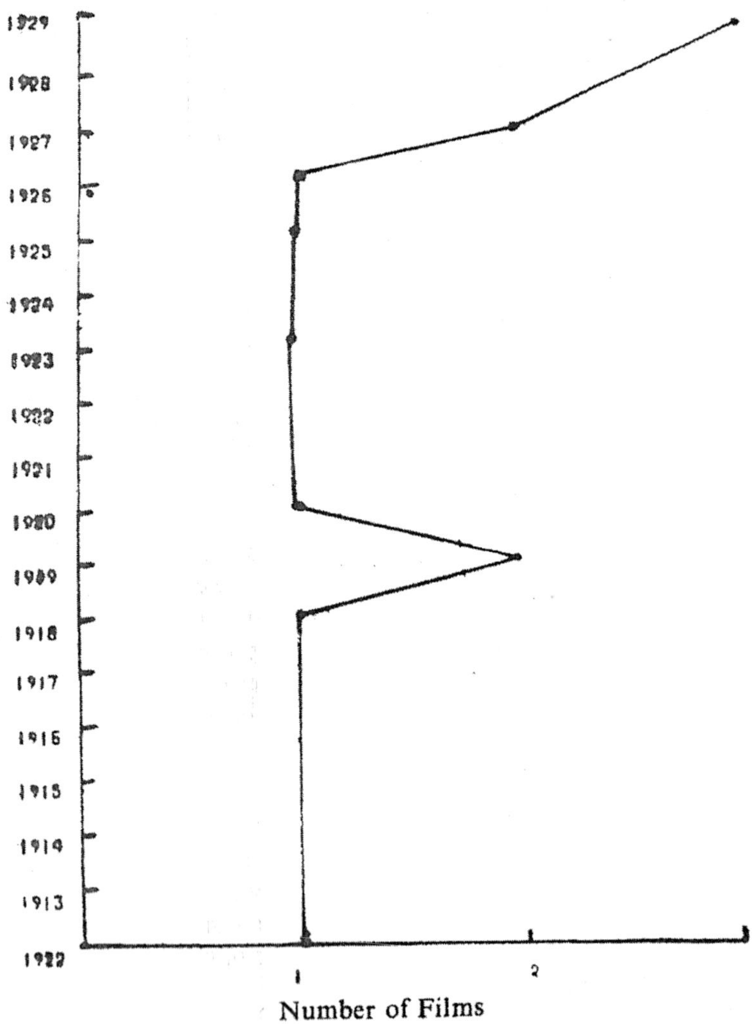

TABLE 1.4

Important Film Making Companies of Punjab Area

S. No.	*Film Institution*	*Year of Establishment*
1.	The Great Eastern Corporation	1924
2.	Pioneer Film Company	1929
3.	United Players Corporation	1928
4.	Punjab Film Company	1929

Contribution of Babu Ram Painter to Indian Cinema

India films generally and Hindi films particularly, got significant contribution from Babu Ram painter in the earlier years. In the words of Dr. Mahendra Mittal—"Babu Ram Painter was the first man, who gave a place to art in the cinema and put an eye on the possibilities of art and commercial folk in the cinema.[45]

This artist produced the first film in his Cinema Company whichwas based on the pages of "Mahabharat" story and named "Sarandhi". It was an artistic film. This film was released in 1919 and it was the first art film of that period. For this film, Mr. Babu Ram Painter got gold award from Lokmanya Balgangadhar Tilak in Poona at Arya Cinema, in a special congregation.

In 1920, Maharashtra Film Company's one of the important film "Singhgarh" was released, it was appreciated both by viewers and critics.

45. Mahendra Mittal, Ibid., p. 33.

Diagram 1.2 : Number of film companies of Bengal areas during 1917-30 in each year

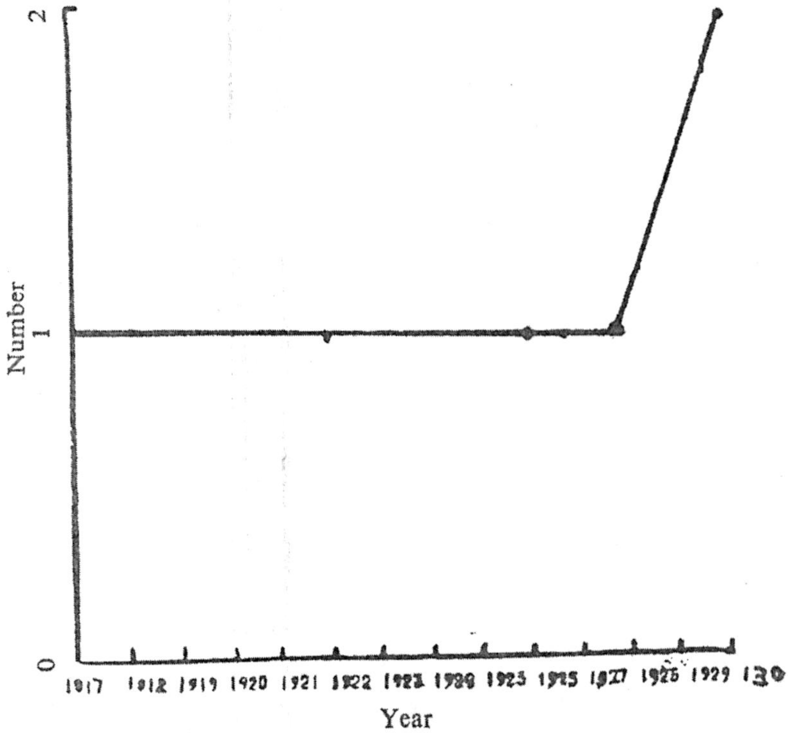

Diagram 1.3: Number of film companies of Madras area during 1921-29 in each year

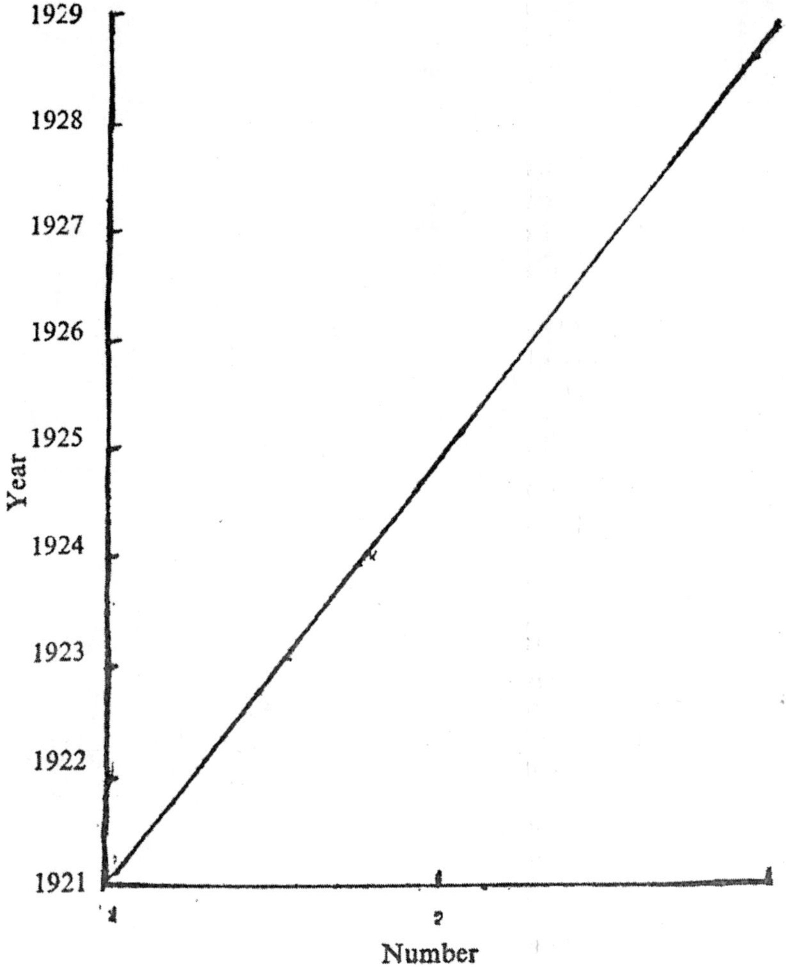

Diagram 1.4 : A comparative view of earlier film companies of all the four areas

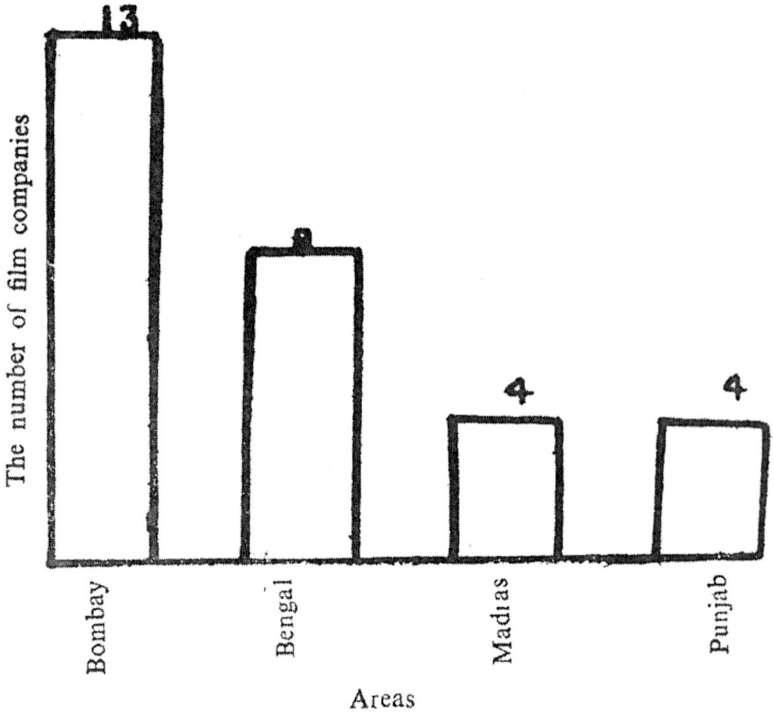

Conclusion

In 1913, Dada Saheb Phalke produced first feature film "Raja Harish Chandra" which brought India on the doorstep of film era. Dada Saheb was a farsighted man and nationalist. It is not an exaggeration to call him, "The Father of India Cinema Industry". He established the film industry, and soon it got attention of many brilliant businessmen and art-lovers. Consequently, the film making took place rapidly in Bombay and excluding it, Calcutta, Madras and Lahore became important centres of film making industry.

PART II

2

Hindi Cinema related to Freedom Movement and Politics

(A) Films about Freedom Movement

The films have influenced all the fields of human life like political, social, cultural and economic. Indian society also touched by its impact. As earlier stated in 1913, after release of "Raja Harish Chandra" the film-era has started in India. Dada Saheb Phalke, the producer of "Raja Harish Chandra" got the pride of being the "Father of Indian Cinema."

It is notable that film-era started in India, at the time when British government had planned to contain the national consciousness. In 1910 the newspapers freedom has been limited by passing "Indian Press Act." In 1911 through "Rebellious Meeting Act," severe punishment had been declared for holding meetings against the then government. In 1913 when "Raja Harish Chandra" film was made and released, in the same year an Act "Criminal Amendment

Ordinance" was accepted to curb the activities of the freedom fighters.[1]

Meanwhile, the preparations for First World War have started, for that political consciousness has increased among the Indian people. One author observed this consciousness among the film makers in the following words:

"Our film makers could not be separated from this consciousness. But in such an environment, it was very difficult to raise the dissident or rebellious voice against the government. Thus, however little, yet the Indian film makers used the power of non-speaking films for the country.

The film makers highlighted such characters, whose qualities were recognised by each Indian. And through them the ideal history of India was revealed. Their object was to inspire the people for the freedom of the country through presentation of the self-sacrifice of such characters."[2]

However, to utilise cinema as a weapon for the freedom struggle was not easy. The government implemented hard censor policy on the films. But the Indian film makers in pre-independent period produced many small and big as well as feature films directly or indirectly related to freedom movement, without caring censor policy. A score of films were made up based on life, personality and ideology of Mahatma Gandhi, but the government did not permit their release through hard censorship.[3] In this respect one author, Mr. Aseem Chakravarty writes,

---

1. Alok Ranjan, "Films and Freedom Movement (Hindi)", *Madhuri*, Fortnightly, Bombay, 5-18 August 1983, p. 18.
2. Ibid., p. 18.
3. Aseem Chakravarty, "Netaji's fight against anti-India campaign" (Hindi), *Amar Ujala*, Daily, Agra, August 15, 1983, p. 4.

"It was 1933. Many well known film companies produced a number of films on Mahatma Gandhi. All these films were speaking and some of these have voice of Gandhiji. The film making companies have arranged these with their regular films for release. In all these films, the contemporary activities of Gandhiji were presented nicely. The owners of these companies have full confidence that these films would have been helpful in freedom movement and thinking it, they planned to show these films in January 1933, in Delhi, with regular films. But a "Press Release" on January 14, 1933 finished all these efforts. The press release was issued by the then Chief Commissioner and he did not permit to release all these films."[4]

But the Indian film makers were not easily defeated. They kept continue their contribution through cinema art. A prominent person among such film makers was producer director Mr. J.B.H. Wadia. He was himself in the Indian National Congress since 1930 to 1938.[5] Due to it, his films have a lot of nationalist ideas. To avoid censorship films were made up based on imaginative stories, but their object was to produce hate in the hearts of viewers against the British government. For example, Wadia Movieton produced a film "Hunter Wali" on this pattern.[6] In this film, a rebellious minister imprisoned the king and increased the grievances of the people. For removal of the deceit minister, the daughter of the king organised the people moving village after village. At last the people changed the whole situation."[7]

In the first sight, it seemed to be a children story, sharpened the people's desire for freedom. The minister's character was a simile to the British, who took over India through deceitful acts.

---

4. Ibid.
5. Alok Ranjan, p. 18.
6. Ibid.
7. Ibid.

Understanding the importance of films, many top leaders of freedom movement showed their interest in the films. Netaji Subhash Chandra Bose had great affection towards films. He had closed relations with producer-director Surendra Nath Sarkar and Himanshu Rai. Aseem Chakravarty writes about Netaji Subhash Bose and his relations with film people:

"Netaji realized that films were a great source of freedom struggle and popular awakening. For this, he showed interest towards films."[8] His interest was the need of the times. Subhash Chandra Bose interest in films also exhibited when he constituted cultural department" with other departments in his "Azad Hind Government." One branch of this department was given the responsibility that it must produce films on the working of Azad Hind Government and scenes of the battles of its army. The branch did this job successfully. After independence, Indian Government got it any way and showed all over India as a short film. The title of this seven thousand feet film was "Netaji Subhash", and as a producer the name of Vallabh Bhai Patel was there. This film was shown sufficiently in the country before independence too. The British government was anxious of the relationship of the film producers and the nationalist leaders. It did not like that any leader be shown at screen. In 1939 just after the Second World War, the British government, through an order issued banned Gandhi, Nehru and other Congress leaders as well as spinning wheel on the screen.[10] The government feared that thus Congress get its propaganda, but even after all these obstructs, Indian films, particularly Hindi films notably contributed for freedom movement.

Based on heroes and incidents of freedom struggle, a number of films have been produced before and after independence, whose national songs influenced the patriotism and

---

8. Aseem Chakravarty, Ibid., p. 4.
9. Ibid.
10. Alok Ranjan, Ibid., p. 19.

awakening of the masses. Balak, Son of India, Jagrati, Haqeeqat, Lambe Haath, Aakraman, Jurm Aur Saza, Shaheed, Hindustan ki Kasam, Leader, Mujhe jeene do, Shaheed-e-Azam, Bhagat Singh, Chandra Shekhar Azad, Subhash Chandra Bose and Anand Math etc. are notable films in this respect.[11]

During freedom movement, the songs of these films and after independence produced films songs influenced the popular mind too much. However it is needed that their higher level must be kept intact.

(B) Political Cinema

The significance of cinema is well known to every man today. Like love affairs, social and family, political films also have great importance. Cinema has been considered one of the powerful medium for the national integration. From this point of view too, political cinema is very useful. Film is an art and as an art its political importance cannot be neglected. One of the important pillar of Turkish political cinema, writer, actor and producer director, late Ilmas Gune, told to an American magazine reporter, in an interview, "Art does not bring revolution itself, but an actor having a right political thinking, who has right political viewpoint towards world, through his work, can establish relations with the people on broad basis. In this meaning, art can be proved fruitful for political resistance and political propaganda."[12] According to him, cinema as a part of art is an important medium for both politics and propaganda. Ilmas Gune produced several films based on Turkish political background. In his films, he presented minutely the "exploitation and torture" scenes. His political films were banned in Turkey. A

---

11. Ashok Grover, (Contributor), *National Songs in Films* (Hindi), Nutan Pocket Books, Meerut, pp. 5-6.
12. Pradeep Saurabh, "Ilmas Gune—End of Political Cinema era", *Nav Bharat Times* (Hindi), New Delhi, October 30, 1984.

journalist suffered imprisonment because he praised one of his film.[13]

Political cinema has its history in India too. Indian people are politically mature and they take great interest in political films. Hence, the people showed significant interest in the recent produced political films.[14] "Tanneer-Tanneer" (Tamil), "Albert Pinto Ko Gussa Kyon Aata Hai", "Aakrosh", "Ardh Satya", "Gandhi", "Inquilab", "Aaj Ka M.L.A. Ram Avtar", "Andha Qanoon" etc. are the main political films released during recent past.

Indian political films and their actors got awards from foreign countries during international film festivals; thus proved their efficiency. Ompuri won 'best actor award' at "Kalavivari Film Festival" for acting in "Ardh Satya."[15] Similarly for another political film "Paar", actor Naseer-uddin Shah got "best actor award" at Venice.[16] In "Ardh Satya"

---

13. Ibid.
14. India Cinema 83-84 writes about these films—"The success of these films has not been lost on the industry. Socially relevant themes are the emergent reality of the popular cinema. Films like "Thenneer (water) have launched a scathing attack on callous officialdom to continuing popular applause. The major trend in "relevance", however relates to women and their position in the society. This may be the compromise between the perceived needs of the audience and the extent to which the industry is willing to challenge the status quo, but its importance can hardly be denied."
    —Uma Da Kunha, (Editor), *Indian Cinema 83/84*, National Films Development Corporation, New Delhi, 1984, p. 23.
15. Ali, "Hindi Cinema—Manthan Ho Raha Hai Amrit Nikal Raha Hai", *Jan Satta*, Hindi Daily, New Delhi, October 5, 1984.
16. Ibid.

politicisation of power is shown.[17] So this film was discussed too much. The presentation of this film was also very effective. For this, its director Govind Nihalini got award from the "Indian Films Directors Association."[18] Some critics of Indian films observed the presentation of international awards to Indian political films as a sign of change in the history of Hindi cinema. In this respect one author comments, "Again the Hindi cinema's history has taken a change. Hindi cinema has not earned such fame at international level before this. The Hindi cinema got new recognition in the world. Before it, the world knows Indian cinema through Satyajeet Ray. After it, a little fame has been received by Mrinal Sen or in socialist countries Raj Kapoor was known. But this time Hindi cinema has taken new direction and added a golden chapter in the history of cinema.[19] In fact, Indian film viewers have been tired of watching love-triangles and beatingful films, and now they take interest in the films based on the problems of people.

For the producers of political films, it is necessary that he must relate his art with the people. In this respect, the director of "Chokh" (Bengali) Mr. Utpalendu Chakravarty said:

"I am not a teacher to the people but a benevolent student of mass community. My art is for the struggling people against torture and exploitation for social political change. . . . In the present system when at every step there are gheraos, ties, and obstructions, yet a powerful film medium can be related by active, living and constructively with the aspirations and struggle of the people, if the wish and vow is there."[20]

---

17. Renu Sharma, "Yatharth" or "Ardh Satya", *Punjab Kesari*, Hindi, Delhi, City Edition, January 13, 1984, p. 1.
18. *Nav Bharat Times*, Hindi Daily, July 23, 1984.
19. Ali, Ibid., p. 5.
20. Sandeep Rai Chaudhry, "Chokh" or "Aankh" or Utplendu Chakravarty, *Amar Ujala*, Hindi Daily, Agra, August 14, 1983.

In fact, the meaningful cinema is that which shows the aspirations and struggle of the people. For example, there is a continuous struggle to finish "bonded labour" in India. The worst feature of this tradition is 'bonded child labour'. Recently, a film "Mundu" has been produced on child bonded labour, it showed the evils of the system.

We can say that Indian political cinema made films on all those subjects which can motivate the Indian people. However, we have not developed a well defined viewpoint of political cinema. It may be a subject of debate, that we must differentiate between political and revolutionary cinema. In our own boundaries what we have like conscious cinema, may be considered as political cinema. It is the tragedy of Indian cinema that out of thousands of films in context of political references, no single personality could be developed. Either there is caste based regional cinema or there is new waves cinema which keeps clothes of modern art to some extent in the structure of film. Unfortunately, disguised in art's name caste jealousy, prejudice, mutual suspicions, and separatism like tendencies have been included in the political cinema as necessary. Some people present their arguments on behalf of such tendencies. In this respect, the famous producer of meaningful cinema, Syam Benegal pointed out, "In my opinion every film is a political film, because the film shows the ethics and behaviour of social structure. Power's social structure is political hence every social film is political."[21] He wants to relate everything political with contextual cinema. However, one other film producer Sayeed Mirza says that whole system is such that no question can be asked. Police-officer, advocates, musicians, film producers, all want to keep the status quo. The system wants that people must not think at all.

Hence, in such circumstances, through the medium of cinema, from where the job of full consciousness can be started

---

21. Anwar Jamal, "Where is the way of political cinema?" *Jan Satta*, Hindi, New Delhi, January 23, 1987, p. 5.

for political change ? To answer this question it may be said that Indian cinema must separate it with adventures, extra-ordinary things and the images of just entertainment, and relate itself with the struggling people closely, but it is only possible when its path passes through politics. The context of the political cinema's path is necessary there, where was no established tradition of film production. Its utility is particularistic in the country like India where there are abundance of emotional—full of dramatic stories, exciting spy incidents, violent and criminal stories films, in the name of tradition.

Main Political Films

In India, particularly in the Hindi language, a score of such films are produced which are based on political background. Here we present four such films analysis for illustration. These films are—Ardh-Satya, Bombay—Hamara Shahar, New Delhi Times, and Inqilab. The stories of all these films are related to the dark sides of our political life.

1. Ardh Satya

Directed by Govind Nihalini and based on the script of Vijay Tendulkar, produced in 1983, "Ardh Satya" is the living illustration of the evils of our society and political system. As per the story of the film Sub-Inspector Anand Valankar (Om Puri) deeply hurts to look upon the close relations of criminal elements with political elements. Due to political pressure, he finds himself unable in taking action against criminal elements and at last he himself commits an offence against the law. The heroine of the film is Jyotsna Gokhle (Smita Patil). The other important actors are—Haider Ali (Shafi Inamdar), Mike Lobo (Naseeruddin Shah), the father of Sub-Insepctor Anand (Amreesh Puri) and Rama Shetti (Sadashiv Amaspurkar) etc. The film's music director is Ajeet Burman.

"Ardh Satya" got many prizes for its best script. In April 1984, thirty-first Film Fair Prizes were announced. In it, "Ardh Satya" got the prize of best film of the year. Excluding it, the same film got prizes for best director (Govind Nihalini), best script writer (D. Padanwalkar), best actor (Sadashiv

Amrapurkar) and best script writer (Vijay Tendulkar) got Film-fare Prizes.[22]

In 1984, at an international film festival at "Karlovi Bary", the main actor of the film, Ompuri got the "Best Male Actor" Prize. Before him at "Karlovi Bary" Nargis Dutt for Mother India and Prithiviraj Kapoor for Aasman Mahal got the prizes for best acting.[23] This film and its actors also got many other international awards.

2. Bombay—Hamara Shahar

In 1984 producer director and editor Anand Patwardhan produced this feature film, which shows the worst living conditions of the forty lakh people who reside in Jhuggi Jhonpris of Bombay. It also illustrates the viewpoints of officers, leaders, capitalists and so called progressives. The film narrates that while Bombay's life cannot sustain without the production capacity of these hut-dwellers, yet there are plans to uproot them, so that their bad smell could not be reached at the bunglows of rich people. The well-to-do citizens wish to keep them in the situation of uprooting. It means that these poor people must construct the skycrapping buildings of the rich people, but they have no right of even two square yards of earth. The film successfully shows that the Inspector-General of Bombay Police and Director of C.R.P. felt sorry because the people did not fear to look uniformed policemen. Why the poor hut-dwellers are raising their voice unitedly against this injustice?

In fact, in the eighty-two minutes, this feature film depicts the awesome condition of hut-dwellers as well as the neglective viewpoint of the government.[24]

---

22. *Navbharat Times*, Hindi Daily, New Delhi, April 12, 1984, City edition, p. 1.
23. *Screen*, Weekly, Bombay, July 27, 1984, p. 1.
24. Anand Swarup Verma, (Interview), "Producer Anand Patwardhan talks to him", *Jan Satta* (Hindi) Daily, City Edition, Sunday, March 30, 1986, pp. 2-6.

This feature film attracted the attention of common people as well as elites, for the solution of the social and political problems of these hut-dwellers. To fulfil political objectives, and to increase the number of hut-dwellers or to uproot them, both are shameful to any civilized society. The film is successfal to convince that without rehabilitation, to uproot hut-dwellers is against the ideal of a welfare state.

3. New Delhi Times

Journalism is one of the most important pillars of democracy. In no country the ideals of democracy and welfare state have any future without free and impartial journalism. The journalists have also the responsibility that they should work impartially in the interest of nation and human welfare.

All these ideas have an expression in the film "New Delhi Times" directed by Ramesh Sharma. Mr. P.K. Tewari produced it in the first half of the 1985. Script-writer is Gulzar. Main actors of the film are Shashi Kapoor, Sharmila Tagore, Ompuri, Kulbhusan Kharbanda, A.K. Mangal, Manohar Singh and A.K. Raina.[25] Based on the story of journalism, the film throws light interestingly on the significance of investigative journalism in the background of present social-political environment. Shashi Kapoor did justice as an ideal journalist in the character role of Vikas Pandey.

In our country, the relations between politicians and journalists are sometimes sweet and sometimes bitter. The ruling party tries to influence the Press while the opposition hopes that the press, in criticism of the ruling party, favour them impartially. In such an environment "New Delhi Times" may inspire ruling party, opposition parties and the Press to keep a balance in their approach towards each other.

---

25. Rangnath Pande, "New Delhi Times", *Navbharat Times* (Hindi) Daily, August 18, 1984, City Edition, p. 7.

4. Inqilab

In this picture of Veeraswami, the true depiction of corrupt politics has been shown. A well known politician "Stanley Waldwik" once said, "politics is the last shelting place of criminal elements". There are some people, in politics, who through false promises, showing crocodiles tears, misguide the people and get the confidence of the people, afterwards exploit the people. For power, such people can commit detested crimes, can leave behind the interests of the country and the society. They can shelter the hard core criminals to make powerful their side and to win the political game, the criminals might have been appliances in the strategy of their chess-board. Such people can initiate riots, looting, dacoities, kidnappings to defame the ruling party and to replace it, so that they can blame the ruling party for such misdeeds.[26] In this film there is good representation of such elements active in ruling as well as opposition parties. The hero of Inqilab is Amitabh Bachchan, and hence it was successful from commercial point of view too. The other roles have been played by Sridevi, Qadar Khan, Utpall Dutt, Ranjeet, and Shakti Kapoor etc.

Conclusion

In 1984, a broad plan was taken up to communicate the general masses through films about the freedom movement. The then information and broadcasting minister, Mr. Harikrishna Lal Bhagat was told by the parliamentary advisory committee of his ministry, in a meeting, that in production of such films the truthfulness and objectivity shall be kept in mind. These shall not be produced from any narrow or party point of view. However the national leaders would be provided proper coverage. In this respect, an editorial board has been

26. Rangnath Pandey, "Revolution against corrupt politics" (Hindi), *Navbharat Times*, Hindi Daily, January 28, 1984.

constituted under the chairmanship of former, old nationalist leader and minister, Pandit Uma Shankar Dikshit, in which historian shall be included. The board shall provide its advice to the government about the script and titles of such films. The Board has done appreciable job and the government produced a score of films based on national movement. However, the need of the time is that such films must be "dubbed" in all languages of India and should be released in the respective regions. These must also be serialised at Television Centre, Delhi, so that the new generation may be taught about freedom movement. It is also necessary for national unity and integrity. As far as is the concern of political fims, it is very critical to produce films based on the stories of corrupt politics. In such films, there should be no direct offence against any political party, in spite of it, the well known points of ordinary corruption must be located. The film has an obvious objective. Thus the political cinema has a meaning.

3

Main Artistes of Hindi Cinema and their Social and Political Contributions

In any film, the hero and the heroine occupy prominent place. In Hindi films, the actors got significant position from earlier days to present times. Their acting has deep impact on the viewers.

(A) Meaning of Film Acting and Different Viewpoints

There is no consensus about the meaning of acting. Theatre acting has a long history of several centuries, but it is very different from film acting.

1. *Meaning of Film Acting*

Acting means copying the working style of the "person" whose role has been provided, through body actions, different impressions and dialogues. But it must be understood well that acting does not just copying. "The actor's activities must express the actions and emotions of the "role" and this expression is possible only when artistic objectives of drama or film have been understood very well."[1] The purpose of a drama or film is to exploit the delicate sentiments of the

---

1. Dinesh, *How to enter in the films* (Hindi), Rangbhoomi Prakashan, New Delhi, 1983, pp. 102-103.

viewers through generalisation and provide extraordinary pleasure. It is possible only when the actor must think himself not as an actor but as an alternate personality of the original character.

Captain A.K. Shinde also expressed similarly about the meaning of acting. He expressed clearly that the stage acting must not be thought out similar to screen acting.[2] In fact,

---

2. "It is difficult to say at which point film acting became a technique on its own, and it is a hesitant,...that is drawn even today between the technique of acting on the stage and that of acting before a film camera. There are obvious divisions, of course. It may generally be said that the actress (or actor) uses her body and her voice to project the character she is playing on the stage, and her eyes and her voice for the screen portrayal.

   It is better to come to screen acting with stage acting experience behind you; it is essential when you act before the camera to reject all that you have learned in a film studio when going back to the stage.

   In the theatre the actress is an entity. The performance she gives, good or bad, is her own. In a film studio she is a part of a vast and complicated mechanism. While she gives her performance, the camera, in the creative hands of the another person is giving its performance too, and that is not all. The final performance she gives, she plays no part in it at all. It is made in the cutting rooms.

   The secret of screen acting is the secret of the imaginative use of realism of the quality of detail which accompanies the magnification of the screen.

   It requires imagination and great self-discipline of body and face to enact subjective feeling in terms of minute objective changes of expression and attitude."—Captain A.K. Shinde (Edited), *Shinde's Dictionary of Cine Art and Film Craft*, Popular Prakashan. Bombay, 1962, pp. 1-2.

during a performance before the camera, the communication power is too much than the acting on the stage. So it must be understood in this context.

2. *Different Viewpoints about Acting*

Some experienced well known persons of this profession have expressed their viewpoints about acting, so that the art of acting can be understood deeply.

Views of Mr. Pudvokin, Film Art Scholar

Mr. Pudvokin has written about the techniques of acting in a theatre and acting before a camera in the following words, "In general condition of real life, there is a definite technique to set human activities. In a stage acting, an actor, compelled by this techninque gives extra meanings to his actions and expression, so that the people sitting in the auditorium may look his expressions very well."[3]

The actors of film cannot be expected that the people can understand their expressions through the medium of camera and microphone, by least of their actions and maximum of control. The special characteristic of the technique of film acting is realism. Thus the mechanical technique provides more facilities to the actors and the actor expresses more naturally in his acting in place of artificiality. Similarly, he needs no extra attention for his make up. However there is need for make up but it needs to express the minute structural details of human figure. In a film, too much make up expressions are assumed as foolish. The reason is that like a stage actor, a film actor has no anxiety of the onlookers. If he will do so his expressions may be defunct and "close up" shall be laughty.

In my opinion, the main element in the acting of an actor is that he must converse with his colleagues without

---

3. Dinesh, Ibid., pp. 104-106.

hesitation and artificiality so that it must be felt just natural in every way. Any actor cannot perform his job just because of his wisdom. The reason for it is that the direction is always present there and he looks that the actor must express his 'role' with real actions.

For constructive acting, any actor, first of all, must get the knowledge about reality. After knowing the reality, the actor can learn acting and put a real impression on the viewers. In any art, my meaning with art is, that it must be nearer to life and express obviously to life, as much as possible.

As a matter of fact, Mr. Pudvokin presented the real picture of an actor in the above mentioned ideas. Any film actor, learning from these teachings, may represent immemorable acting.

Views of Hindi Film Actors and Actresses

Well known film actors of Hindi cinema have also expressed their opinions and views about acting. Dilip Kumar, Raj Kapoor, Meena Kumari, Nargis Dutt etc. expressed that any body after regular practice can bring peculiarity in his acting.

One of the famous actor of Hindi cinema late Balraj Sahni did not agree that acting relates to hereditary character. In this respect he has written in his "autobiography" that "... the art of acting is also like any other worldly profession. A carpenter after making up a table or a chair and an engineer after making up a machine, fulfils any physical need of the humans. Similarly, a dramatist writing up a drama or an actor playing a role of any character, fulfils the mental need of the humans. Both kind of jobs are pious and worthy of appreciation.

In our country, there is an attitude, that art is a Divine reward. An artist cannot make, but he got it by birth. He gets inspiration from God and he is a supernatural person.

Now I have finished my belief in this attitude. I think it happened right. To bring spiritualism in art is only harmful, there is no use out of it.

We watch a score of American films every year. Not only the main character, but each, however little character, used to be presented so beautifully that no error looks anywhere in these films. But in our Indian films, leaving just two or four characters, the roles played by the rest actors do not seem good. It also happens sometime that a well-known actor works in twenty films simultaneously, brings his standard of acting at a low level.

If acting is a Divine reward, it is surprising that in Western countries, where religion has no particular significance, this reward has been got easily, but in our country just a little persons got it.

Acting is not only an art, it is also science. Studying scientifically and after regular practice, any person can become a good actor.

However it is wrong to say that any person did not get anything by birth. Everybody has different hereditary characteristics. Somebody takes birth, with particular qualities to become scientist or mathematician, or player or musician or painter or actor. The person get, full development, whose qualities get flourishing environment from childhood. But how many persons get such facilities in our country? Due to poverty, illiteracy and many other lacks, the expectations of many persons may be crumbled in the childhood.

To become an actor it is necessary to have an imagination power of highest expectations. Some children have sharp imagination which can be traced by their parents or teachers. Such children, after being adult, can touch the climax of art. Anybody can become good actor but there are few persons who can become the great actor.

However, who can say that any actor shall be a great actor or will remain an ordinary actor. It is appropriate, that the man thinks himself ordinary in place of extraordinary and must rely upon his own regular practice and hard work in place of Divine inspiration and hereditary character."[4]

In fact, the opinions of Balraj Sahni are appropriate. To be a film actor or actress it is necessary that in place of hereditary character, one must continue the regular practice and hard work. The history of Hindi cinema testifies to this fact that many artists who were unsuccessful in their debut films, established new records in the field of acting, after some time.

Prominent Actors of Modern Hindi Films

The list of prominent actors of modern Hindi films is very lengthy. The area for production of Hindi films is Bombay, so all the film actors reside there permanently.

The prominent Hindi film actors and their qualities of acting are following:

1 Amitabh Bachchan

In modern Hindi films, the name of Amitabh Bachchan is notable. He is assumed as "Super Star." The close up of Amitabh Bachchan is as follows:

1. Date of birth	October 11, 1942
2. Father's name	Dr. Harivansh Rai Bachchan
3. Mother's name	Shrimati Teji Bachchan
4. Wife's name	Shrimati Jaya Bachchan
5. Primary Education	Sherwood School, Nainital
6. Higher Education	B.Sc.
7. Hobbies	Studies, Sitar Playing

4. Balraj Sahni, *My film autobiography* (Hindi), Star Pocket Books, New Delhi, 1962, pp. 105-107.

8. Languages known — Hindi, English, Bangla, Punjabi, Urdu and Bhojpuri
9. Beloved Author — Khuswant Singh and Hadley Chase

The first released film of Amitabh Bachchan was "Saat Hindustani" directed by Khwaja Ahmad Abbas. It was produced in 1969. Since then he had acted in a score of films. In the field of acting he secured charismatic success and highest popular appreciation.

TABLE 3.1

Super Hit Films of Amitabh Bachchan

S. No.	*Year*	*Super Hit Films*
1.	1974	Zanjeer, Roti Kapra aur Makan
2.	1975	Deewar, Sholay
3.	1976	Hera Pheri, Kabhi-Kabhi
4.	1977	Amar-Akbar-Anthony, Parvarish
5.	1978	Anusandhan (Bengali)
6.	1981	Lawaris
7.	1982	Namak Halal

TABLE 3.2

Hit Films of Amitabh Bachchan

S. No.	*Year*	*Hit Films*
1.	1971	Anand
2.	1973	Bombay to Goa, Abhiman, Namak-Haram
3.	1974	Kasauti
4.	1977	Chupke-Chupke, Khoon-Paseena
5.	1978	Ganga Ki Saugandh, Kasme-Wade
6.	1979	Mr. Natwar Lal, Suhag, Jurmana
7.	1980	Dostana
8.	1981	Naseeb, Kalia, Yarana
9.	1982	Satte Pe Satta, Bemisal, Desh-Premi, Khuddar

TABLE 3.3

Amitabh Bachchan's Flop (Unsuccessful) Films

S. No.	*Year*	*Flop Films*
1.	1969	Sat Hindustani
2.	1971	Reshma aur Shera, Pyar Ki Kahani, Parwana
3.	1972	Ek Nazar, Sanyog, Bansi Birju, Raste Ka Patthar
4.	1973	Bandhe Haath, Gehri Chaal, Saudagar, Benam
5.	1974	Mazboot
6.	1975	Farar, Zameer
7.	1976	Iman Dharam, Do Anjane
8.	1977	Alap
9.	1978	Besharm
10.	1979	Kala Patthar, Manzil, The Great Gambler
11.	1980	Do aur Do Panch, Ram Balram, Shan
12.	1981	Barsat Ki Ek Raat, Silsila

The above mentioned tables explicit that before 1974, when Zanjeer was released, all of his films were a failure at Box Office. But, the sudden success of Zanjeer changed the fortunes of Amitabh Bachchan and he reached at the position of "Super Star."

Prominent Amitab Bachchan's Film Heroines (Actresses)

Amitab Bachchan has played as a hero in many Hindi films with prominent heroines and actresses. Rekha, Rakhi, Hema Malini, Jaya Bhaduri, Waheeda Rehman, Zeenat Aman, Parveen Bobby, Jaya Prada, and Shridevi are included among the actresses who worked with Amitabh Bachchan in many films.

Diagram 3.1 : Number of Super Hit films of Amitabh Bachchan during 1974-82 in each year

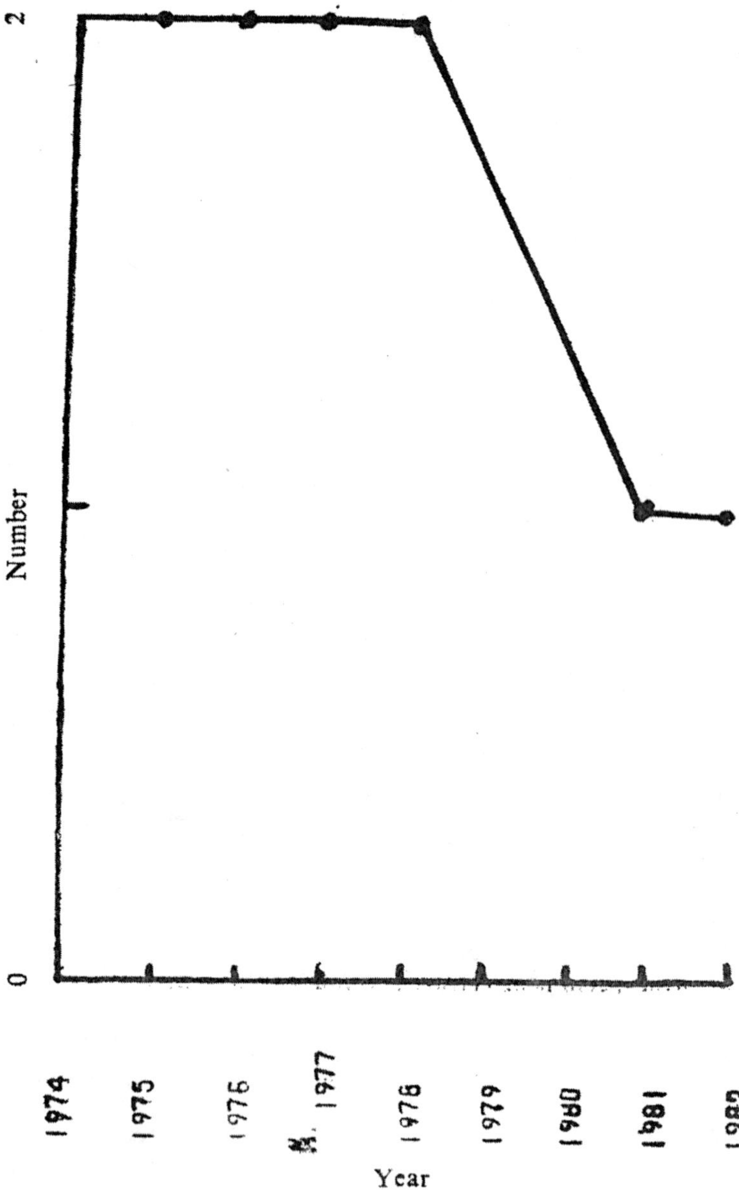

Diagram 3.2 : Number of Hit films of Amitabh Bachchan during 1971-82 in each year

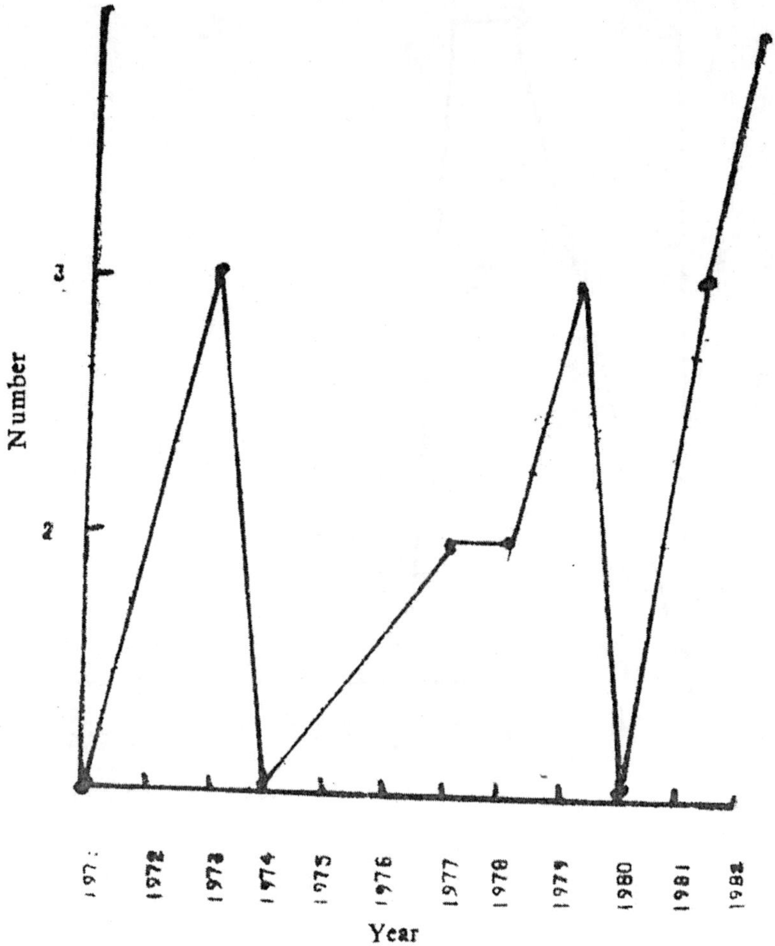

Diagram 3.3 : Number of flop films of Amitabh Bachchan during 1969-81 in each year

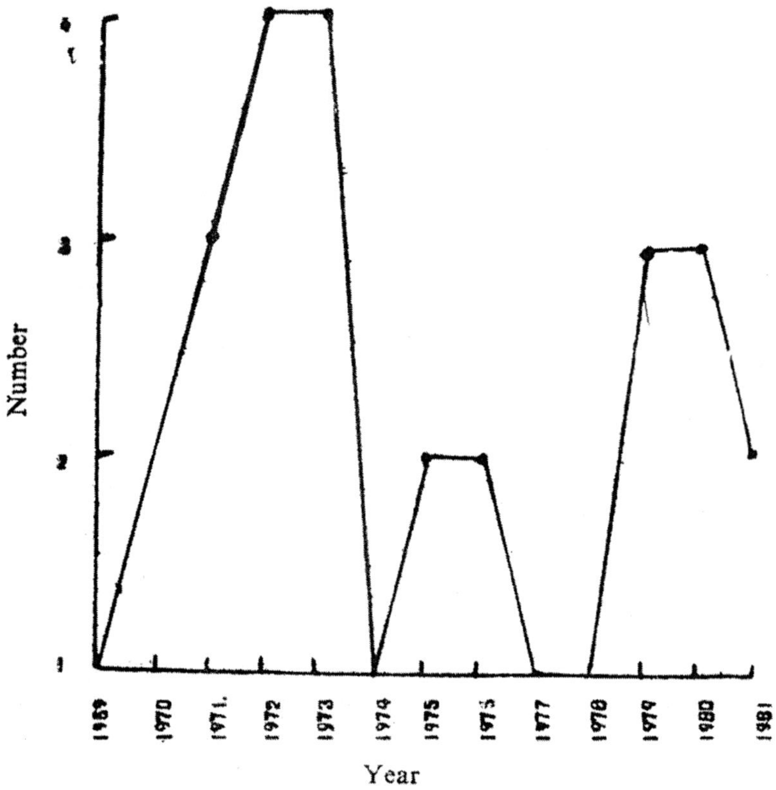

TABLE 3.4

Amitabh Bachchan's Films with Prominent Actresses

S. No.	*Actresses*	*Films*
1.	Jaya Bhaduri	Bansi Birju, Ek Nazar, Abhiman, Zanjeer, Mili, Sholay, Chupke-Chupke, Silsila
2.	Zeenat Aman	Dan, The Great Gambler, Lawaris, Dostana
3.	Rakhi	Kabhi-Kabhi, Muqaddar Ka Sikandar, Trishul, Kala Patthar, Barsat Ki Ek Raat, Jurmana, Bemisal, Anusandhan (Bangla)
4.	Hema Malini	Gehri Chaal, Kasauti, Naseeb, Satte Pe Satta
5.	Rekha	Do Anjane, Iman Dharam, Aalap, Khoon Paseena, Ganga Ki Saugandh, Muqaddar Ka Sikandar, Mr. Natwarlal, Suhag, Ram Balram, Silsila
6.	Neetu Singh	Adalat, Parvarish, The Great Gambler, Yarana
7.	Parveen Bobby	Majboor, Deewar, Amar-Akbar-Anthony, Do aur Do Panch, Kalia, Khuddar
8.	Mausami Chatterji	Be-nam, Manzil
9.	Sharmila Tagore	Farar, Besharm, Desh Premi
10.	Waheeda Rehman	Adalat, Kabhi-Kabhi
11.	Aruna Irani	Bombay to Goa, Sanjog
12.	Shahnaz	Saat Hindustani
13.	Mumtaz	Bandhe Haath
14.	Mala Sinha	Sanjog

Diagram 3.4 : Number of main films of Amitabh Bachchan with main heroines

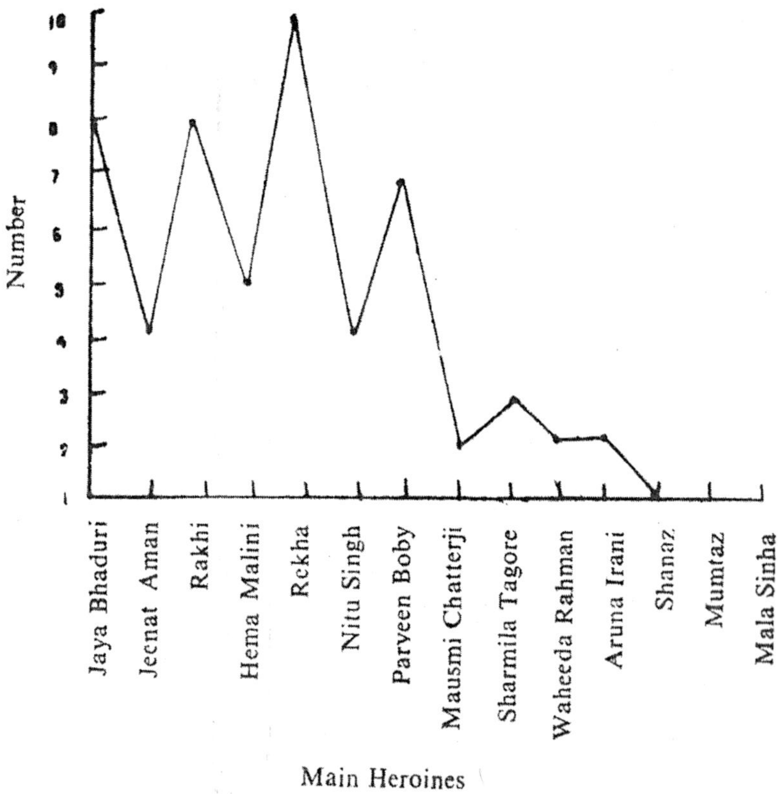

In recent times, Amitabh Bachchan played as hero in many films and with him Jaya Prada, Shridevi, Padmini Kolhapure and Rati Agnihotri have also worked as heroines or prominent actresses.

Directors of Amitabh Bachchan's Films

In his film life Amitabh Bachchan had worked as an actor and hero under the directorship of all important directors.

TABLE 3.5

Amitabh Bachchan's Films and Directors

S. No.	*Director*	*Films*
1.	Rishikesh Mukherji	Anand, Abhiman, Namak Haram, Chupke-Chupke, Mili, Alaap, Jurmana, Bemisal
2.	Yash Chopra	Deewar, Kabhi-Kabhi, Trishul, Kala Patthar, Silsila
3.	Prakash Mehra	Zanjeer, Hera Pheri, Muqaddar Ka Sikandar, Lawaris, Namak Halal
4.	Manmohan Desai	Amar Akbar Anthony, Parvarish, Suhag, Naseeb, Deshpremi
5.	Rakesh Kumar	Khoon Paseena, Mr. Natwarlal
6.	Shakti Samant	Do aur Do Panch, Yarana, The Great Gambler, Barsat Ki Ek Raat, Anusandhan (Bangla)
7.	Ravi Tandon	Khuddar
8.	Ramesh Sippi	Sholay, Shan
9.	Narendra Bedi	Benam, Adalat

(*Contd.*)

S. No.	Director	Films
10.	Khwaja Ahmad Abbas	Saat Hindustani
11.	Sunil Dutt	Reshma aur Shera
12.	Jyoti Swarup	Parwana
13.	Ravi Nagaich	Pyar ki Kahani
14.	S.S. Balan	Sanjog
15.	S. Ramanathan	Bombay to Goa
16.	B.R. Ishara	Ek Nazar
17.	Prakash Verma	Bansi Birju
18.	O.P. Goyal	Bandhe Haath
19.	Mukul Dutt	Raste Ka Patthar
20.	Shri Dhar	Gehri Chaal
21.	Arvind Sen	Kasauti
22.	Manoj Kumar	Roti Kapra aur Makan
23.	Shankar Mukherji	Farar
24.	Ravi Chopra	Zameer
25.	Dulal Guha	Do Anjane
26.	Desh Mukherji	Iman-Dharam
27.	Sultan Ahmad	Ganga Ki Saugandh
28.	Deven Verma	Besharm
29.	Chandra Barot	Don
30.	Ramesh Bahal	Kasme-Wade
31.	Basu Chatterji	Manzil
32.	Vijay Anand	Ram Balram
33.	Raj Khosla	Dostana
34.	Tinu Anand	Kalia
35.	Raj N. Sippi	Satte Pe Satta

Diagram 3.5 : Number of Films and names of directors who have directed more than one film of Amitabh Bachchan

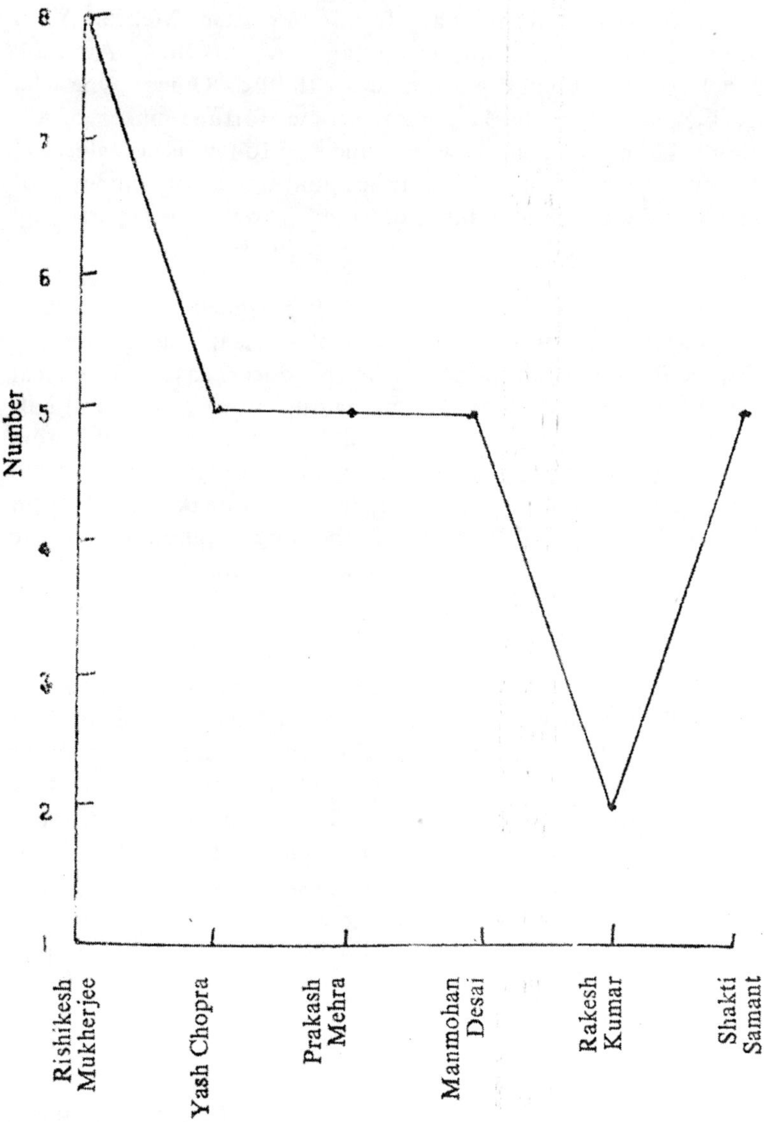

Any director feels pride to work with Amitabh Bachchan because his name is guarantee for success. In the film-world a successful actor used to be worshipped. Rupa Gupta writes in this respect: "Manmohan Desai, Prakash Mehra, Yash Chopra and Ramesh Sippi are his fan. At this time, Amitabh Bachchan is the biggest guarantee for the Box Office. One who was kicked till yesterday, has become fortune-maker of all, today. Here rising sun is worshipped. Money is greatest of all. When Amit has become a guarantee for money, all started to dance just on his pointing, however till yesterday he was called a tall boy, a ziraffe, or a horse.

Today, if anyone has a paper signed by Amitabh Bachchan, he can make a film without a paisa. The distributors can give him as much money as he (producer) says. The local cinema owners can advance money upto one or one and half lakh rupees for Amitabh Bachchan's film. The distributors have acquired money upto two lakh rupees in advance from the cinema owners for "Shaan", "Namak-Halal" and "Naseeb". Amitabh Bachchan is the biggest guarantee in the film world and he is most valuable appliance of the chess game."[5] Though some critics may say that this statement is an exaggeration, yet it has a lot of truth.

There are a lot of directors, to whom Amitabh Bachchan provided "stability" in their career through acting in their debut films. Film critic Ashok Chopra writes, "the famous actors do not like to act in their debut films. Dilip Kumar was hesitating for acting in the third film of Ravi Chopra named "Mazdoor", but Amitabh has acted in Ravi's debut film, "Zameer". Similarly when Desh Mukherji decided to become director, previously he was art-director, in his first film "Iman-Dharm", Amitabh Bachchan agreed for acting. Rakesh Kumar initiated his career in "Khoon-Paseena" with Amitabh Bachchan. "Don" was the first film of Chandra Barot

---

5. Rupa Gupta, *Rebellious actor Amitabh Bachchan* (Hindi), pp. 110-111.

and its hero was Amitabh Bachchan. When writer-actor Qadir Khan took a decision to be director, his film "Jahil" got Amitabh Bachchan as a hero."[6]

Amitabh Bachchan struggled hard in the earlier days of his film-career, hence he thinks to help a new director as his duty. He also believes that his films get popularity because of his name, it makes no difference whether the director is new or old one.

Social and Political Contribution

In most of the films Amitabh Bachchan played the role of an "angry young man." Hence he is described as "the symbol of youth aggressiveness."[7]

After independence, a significant change has been taken place in the social and political life of India. The expectations of the youth have increased. When these expectations do not get fulfilments, these turned into angerness. Amitabh Bachchan represents this angerness in Hindi films. However, most of the films of Amitabh Bachchan are professional, whose only purpose is entertainment, in which social and political message exists least. Thus Amitabh Bachchan did not get any occasion for contribution in social and political field. However his contribution as a member of parliament is quite obvious.

The contribution of Amitabh's professional entertaining films cannot be minimised as he made the Indian youth "modern." Though it is said that Amitabh's films are full of violence, yet our society is passing through such crises,

---

6. Ashok Chopra, *Story of Amitabh Bachchan through pictures* (Hindi), p. 32.
7. Kailash Chandra Sharma, "The Symbol of Youth Aggressiveness—Amitabh" (Hindi), *Daily Navjyoti*, Jaipur, Sunday Special, December 11, 1983.

that watching such films provides a layout to their violent sentiments. We cannot forget Amitabh's this social and political contribution.

2. Rajesh Khanna

Rajesh Khanna is an important film star of Hindi films. Before Amitabh Bachchan, he was supposed as "Super Star." Rajesh Khanna influenced the young generation through his romantic roles.

Films of Rajesh Khanna

Rajesh Khanna took his debut in Hindi films through "Aakhri Khat" produced by Chetan Anand. Since then he has played roles in many films. Once he was supposed "Super Star." But, like Amitabh, most of his films were entertaining not artistic.

Since 1980, Rajesh Khanna is working in films regularly. Since 1981 a score of Rajesh Khanna's films have been released. Well known of these are "Chamatkar", "Ham Donon", "Rajput", "Bain Haath Ka Khel", "Dharam Kanta", "Dard", "Dil-e-Nadan", "Fify-Fifty", "Gora", "Janwar", "Nishan", "Nasihat", "Wapsi", "Zamana", "Dushman Dost", "Dhanwan", "Qudrat", "Aaj Ka M.L.A. Ramavtar", "Avtar", "Sautan" etc.

Social-Political Contribution of Rajesh Khanna as a Film-Actor

Most of the Rajesh Khanna's films are entertaning, and he played romantic role in them. As an actor and hero he influenced deeply to the Indian youth generation. This impact is on every field of individual life of youngmen.

"Aaj Ka M.L.A. Ram Avtar" is one of the memorable political film of Rajesh Khanna. The viewers praised his role in the film. Rajesh Khanna presented a character of corrupt politician and how he gets success for "Power" has been resembled in this film. He is successful acting as a politician.

During 1966-1980 Rajesh Khanna acted in the films as mentioned below:[8]

TABLE 3.6

Description of Rajesh Khanna's Important Films during 1966-1980

S. No.	*Year*	*Film*	*Producer*	*Director*	*Music Director*	*Other Artists*
1	*2*	*3*	*4*	*5*	*6*	*7*
1.	1966	Aakhri Khat	Chetan Anand	Chetan Anand	Khayyam	Indrani Mukerji, Bunti
2.	1967	Aurat	S.S. Balan	S.S. Balan	Ravi	Padmini, Feroze Khan, Pran
3.	1967	Raj	J.P. Sippi	Ravindra Dube	Kalyanji Anandji	Babita, I.S. Johar, Rahul
4.	1967	Baharon ke Sapne	Nasir Hussain	Nasir Hussain	R.D. Burman	Asha Parekh, Prem Nath, Madanpuri
5.	1969	Bandhan	J.P. Sippi	Narendra Bedi	Kalyanji Anandji	Mumtaz, Aruna, Jeevan

8. *Film Mirror*, English Monthly, May 1981, pp. 43-45.

(*Contd.*)

1	2	3	4	5	6	7
6.	1969	Do Raste	Raj Khosla	Raj Khosla	Laxmikant Pyare Lal	Mumtaz, Prem Chopra, Bindu
7.	1969	Doli	Hargobind	A. Subbarao	Ravi	Babita, Prem Chopra, Nazima
8.	1969	Ittafaq	B.R. Chopra	Yash Chopra	Salil Chaudhry	Nanda, Bindu, Madanpuri
9.	1969	Aaradhna	Shakti Samant	Shakti Samant	S.D. Burman	Sharmila, Farida, Sujit Kumar
10.	1969	Khamoshi	Hemant Kumar	Asit Sen	Hemant Kumar	Waheeda, Snehlata, Lalita
11.	1970	Aan Milo Sajna	Jagdish Kumar	Mukul Dutt	Laxmikant Pyarelal	Aasha Parekh, Vinod Khanna, Aruna
12.	1970	Aanand	Rupam Chitra	Rishikesh Mukerji	Salil Chaudhry	Amitabh, Sunita Sanyal, Ramesh Dev
13.	1970	Kati Patang	Shakti Samant	Shakti Samant	R.D. Burman	Aasha Parekh, Prem Chopra, Bindu
14.	1970	Sachcha Jhuta	Doki Desai	Manmohan Desai	Kalyanji Anandji	Mumtaz, Vinod, Farial

15.	1970	Safar	Musheer Riaz	Asit Sen	Kalyanji Anandji	Sharmila, Ferozekhan
16.	1970	The Train	Ramesh Bahal	Ravi Nagaich	R.D. Burman	Nanda, Helen, Aruna, Madanpuri
17.	1971	Amar Prem	Shakti Samant	Shakti Samant	R.D. Burman	Sharmila, Vinod Mehra, Farida
18.	1971	Choti Bahu	Daris Gotia	K.B. Tilak	Kalyanji Anandji	Sharmila, Shashikala, I.S. Johar
19.	1971	Dushman	Premji	Dulal Guha	Laxmikant Pyarelal	Mumtaz, Meena Kumari, Rehman
20.	1971	Hathi Mere Saathi	Dewar	M.A. Thirumugam	Laxmikant Pyarelal	Tanuja, Sujeet, K.N. Singh
21.	1971	Mahboob Ki Mehndi	H.S. Rewal	H.S. Rewal	Laxmikant Pyarelal	Leena, Pradeep Kumar, Manorama, Sunder
22.	1971	Maryada	Arvind Sen	Arvind Sen	Kalyanji Anandji	Mala Sinha, Raj Kumar, Pran
23.	1972	Apna Desh	Olympic Pictures	Jambu	R.D. Burman	Mumtaz, Madanpuri, Om Prakash

(*Contd.*)

1	2	3	4	5	6	7
24.	1972	Dil Daulat Duniya	P.N. Arora	P.N. Arora	Shankar Jaikishan	Ashok, Sadhna, Helen, Agha
25.	1972	Bawarchi	Rupam Chitra	Rishikesh Mukherji	Madan Mohan	Jaya Bhaduri, Durga Khote, Asrani
26.	1972	Joru Ka Ghulam	United For	A. Bhim Singh	Kalyanji Anandji	Nanda, Sharad Kumar, Manisha, Ramesh Dev
27.	1972	Mere Jeevan Saathi	Shilpkar	Ravi Nagaich	R.D. Burman	Tanuja, Bindu, Helen. Utpal Dutt
28.	1972	Shahzada	Surendra Kapoor	K. Shankar	R.D. Burman	Raakhi, Madanpuri, Karan Diwan
29.	1972	Maalik	Wash Menon	A. Bhim Singh	Kalyanji Anandji	Sharmila, Devan Verma, Sonia
30.	1973	Aavishkar	Basu Bhatta-charyaji	Basu Bhatta-charyaji	Kanurai	Sharmila Tagore, Meena, Satyan Kappu
31.	1973	Namak Haram	Waglai Pandya	Kesh Mukherji	R.D. Burman	Amitabh, Rekha, Simmi, Asrani

32.	973	Dagh	Yash Chopra	Yash Chopra	Laxmikant Pyarelal	Sharmila, Rakhi, Padma Khanna
33.	1973	Rajarani	Jagdish Kumar	Sachin Bhaumik	R.D. Burman	Sharmila, Raj Mehra, Iftikhar
34.	1974	Aap Ki Kasam	J. Om Prakash	J. Om Prakash	R.D. Burman	Mumtaz, Sanjeev, Asrani
35.	1974	Ajnabi	Girija Samant	Shakti Samant	R.D. Burman	Zeenat, Yogita Bali, Prem Chopra
36.	1974	Hamshakal	Olympic Pictures	Jamboo	R.D. Burman	Tanuja, Mausami, Asrani, Aruna
37.	1974	Prem Nagar	U.D. Ramanaidu	K. Prakash Rao	S.D. Burman	Hema, Ashok, Prem Chopra, Asrani
38.	1974	Roti	Rajni Desai	Manmohan Desai	Laxmikant Pyarelal	Mumtaz, Nripurai, Jagdeep
39.	1975	Prem Kahani	Raj Khosla	Raj Khosla	Laxmikant Pyarelal	Mumtaz, Shashi Kapoor, Vinod Khanna
40.	1976	Mahachor	Narendra Bedi	Narendra Bedi	R.D. Burman	Neetu, Prem Chopra, Aruna Irani

(*Contd.*)

1	2	3	4	5	6	7
41.	1976	Mehbooba	Musheer Riaz	Shakti Samant	R.D. Burman	Hema Malini, Prem Chopra, Asrani
42.	1977	Aashiq Hoon Baharon Ka	Talwar Bathija	J. Om Prakash	Laxmikant Pyarelal	Zeenat, Danny, Asrani, Rehman
43.	1977	Anurodh	Girija Samant	Shakti Samant	Laxmikant Pyarelal	Ashok, Simple, Asrani
44.	1977	Chalta Purza	Bhappi Soni	Bhappi Soni	R.D. Burman	Parveen Bobby, Ajeet
45.	1977	Karam	B.R. Chopra	B.R. Chopra	R.D. Burman	Vidya, Asrani
46.	1977	Chhela Babu	Shomu Mukherji	Jai Mukherji	Laxmikant Pyarelal	Zeenat, Padma Khanna, Asrani
47.	1977	Palkon Ki Chaon Mein	Nav Sampati Production	Mairaj	Laxmikant Pyarelal	Hema, Amjad, Farida, Asrani
48.	1977	Bandal Baj	H.A. Nadiawala	Shammi Kapoor	R.D. Burman	Sulakshna, Shammi Kapoor, Ranjeet
49.	1978	Bhola-Bhala	B. Gopal Krishna	Sat Pal	R.D. Burman	Rekha, Mausami, Jogindar, Deven Verma

50.	1978	Prem Bandhan	R.R. Nanda	Ramanand Sagar	Laxmikant Pyarelal	Rekha, Joginder, Vikram, Prem Narayan
51.	1978	Naukari	R.K. Production	Rishikesh Mukherji	R.D. Burman	Raj Kapoor, Zahira, Nadira
52.	1979	Amar Deep	K. Balaji	Vijayan Krishna-murti	Laxmikant Pyarelal	Shabana, Bindu, Vinod Mehra
53.	1979	Chakravyuh	Yosuf Hasan	Bamu Chatterji	Laxmikant Pyarelal	Neetu Singh, Simple, Vinod Mehra
54.	1980	Janata Hawaldar	Chhabria Jai Singh	Mehmood	Rajesh Roshan	Ashok, Hema, Yogita
55.	1980	Red Rose	M.P. Jain Ravi Kumar	Bharti Raja	R.D. Burman	Poonam, Satyan, Kappu
56.	1980	Thori See Bewafai	Konark Combine	Ismail Sarraf	Khayyam	Shabana, Padmini Kolha Pure, Sushant Rai
57.	1980	Phir Wohi Raat	M.N. Sippi	Danny	R.D. Burman	Kimi, Danny, Shashikala, Tamanna
58.	1980	Bandish	D. Ramanaidu	K. Bapayya	Laxmikant Pyarelal	Hema, Danny, Asrani
59.	1980	Aanchal	Guha Chatterji	Anil Ganguli	R.D. Burman	Rakhi, Rekha, Amol, Prem Chopra

Diagram 3.6 : Number of main films of Rajesh Khanna during 1966-80 in each year

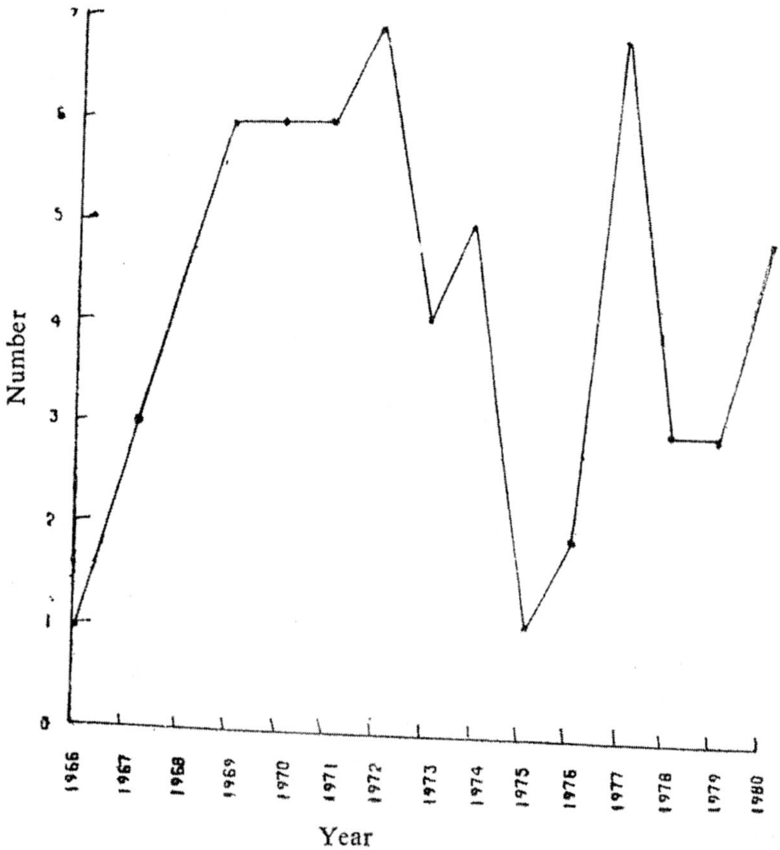

Due to impact of this film the sale of Khadi decreased. As per one news, hundreds of people who used to wear Khadi, left it because in their travel via Lucknow-Kanpur, they were called as "Ramavtar" by fellow travellers. They could not bear it. In other areas, such incidents also took place.

In many films of Rajesh Khanna, social problems have been dealt. He attracted the attention of people through his acting in such films.[9]

3. Raj Kapoor

The Kapoor family has a prominent place in the history of modern Hindi cinema. Raj Kapoor's father late Prithiviraj Kapoor was a well known actor of Hindi cinema. He was active in films for forty years.[10] For his contribution in the film industry and art Prithiviraj Kapoor was nominated as the member of Rajya Sabha.

Whole of the Raj Kapoor family has been active in the films. Both of his brothers Shammi Kapoor and Shashi Kapoor and three sons Randheer Kapoor, Rishi Kapoor and Rajiv Kapoor are also active in films. Not only this, two daughter in laws of Raj Kapoor Babita and Nitu Singh are also famous artists of Hindi cinema.[11] One of the film critics said rightly that Kapoor family is "Filmdom's First Family."[12]

Raj Kapoor was awarded "Dada Saheb Phalke Award" for 1987. His father, Prithiviraj Kapoor was also rewarded

---

9. *Punjab Kesari*, Hindi Daily, New Delhi, City Edition, April 5, 1984, p. 1.
10. Rama Shankar, "Chanchal", "Leader of acting—Prithivi Raj Kapoor", *Amar Ujala*, Hindi Daily, December 30, 1983.
11. Shakuni, "Family occupation on films", *Amar Ujala*, Feb. 8, 1984.
12. Sunil Sethi, "The Kapoor's Filmdom's First Family, *India Today*, New Delhi, 15th August 1982, p. 120.

by this award. Thus Raj Kapoor proved that he was a brilliant son of a brilliant father. Raj Kapoor breathed his last in New Delhi just after some days of receiving this reward.

Diagram 3.7: Raj Kapoor's Family Map

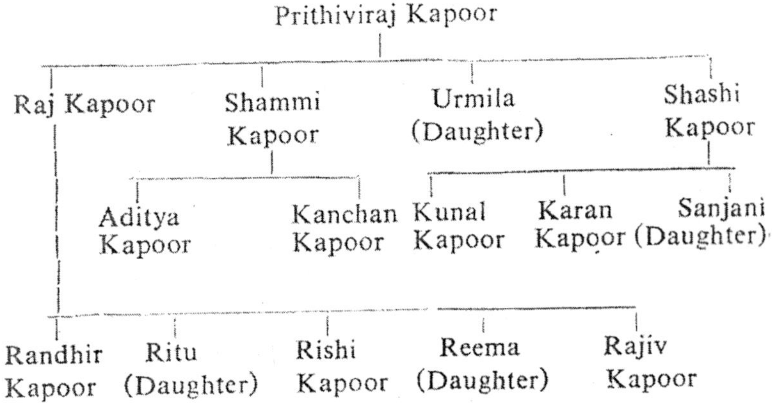

Raj Kapoor's Films

Raj Kapoor was a well known actor, producer and director of Hindi cinema. Thus there is an interesting study aspects in his produced, directed and acted films. Raj Kapoor proved his expertness in all aspects of cinema arts. As an able director, he looked upon minutely to his films, is notable. Here it is a fact, like the unwritten constitution of Britain, the script of his films also used to be unwritten. During the production of his films, all scenes used to be in his mind, not on the paper. Due to it, we find "multiplity full of unity" among his directed films. As a matter of fact, his films have become immortal, and we will remember his name for ever.

TABLE 3.7

Well-known Films of Raj Kapoor

S. No.	*Year*	*Film*	*Heroine*	*Director*	*Report*
1	*2*	*3*	*4*	*5*	*6*
1.	1943	Hamari Baat	Devika Rani	—	Flop
2.	1946	Balmik	Shanta Apte	Bhalaji Pithaskar	100 days or more
3.	1946	Neel Kamal	Madhu Bala	Kedar Sharma	Silver Jubilee
4.	1946	Chittor Vijay	Madhu Bala	Mohan Sinha	100 days or more
5.	1946	Dil Ki Rani	Madhu Bala	Mohan Sinha	100 days or more
6.	1946	Jail Yatra	Kamini Kaushal	Gajanan Jagirdar	100 days or more
7.	1948	Aag	Nargis	Raj Kapoor	100 days or more
8.	1948	Amar Prem	Madhu Bala	N.M. Kelkar	100 days or more
9.	1948	Gopi Nath	Tripti Mitra	Mahesh Kaul	100 days or more

(Contd.)

1	*2*	*3*	*4*	*5*	*6*
10.	1949	Andaz	Nargis	Mehboob	Golden Jubilee
11.	1949	Barsat	Nargis	Raj Kapoor	Diamond Jubilee
12.	1949	Sunhre Din	Rehana	Satish Nigam	100 days or more
13.	1950	Bhanwra	Nimmi	G. Rakesh	Flop
14.	1950	Bawre Nain	Geeta Bali	K.N. Sharma	100 days or more
15.	1950	Dastan	Suryya	A.R. Kardar	Silver Jubilee
16.	1950	Jan Pehchan	Nargis	Ali Mistri	Flop
17.	1950	Pyar	Nargis	B.M. Bayas	Flop
18.	1950	Sargam	Rehana	P.L. Santoshi	Silver Jubilee
19.	1951	Awara	Nargis	Raj Kapoor	Golden Jubilee
20.	1952	Ambar	Nargis	Jayant Desai	Silver Jubilee
21.	1952	Anhoni	Nargis	K.A. Abbas	Flop
22.	1952	Ashiana	Nargis	B. Trilochan	100 days or more
23.	1952	Bewafa	Nargis	M.L. Anand	100 days or more
24.	1953	Aah	Nargis	Raja Nawabe	100 days or more

25.	1953	Dhun	Nargis	Kumar	Flop
26.	1953	Papi	Nargis	Chandulal Shah	Flop
27.	1954	Boot Polish	Nargis	Prakash Arora	Silver Jubilee
28.	1955	Shri Charsobees	Nargis	Raj Kapoor	Silver Jubilee
29.	1956	Chori-Chori	Nargis	Anant Thakur	Silver Jubilee
30.	1956	Jagte Raho	Nargis	Som Mitra & Amit Mitra	100 days or more
31.	1957	Sharda	Meena Kumari	L.V. Prasad	Silver Jubilee
32.	1958	Parvarish	Mala Sinha	S. Banerji	100 days or more
33.	1958	Phir-Subah	Mala Sinha	Ramesh Sehgal	Flop
34.	1959	Anari	Nutan	Rishikesh Mukerji	Silver Jubilee
35.	1959	Char Din Char Rahen	Meena Kumari	K.A. Abbas	Flop
36.	1959	Do Ustad	Madhu Bala	Tara Harish	100 days or more
37.	1959	Kanahyya	Nutan	Om Prakash	100 days or more
38.	1959	Main Nashe Mei Hoon	Mala Sinha	Naresh Sehgal	100 days or more

(*Contd.*)

1	2	3	4	5	6
39.	1960	Chalia	Nutan	Manmohan Desai	100 days or more
40.	1960	Jis Desh Mein Ganga Bahti Hai	Padmini	Radhu Karmarkar	Silver Jubilee
41.	1960	Shriman Satyavadi	Padmini	Radhu Karmarkar	Silver Jubilee
42.	1961	Nazrana	Vijyanti Mala	Radhu Karmarkar	Silver Jubilee
43.	1962	Aashiq	Padmini	Rishikesh Mukherji	100 days or more
44.	1963	Dil Hi to Hai	Nutan	P.A. Santoshi & C.L. Rawal	100 days or more
45.	1963	Ek Dil So Afsane	Waheeda Rehman	R.C. Talwar	100 days or more
46.	1964	Dulha Dulhan	Sadhna	Ravindra Dube	100 days or more
47.	1964	Sangam	Vijyanti Mala	Raj Kapoor	100 days or more
48.	1966	Tisri Kasam	Waheeda Rehman	Vasu Bhattacharya	Flop
49.	1967	Around The World	Raj Shree	Pachchi	100 days or more
50.	1967	Diwana	Saira Bano	Mahesh Kaul	100 days or more
51.	1968	Sapno Ka Sodagar	Hema Malini	Mahesh Kaul	100 days or more
52.	1970	Mera Naam Joker	Simmi, Chan-Rabinkina, Padmini	Raj Kapoor	Flop

53.	1972	Kal Aaj Aur Kal	Babita	Randheer Kapoor	Flop
54.	1973	Bobby	Dimple Kapadia	Raj Kapoor	Golden Jubilee
55.	1975	Dharam-Karam	Rekha	Randheer Kapoor	100 days or more
56.	1978	Satyam Shivam Sundram	Zeenat Aman	Raj Kapoor	Silver Jubilee
57.	1982	Prem Rog	Padmini Kolhapure	Raj Kapoor	Golden Jubilee
58.	1985	Ram Teri Ganga Meli	Mandakini	Raj Kapoor	Golden Jubilee

Diagram 3.8 : Main twelve film Heroines of Raj Kapoor and his successful films with them

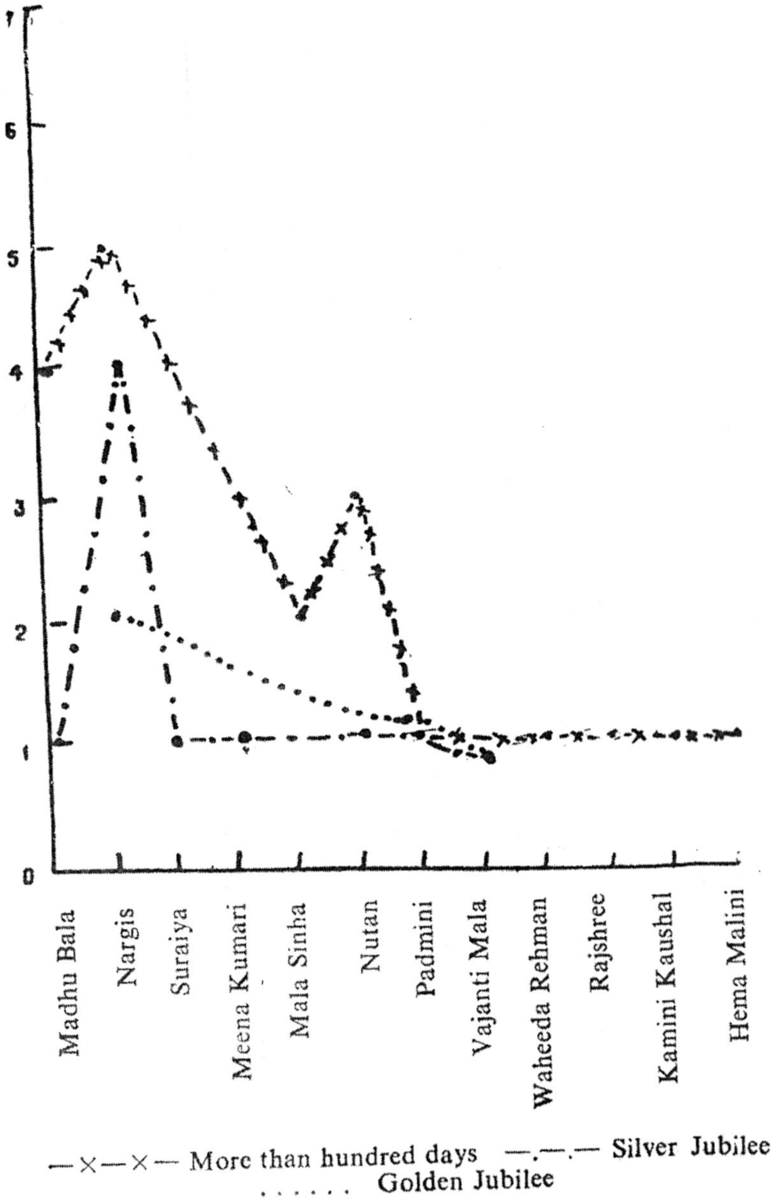

In the above mentioned table there are films like "Bobby", "Dharam-Karam", "Satyam-Shivam-Sundram", "Prem Rog", and "Ram Teri Ganga Meli", in which Raj Kapoor himself did not act.

Among the above described films, the films in which **Raj Kapoor acted with Nargis, were particularly a subject** of discussion. There was a time when Raj Kapoor-Nargis match was the most popular pair of Hindi films. Raj Kapoor also established R.K. Studio, Bombay and founded "R.K. Films" as a film production company.

Social and Political Contribution of Raj Kapoor as a Cinema Actor and Film Producer

Raj Kapoor was a successful producer director. In this respect, one author has written, "Raj Kapoor is a successful tonic director, his critics cannot refuse about it. He has acquired credit in an industry where box-office success is sole criteria. It is not easy to break the failed image of initial period. Raj Kapoor is not an exception. Raj Kapoor moved ahead with image. Sometimes, this quality is considered as his particularity. It is useful to have an image in the cinema. The characteristics of Raj Kapoor are searched among the films produced under the banner of R.K."[13] As a matter of fact the image of Raj Kapoor influenced the social life of people seriously. **Raj Kapoor was full of confidence. When** he initiated the production of "Aag", he did not possess any finance.[14] Yet he made his place due to his confidence. Raj

---

13. Madhur Chaturvedi, "Imprisoned in Success: Raj Kapoor" (Hindi), *Navbharat Times*, Hindi Daily, New Delhi, Nov. 30, 1985, p. 5.
14. In this respect Raj Kapoor said, "When I started my first movie "Aag" it was without any money at all. But **I had a proper "muhurat" with a proper first shot and all the paraphernalia of starting a movie.** I remember my mother saying to my father, in a sarcastic Punjabi phrase, that you cannot fry 'Pakoras' in spit, meaning that I would never be able to make the film without any resources. He just turned around to her and said, "you

Kapoor raised a lot of social problems. In "Prem-Rog" he presented the problems of widows. "Boot-Polish", however, an art film, was also successful at Box-Offices. Through this film, Raj Kapoor tried to implement the dream of late Pt. Jawahar Lal Nehru, who said "today's children are tomorrow's leaders."[15] They must not beg. In this children film, though Raj Kapoor did not act, yet in a scene he is shown passing in a train and children cried out, "Raj Kapoor is going."

Raj Kapoor worked in foreign countries like an unofficial ambassador of India. It is his important political contribution. The foreign people looked upon him with great respect. In Soviet Union he was considered most popular Indian after Pt. Jawahar Lal Nehru.

Many social problems got good representation in Raj Kapoor's films. He was awarded "Padam Bhushan" in 1972 because of a conscious film maker.[16] It is the significance of Raj Kapoor's art that he fills social objectives in the entertaining films. Raj Kapoor had acquired too much influence among the political circles too, due to it film censor board alway took a liberal view of his films. In this respect, one film critic has written about his influence, "The truth is that whole of the film industry is zealous of Raj Kapoor. It is not because he is a good director and a successful film producer. It is also not because he is very successful professionally, the reason of their zealousy is to think that the Censor Board takes a partial view on his films. The Board becomes too much

---

wait and watch. The boy will make the film. He has the confidence and the conviction." I could not forget those words, and have not, because that is all you need in this business. But the point is that he believed in each one of us." Sunil Sethi, Ibid article, p. 124.

15. Mahavir Singh Chauhan, *Great Showman—Raj Kapoor*, Star Pocket Books, New Delhi, 1983, pp. 20-21.
16. Pradeep Sardhana, "Ups and downs of Raj Kapoor's long journey" (Hindi), *Navbharat Times*, Hindi Daily, Feb. 25, 1984, p. 5.

liberal examining his films, consequently Raj Kapoor can show what he wishes, how he wishes in his films. There used to be no objection and no censor scissors run against it.

The truth is that the personality of Raj Kapoor is so influential that Censor Board's scissors stop itself. The member of his panel, hardly consists of anyone who have not seen his films, who does not know his popularity or who would not have been influenced by his previous films. When the people examine bis films, they feel what should be examined? The person has more knowledge about the subject who created the creature. This is that complex, which imprisons the examiners."[17]

In fact, Raj Kapoor have acquired that position in the social and political life of India, that most of the people have become his fans.

4. Other Important Hindi Cinema Actors

The list of Hindi film actors is too much lengthy. But out of these actors, there are few actors, whose acting art was full of different aspects and who influenced the people's consciousness deeply.

An analytical study of different Hindi's modern film actors and their social-political contribution is following.

Devanand

Devanand used to be considered as "ever blossom hero" of Hindi cinema. With the release of "Ham Naujawan", Devanand has completed one hundred films as an actor.[18] It is the hundredth film in which he played a role.

Devanand was born on September 26, 1923 in the Gurdaspur district of Punjab.[19] His full name is Dharam Dev

---

17. B. Sushila, "Censor Board and Raj Kapoor films" (Hindi), *Saptahik Hindustan* (Weekly Hindi); New Delhi, December 22-28, 1985, p. 11.
18. Subhash Shirdonkar, "Devanand : A Century of Acting" (Hindi), *Punjab Kesari*, Ibid, April 5, 1986.
19. Ibid, p. 1.

Anand. His wife Kalpna Kartik was a well known heroine in old days. Kalpna Kartik and Devanand worked together in "Baazi", "Aandhiyan", "Ham Safar", "Taxi Driver", "Makan No. 44", and "Nau Do Giyarah" etc.

Devanand's Films

The first film of Devanand was "Ham Ek Hain" and it released in 1946.[20] Devanand has had to work hard for entering in the films. About it, Shri Subhash Shirdonkar writes, "Just some years before the independence of the country, Dev Saheb arrived Bombay. His elder brother, Mr. Chetan Anand had been busy in films, hence it was but natural to work in the films, in the heart of Devanand. But Chetan Anand never provided any chance for him. In spite of it, he used to say that Devanand would never become successful in the films, however, Dev Anand kept his struggle continue for entering in the films. He used to pass his evening in a restaurant where many such struggling heroes used to visit. On one such evening, he met producer P.L. Santoshi. For "Ham Ek Hain" P.L. Santoshi was in search of a new hero. Devanand was selected for five years for five hundred rupees per month as contract. The heroine, with Devanand, in this film was Kamla Kotnis. This film was released in December 1946.[21]

After "Ham Ek Hain", Devanand appeared in "Ziddi" and "Vidya" released in 1947. Soon after "Jeet", Shayad", "Afsar", "Do Sitare" and films like "Sanam" were appeared and Devanand established firmly in cinema industry. As a producer, in 1950, his first film "Afsar" was released. About eighteen years ago he directed "Prem Pujari". Though he had not done notable service as director, yet, some of his films proved super hit.

In his forty years career of film acting, he worked in 28 films. His acting in "Guide" is immemorable.

---

20. Madhur Chaturvedi, "Devanand—step up only ahead", *Navbharat Times*, Dec. 14, 1985, p. 7.
21. Subhash Shirdonkar, Ibid, p. 1.

TABLE 3.8

Main Films of Devanand

S.No.	*Year*	*Film*
1.	1946	Ham Ek Hain
2.	1951	Bazi
3.	1956	Fantoosh
4.	1960	Ham Donon
5.	1966	Guide
6.	1972	Hare Rama Hare Krishna
7.	1974	Heera Panna
8.	1975	Ishq-Ishq-Ishq
9.	1978	Desh-Pardesh
10.	1980	Lootmar
11.	1983	Swami Dada
12.	1984	Anand aur Anand
13.	1986	Ham Naujawan

Social and Political Contribution of Devanand as a Film Actor

Majority of Devanand's films was entertainment providing. However, he did not influence people through his films, for solving social problems, yet his romantic image modified the consciousness of viewers. In this respect, one author said that Devanand is one of the fantastic personality of film industry. For forty years he is working in the cinema world. As a producer-director and actor, Devanand's courage, work and dedication is up to date even today. Devanand has crossed sixty-six years of his life, but in spite of it he has extraordinary activitities. Devanand is one of the Hindi stars who have passed a long journey of success. He kept himself on the climax of popularity for forty years. His popularity never diminished due to the smoke of time.[22]

Devanand got many awards for his films. Devanand also activised himself politically. In 1977, he campaigned independently for Janata Party. In 1980, when film stars established a political party called "national party", he was one of his founder member. He contributed so much in the political field because of his respect gained in the films.

There are no two opinions that there is no alternative for Devanand. It may be happened that viewers might have not looked upon his films enthusiastically, however, his youthfulness, his speedy actions, dedication and courage are praise worthy.

Late Sanjeev Kumar

In the history of Hindi films, late Sanjeev Kumar's name shall be immortal He is known as "Indian Marlyn Brando."[23] For a long period, he remained one of the popular hero of Hindi films. Unfortunately, at an early age of forty-seven years, he breathed his last on November 6, 1985.[24] But his films shall be remembered for ever for his top acting performance.

Films of Sanjeev Kumar

Sanjeev Kumar worked in stage dramas before films. He had had to struggle fast for entering into films. Initially, he got stunt films but soon he has become one of the popular actor of social films. He took his debut into the films in 1964 with "Ham Hindustani."[25] Sanjeev Kumar performed nine different

22. Ibid.
23. Rajpal Raje, *Navbharat Times*, Ibid, Dec. 7, 1985, p. 5.
24. Sarosh Modi, "The Sanjeev Kumar I knew". *Screen*, English Weekly, Bombay, December 6, 1985, p 8.
25. Rajpal Raje, Ibid, p. 5.

character roles in "Naya Din Nai Raat".[26] The well known artist worked one after another in many memorable films.

It so happens in Hindi film industry that one actor artist used to become "typed". Sanjeev Kumar broke up this tradition and he appeared in different character roles in "Anokhi Raat", "Ashirvad", "Gauri", "Raja aur Rank". He slowed his artistic talents everywhere. He was co-hero in "Shikar" with Dharamendra and won Filmfare award. In the same year i.e. in 1968, Sanjeev Kumar surpassed Dilip Kumar and Balraj Sahni in "Sangharsh". For this role he became famous overnight. In a short role in "Sangharsh", sitting on the chessboard, with his satiric laugh, defeats Dilip Kumar. Similarly in the film titled "Dharti Kahe Pukar ke", in spite of short role, the viewers used to weep in the last scene. The characteristic of Sanjeev Kumar's art was that either the role was lengthy or short, he used to be felt extremely present. "Chanda Aur Bijli", "Gustakhi Maaf", "Insaf Ka Mandir", "Jyoti", "Sachchai" and "Satya Kam" were such films that in spite of secondary role his presence was felt by the viewers.

---

26. Faujia Khasai Shiraji writes about the role of Sanjiv Kumar in 'Naya Din Nai Raat' :
"The most fantastic, the most superb thing to happen to Sanjeev, the actor, the creative artist, was a film titled 'Naya Din Nai Raat". In this film he dared to play nine different roles, each a different character with a different temperament, habit and style. This is by far the greatest achievement any actor could have dreamt of. This film was introduced by another film actor Dilip Kumar, who showered genuine praise on his fellow actor Sanjeev. I do not think any actor in India or abroad can claim such as achievement which is unsurpassed in the history of films. We still remember the leper in the film as we do the dramatist who has a feminine voice and manners and who repeats the words "Lucha Kahin Ka" every now and again with the charm he alone could have lent to it." F.K. Shiraji, *Screen*, Weekly, November 29, 1985, p. 12.

TABLE 3.9

Main Films of Sanjeev Kumar

S No.	*Film*
1.	Dastak
2.	Khilona
3.	Kaushish
4.	Parichaya
5.	Aandhi
6.	Mausam
7.	Namkeen
8.	Angoor
9.	Anhoni
10.	Manchali
11.	Vishwasghat
12.	Mukti
13.	Papi
14.	Shatranj ke Khilari
15.	Chehra Pe Chehra
16.	Sholay
17.	Trishul
18.	Silsila
19.	Naukar
20.	Yehi Hai Zindigi
21.	Arjun Pandit
22.	Zindigi
23.	Iman-Dharam
24.	Be-Reham

While Sanjeev Kumar also played a score of roles in second grade films, however, his acting talent remained high up. He believed that for an artist his artistic talent and hard work are important rather than the lower or higher standard of the film.

Social and Political Contribution of Sanjeev Kumar as an Film Actor

Sanjeev Kumar got opportunities in acting many films whose stories were based on social problems.

In our society, the life of physically handicapped people is highly neglective. In a film titled "Kaukish", Sanjeev Kumar played the role of a dumb and deaf person. In this film, through his higher acting, he showed how a deaf and dumb person can make his position in the society on marching the road of progress. In an another film "Khilona", he played the role of "a mad young man". He acted extremely artisticly how a mad man used to feel, express, think, talk, walk, sing and love.

His political contribution as an actor was expressed in the two films titled as "Aandhi" and "Shatranj Ke Khilari". These two films helped him in reaching on the climax level of acting. "Aandhi" was directed by Gulzar. In this film, Sanjeev Kumar played the role of a husband, whose wife used to be busy in political activities. Due to busy life of the wife, in this film, he separated from his wife, but whenever he met her, met in an another way.[27] A lot of debate took place on this film. Some critics viewed that conversion of the story of this film into political was absolutely wrong. The second political film was "Shatranj Ke Khilari". In this film the script described how one state after another state was occupied under the British control. In the same process "Avadh" was also occupied by the British. The acting of Sanjeev Kumar under Satyajeet Ray's direction was extremely appreciable.

Sanjeev Kumar acted in many social fims. For his role in "Dastak" he was awarded by the "National Film Prize" for best acting. Again, for his work in "Kaushish", he was awarded by the same prize for his best acting.

---

27. Rajpal Raje, Ibid, article, p. 5.

Dara Singh

Dara Singh is one of the actor of Hindi films, who is also a wrestler. So far he had worked in more than one hundred films.

Films of Dara Singh

Born on November 19, 1928 at 'Dharam Chak' village of Amritsar district, the first film titled as "Dara Singh" was released in 1962.[28] Though Dara Singh did not get such success that may make him 'Star', yet he is regularly working in the films. He had done acting job in more than one hundred films.[29]

TABLE 3.10

A Hundred Films of Dara Singh

S.No.	*Film*
1	*2*
1.	King Kong
2.	Rustam-e-Baghdad
3.	Ek Tha Ali Baba
4.	Faulad
5.	Awara Abdullah
6.	Samson
7.	Dara Singh
8.	Rustam-e-Rome
9.	Badshah
10.	Aandhi Aur Toofan

28. Ali Peter Jan, "So Strong and Yet So Soft: Seven Hundred Fights, Twenty Five Years; A Hundred Films and Still Going Strong", *Screen*, Weekly, July 7, 1985, p. 12.

29. Ibid.

1	*2*
11.	Aaya Toofan
12.	Herculas
13.	Jagga
14.	Veer Bhimsen
15.	Sangram
16.	Sher Dil
17.	Boxer
18.	Ham Sab Ustad Hain
19.	Mahabharat
20.	Raka
21.	Khakan
22.	Lutera
23.	Sat Sumandar Paar
24.	Torzan
25.	Rustam-e-Hind
26.	Insaaf
27.	Sikandar-e-Azam
28.	Jawan Mard
29.	Thakur Jarnail Singh
30.	Khoon Ka Khoon
31.	Dada
32.	Daku Mangal Singh
33.	Naujawan
34.	Shankar Khan
35.	Sardar
36.	Naseehat
37.	Do Dushman
38.	Watan Se Door
39.	Jang Aur Aman

(*Contd.*)

1	2
40.	Balram Shri Krishna
41.	Sangdil
42.	Darun Ka Ghulam
43.	Dulabhati
44.	Chalbaaz
45.	Thief of Baghdad
46.	Toofan
47.	Killers
48.	Jalsaaz
49.	Danka
50.	Bekasoor
51.	Apna Khoon
52.	Apna Dushman
53.	Ham Ek Hain
54.	Choron Ka Chor
55.	Gunahon Ke Raste
56.	Ilzam
57.	Nanak Dukhya Sab Sansar
58.	Sher-e-Watan
59.	Tulsi Vivah
60.	Daku Man Singh
61.	Ramu Ustad
62.	Lalkar
63.	Sultana Daku
64.	Male Mitre De
65.	Criminals
66.	Mera Shikar
67.	Mera Desh Mera Dharam
68.	Phir Aaya Toofan
69.	Har Har Mahadev
70.	Dhana Jat

1	2
71.	Kisan aur Bhagwan
72.	Warrant
73.	Dharmatma
74.	Zehreela Insan
75.	Dharam Karam
76.	Rakhi Aur Rifle
77.	Bajrang Bali
78.	Ali Baba
79.	Sava Lakh Se Ek Laraun
80.	Ram Bharose
81.	Veeru Ustad
82.	Dhyanu Bhagat
83.	Bhakti Mein Shakti
84.	Sone Ka Dil Lohe Ke Haath
85.	Nalayaq
86.	Chambal Ki Rani
87.	Van Manush
88.	Shiv Shakti
89.	Lamberdarni
90.	Khel Muqaddar Ka
91.	Guru Suleman Chela Pahlwan
92.	Main Intaqam Loonga
93.	Rustam
94.	Bhulekha
95.	Aan aur Shaan
96.	Maya Bazar
97.	Veer Bhimsen
98.	Mera Naam Joker
99.	Vala Namori
100.	Mard

In the above mentioned films Dara Singh played different roles. In many films he played the role of a "wrestler". He was successful as film producer-director, though his films did not prove superhit yet these were not failures on box-offices.

Before being film producer he deeply studied this subject.[30] Dara Singh also produced Punjabi films.

Social and Political Contribution

Dara Singh is basically a wrestler. It is a matter of pride for the country and society. He defeated many wrestlers in the young age of 28 years. Hereafter he prepared for world championship. In 1959, he became Commonwealth Champion. After it, in the same year, defeating British wrestler Luthas, he became World Champion.[31] At the age of 32 he has become the top wrestler of the world.

As a wrestler, his contribution to society was appreciable. Subhash Shirdhonkar writes, "Dara Singh not only worked in films, but kept on continue his wrestling matches too. Meanwhile, he went on the climax of fame at Colombo, Madras and Lahore. His wrestling match with the Pakistani wrestler "Abdul Majeed Akkara" has been very popular. In that wrestling match one of the arm of Abdul Majeed Akkara got fractured and afterwhile he breathed his last due to it.[32] In any society, games have an important place. There was

---

30. In this respect Ali Peter Jan writes—"Dara soon learned all amount of film business and made his debut as a full-fledged film maker after thirty-six films as an actor. 'Nasihat' made in 1967 was the first of his films. He went on to make (produce and direct) 'Nanak Dukhiya Sab Sansar' (Punjabi), "Mera Desh Mera Dharam", "Dhana Jat', (Punjabi), "Kisan aur Bhagwan", 'Dhayanu Bhagat", "Rustam" and "Unkhilee Mutiyar", which is still to be released. He put all that he earned into his films. He started Dara studio in Punjab where he shot all his films and which gave a new impetus to the Punjabi film movement." (Ibid).
31. Subhash Shirdhonkar, "Returning of a wrestler actor" (Hindi), *Navbharat Times*, city edition, December 28, 1985, p. 5.
32. Ibid.

scarcity of films on this topic. Dara Singh paid attention towards it. He produced "Rustam" in 1983 on this subject. The film was so much contextual and interesting, that it declared tax free.

However, Dara Singh always remained at a distance from political affairs, yet he has kept good relations with Nehru family.

One of the social contribution of Dara Singh is that he provided opportunities in the films to a score of people.[33] It shows his social responsibility and broad mindedness. There are just few persons in the film-world who welcome new comers. Our society needs such individuals.

Dilip Kumar

The place occupied by Dilip Kumar in the history of Hindi cinema is extremely notable. He is called "King of Tragedy Acting".[34] Although, the list of Dilip Kumar films is not lengthy, but his acting art cannot be compared with anyone.

Films of Dilip Kumar

Dilip Kumar, as a hero, appeared in the film titled "Jawar Bhata" in the year of 1944. Appreciating his acting

---

33. Ali Peter Jan writes in this concern—"His coming to films showed many a new way. Producers who did not know what to do, what kind of films to make and with whom to make them saw new hope in Dara Singh. Directors, music directors, technicians and casual workers who were unemployed found new opportunities. The new Dara Singh factor also gave work to a number of actresses and character artists."
—Ali Peter Jan, Ibid article, p. 12.
34. Dharmendra Gaur, "King of Tragedy Acting: Dilip Kumar" (Hindi), *Amar Ujala*, Hindi Daily; December 23, 1983, p. 8.

performance in the debut film, the famous hero of that period Moti Lal commented, "At last an artist has arrived to occupy my place".[35] Born on December 11, 1923 at Peshawar (Pakistan), Dilip Kumar (Yosuf Khan) secured his position in Hindi films very soon.

TABLE 3.11

Main Films of Dilip Kumar

S.No.	*Year*	*Film*
1.	1944	Jawar Bhata
2.	1946	Milan
3.	1947	Jugnu
4.	1948	Mela, Shaheed
5.	1948	Nadia Ke Paar
6.	1949	Shabnam
7.	1950	Jogan
8.	1950	Aarjoo
9.	1951	Deedar
10.	1954	Footpath
11.	1955	Devdas
12.	1955	Azad
13.	1958	Yahudi
14.	1959	Paigham
15.	1960	Kohinoor
16.	1960	Mughal-e-Azam
17.	1961	Ganga-Jamuna
18.	1964	Leader
19.	1964	Ram aur Shyam
20.	1974	Sageena

35. Bharat, "Dilip Kumar—Kal, Aaj aur Kal", Ibid daily, November 18, 1983, p. 6.

Diagram 3.9 : Number of well-known films of Dilip Kumar during 1944-48, 1949-54, 1955-59, 1960-64, 1965-69 and 1970-74

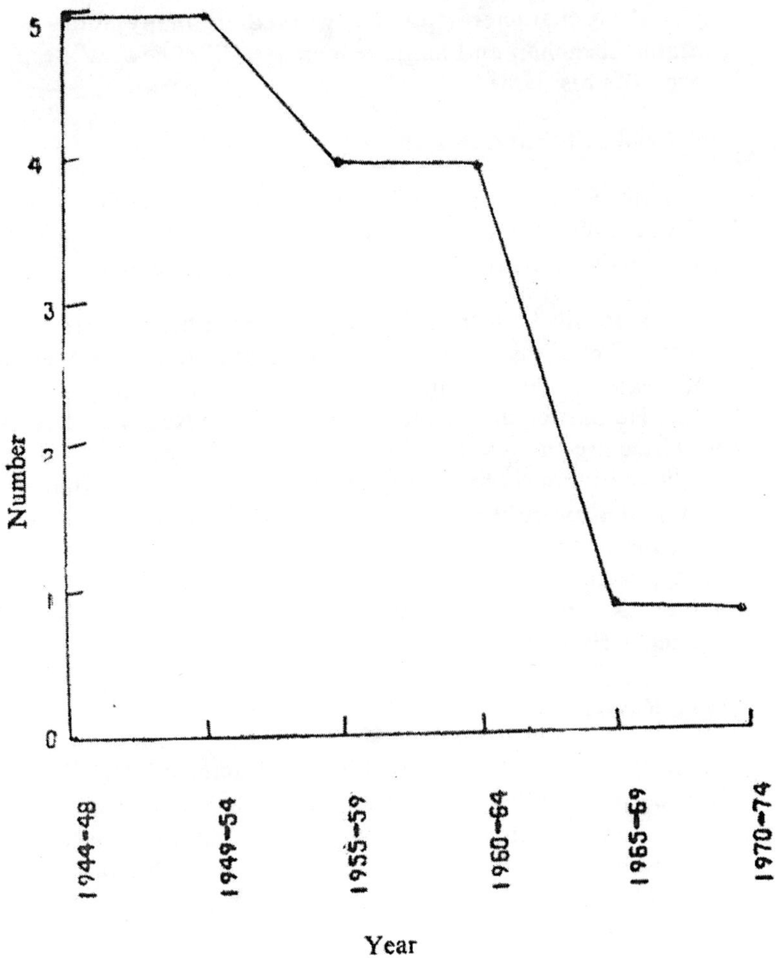

Each of Dilip Kumar's film got unexpected success at Box-offices. He used to be extremely successful in tragedy based roles.

Recently, Dilip Kumar made up his image as a character artist. As a character actor he worked in many films with Amitabh Bachchan and Sanjeev Kumar. The viewers keep a "craze" for his name.

Social and Political Contribution

Dilip Kumar is one of those film actors of Hindi cinema who not only worked in films which raised social issues, he always participated in many social service programmes.

His political contribution is also significant. He kept friendship relations with Maulana Azad, Krishna Menon, Rajni Patel, Mohan Kumar Mangalam and Shah Nawaz Khan. He participated overwhelmingly for Nehru's canvassing. These are the reasons that after the death of Nargis Dutt, there were rumours for Dilip Kumar being nominated for Rajya Sabha to fill her vacant place. Dilip Kumar also took part in the historical "padyatra" (walk on feet) of Chandrashekhar, with his wife. He also nominated "Sheriff" of Bombay and being Sheriff he participated in many social and political activities.

Manoj Kumar

Manoj Kumar is one of those hero actor of Hindi films who used to be called "Bharat Kumar". He is also a producer-director. About the success of Manoj Kumar, an author Promod Laitu writes, "Manoj Kumar is one of the well known name of Hindi films. Not only in the area of acting, but as a writer-director he also proved his extraordinary capabilities in many films, these films were appreciated by the masses, and with commercial success, these films are also praised by intellectuals and thus Manoj Kumar became famous in film production and acquired praise from all corners of society. As a matter of fact, he started his career as an actor, but it got concentration on self, as he became script writer, dialogue writer, producer and director. Thus he made few agreements for film acting with other people. He himself founded a film making institution, through it a score of highly discussed and successful films have been produced, consequently Manoj Kumar's fame increased many times."[36]

His Films and Socio-political Contribution

There is no doubt that Manoj Kumar mostly produced patriotic films. Whether it is "Shaheed Bhagat Singh" film or film titled as "Purab-Paschim", "Upkar", or "Roti, Kapra aur Makan", in all films presentation explicits the qualities of Manoj Kumar as an able author, and producer.

Manoj Kumar's film titled as "Upkar" was based on the slogan of Late Prime Minister Lal Bahadur Shastri, "Jai Jawan Jai Kisan". That film brought patriotic sentiments in the hearts of people. The importance of a former was magnified on that time when India had had to import foodgrains in huge quantity.

In Indian society, the blind imitation of Western culture has increased too much. It is one of the significant social contribution of Manoj Kumar that through his "Purab-Paschim" he proved that Indian culture has also many good elements and copying of West is not appropriate from any point of view.

Manoj Kumar's film titled "Kranti" was based on freedom movement. It is necessary that the young generation must be aware about the freedom movement. Manoj Kumar's this film fulfils that purpose.

Though Manoj Kumar acted and produced in few films, yet his contribution for social and political consciousness is sufficient.

---

36. Promod Laitu, "Professional due to times" (Hindi), *Punjab Kesari* (Hindi) Daily, November 23, 1985, p. 1.

There are two such film actors of Hindi cinema Naseeruddin Shah and Ompuri, who worked in art films and there are hopes for their good performances in future. Now the highly rich families boys are entering into Hindi cinema. The grandson of former President of India, Giani Zail Singh, Mr. Inderjit Singh has also entered into Hindi filmdom.[37] He wishes to grasp position through his hard work in Hindi films. He said in an interview, "Truly speaking, those who meet me they came because I am related to the President of India, I hate it. I am myself. I want to live with my name. The people must know me with my name, hence I joined films not joined the politics.[38] However, with the entrance of youth like Inderjeet Singh, the relations between "film and politics" in India shall become more deep.

5. An Analysis of Hindi Film Actor's Films during 1984 and 1985

In the years of 1984 and 1985 a score of films were released. Some new actor's films were successful professionally, though many old actor's films have had to face 'flop'.

The table on p. 85 presents the professional success of main actors during 1984.[39]

The analysis of this table explicits that in 1984, the most successful heroes were Jitendra and Rajesh Khanna. Although there were twenty-six hero actors but none of their film got professional success.

---

37. Sharad Rai, "Inderjeet Singh (Interview)" Hindi, *Movie Jagat*, Hindi Weekly, N. Delhi, 23-29 September, 1983, p. 1.
38. Ibid.
39. Mohan Siroya, "1984—Trends in Hindi Cinema", *Screen*, Ibid, February 15, 1985, p. 12.

TABLE 3.12

Professional Success of Main Actors in 1984

S.No.	*Actor's Name*	*Number of Films released*	*Successful Films*	*Names of successful Films*
1.	Jitendra	8	3	Tohfa, Maqsad, Qaidi
2.	Rajesh Khanna	7	2	Papi Pet Ka Sawal Hai, Maqsad
3.	Amitabh Bachchan	2	1	Sharabi
4.	Mithun Chakravarty	10	1	Ghar Ek Mandir
5.	Raj Babbar	7	1	Aaj Ki Awaz
6.	Shashi Kapoor	3	1	Ghar Ek Mandir
7.	Naseeruddin Shah	4	1	Sparsh
8.	Anupam Kher	2	1	Saransh
9.	Dharmendra	7	—	—
10.	Kamal Hasan	6	—	—
11.	Rishi Kapoor	4	—	—
12.	Anil Kapoor	4	—	—
13.	Rajni Kant	4	—	—
14.	Raj Kumar	3	—	—
15.	Sunni Deol	3	—	—
16.	Mohnish Bahl	3	—	—
17.	Farooq Sheikh	3	—	—
18.	Sanjay Dutt	2	—	—
19.	Kumar Gaurav	2	—	—
20.	Sunil Dutt	2	—	—
21.	Devanand	1	—	—
22.	Sunil Anand	1	—	—
23.	Jatin Malhotra	1	—	—
24.	Rajiv Kapoor	1	—	—
25.	Jackey Shroff	1	—	—
26.	Karan Shah	1	—	—

Diagram 3.10 : Twelve professionally successful main actors and number of their total films in 1984

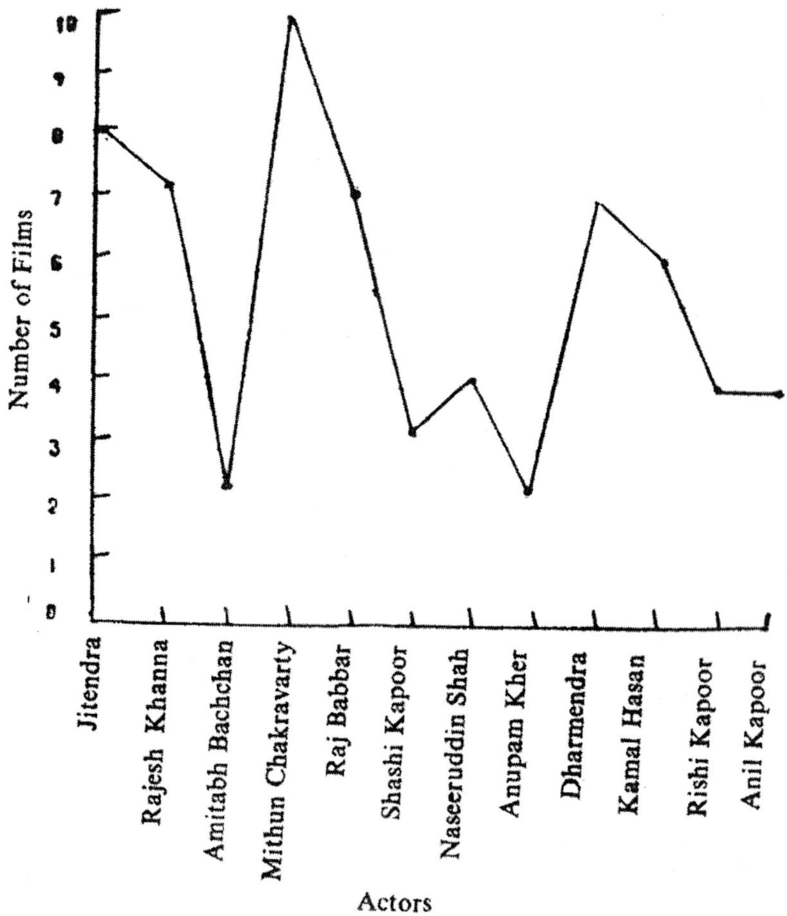

Diagram 3.11 : Professionally successful actors and their successful films in 1984

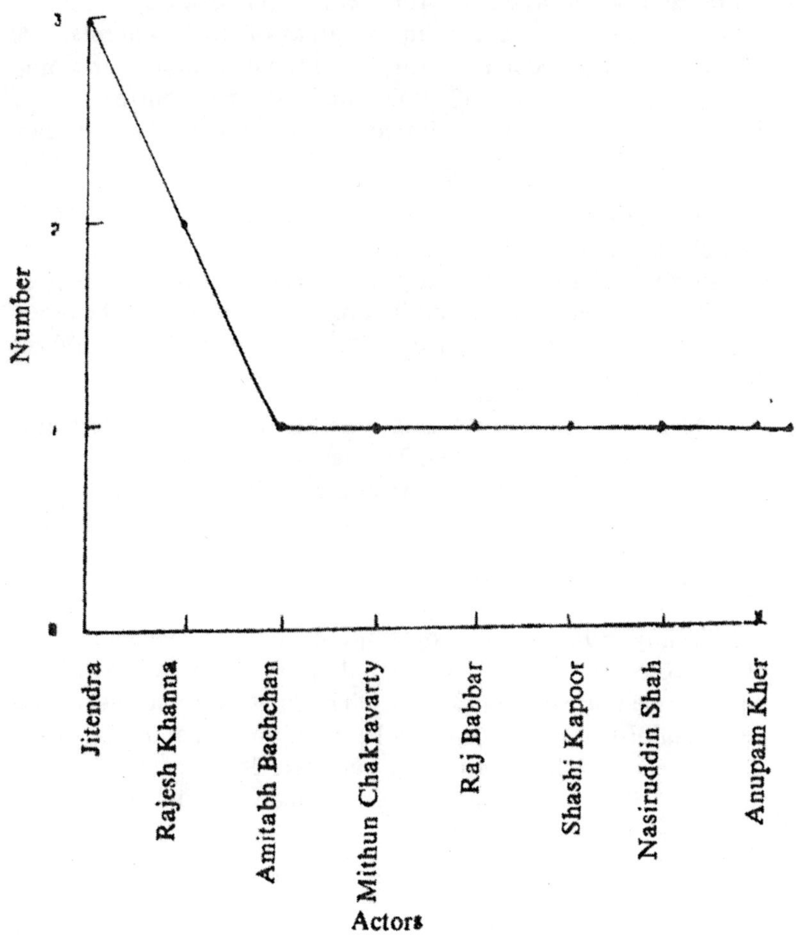

Professional Success of Main Heroes in the year 1985

The 1985 year proved a revolutionary year for Hindi films. The new heroes got more success this year.[40]

For some years, many star-sons are appearing in Hindi cinema. They tried to show their talents. It is but natural to adopt acting as a career for them. It is assumeed that the children got more success in the areas of their parents. A doctor's son can become doctor, a politician's son can become politician, businessman's son can become business and establishes new records, similarly why not star's son can become star ?

The study of Table 3.13 presents that in the year 1985, Amitabh Bachchan's films got cent per cent success, however, Rajesh Khanna's films got only eleven per cent success. Interestingly, the new hero actor, Anil Kapoor's released all the four films were successful at Box-Office. Thus he got highest position.

Hence the rise and fall among Hindi film actors and heroes is a continous process. The new generation gives priority to the new actors. When new generation is leading in all spheres of life, why not they lead in films. To act in Hindi films has become so profitable that international fame acquired actors have tried for it.[41]

Many ruling and opposition parties leaders have played roles in films.[42] In South India, film actor and politician has become two sides of a coin. The kind of relationship has been established in South India between politics and acting, it gives a clue to the South Indian culture. But it cannot happen in the North India because there are many prejudices against actors in the minds of people.

---

40. Mohan Siroya, 1985—A Survey—A Year of Revival and Consolidation for Hindi Cinema", *Screen*, Weekly, January 3, 1986, p. 20 and *Screen*, January 24, 9986, p. 6.
41. *Screen*, Ibid Weekly, February 28, 1986, p. 1.
42. Ibid.

TABLE 3.13

Professional Success of Main Actors in 1985

S.No.	Name of Main Actor	Number of released films	Successful Films		Percentage of successful Films
			Number	Names	
1	2	3	4	5	6
1.	Anil Kapoor	4	4	Sahib, Yudh, Mohabbat, Meri Jang	100
2.	Amitabh Bachchan	2	2	Giraftar, Mard	100
3.	Amol Palekar	1	1	Ankahi	100
4.	Kamal Haasan	3	2	Giraftar, Saagar	66
5.	Sunni Deol	2	1	Arjun	50
6.	Rajni Kant	2	1	Giraftar	50
7.	Jackey Shroff	7	3	Shiv Ka Insaf, Yudh, Teri Mehrbanian	43
8.	Rishi Kapoor	5	2	Tawaif, Saagar	40

(Contd.)

1	2	3	4	5	6
9.	Mithun Chakravarty	12	4	Pyar Jhukta Nahin, Pyari Behna, Aandhi Toofan, Ghulami	33
10.	Dharmendra	3	1	Ghulami	33
11.	Shashi Kapoor	6	2	Aandhi Toofan, Utsav	33
12.	Naseeruddin Shah	5	1	Ghulami	20
13.	Rajiv Kapoor	5	1	Ram Teri Ganga Meli	20
14,	Jitendra	8	1	Patal Bhervi	12.5
15.	Shatrughan Sinha	8	1	Aandhi Toofan	12.5
16.	Rajesh Khanna	9	1	Aakhir Kyon?	11
17.	Raj Babbar	10	1	Durga	10
18.	Farooq Sheikh	3	—	—	—
19.	Late Sanjeev Kumar	2	—	—	—
20.	Kumar Gaurav	2	—	—	—
21.	Rajan Sippi	2	—	—	—
22.	Sanjay Dutt	2	—	—	—
23.	Sandeep Patil	1	—	—	—
24.	Rohan Kapoor	1	—	—	—

Diagram 3.12 : Twelve professionally successful actors and number of their released films in 1985

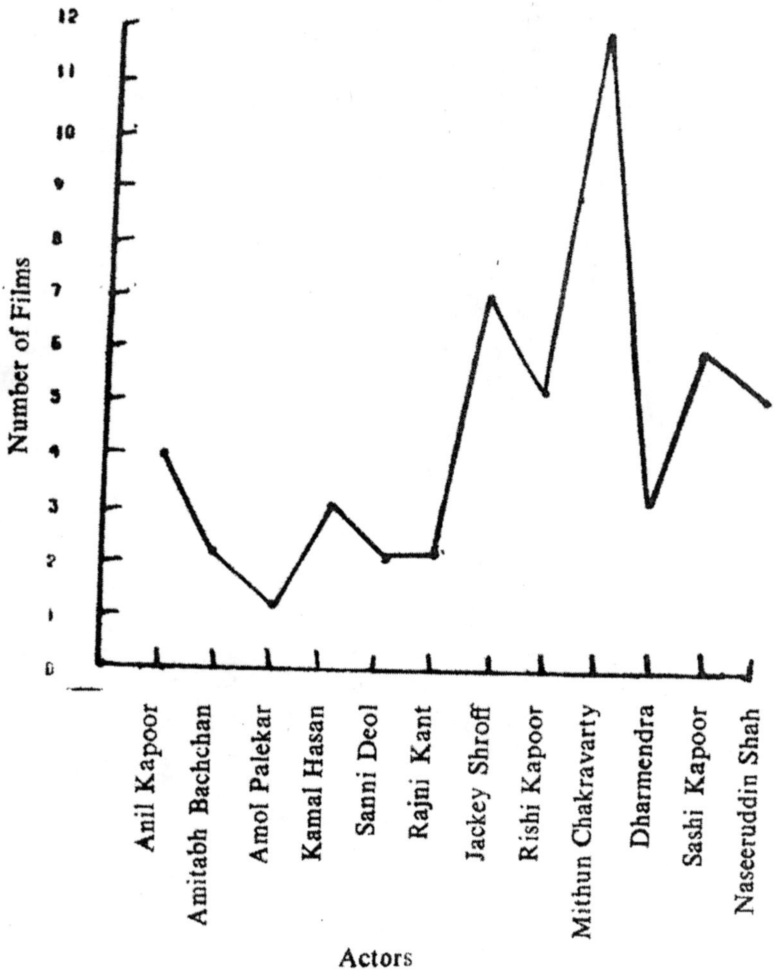

Diagram 3.13 : Twelve professionally successful actors and number of their successful films in the year 1985

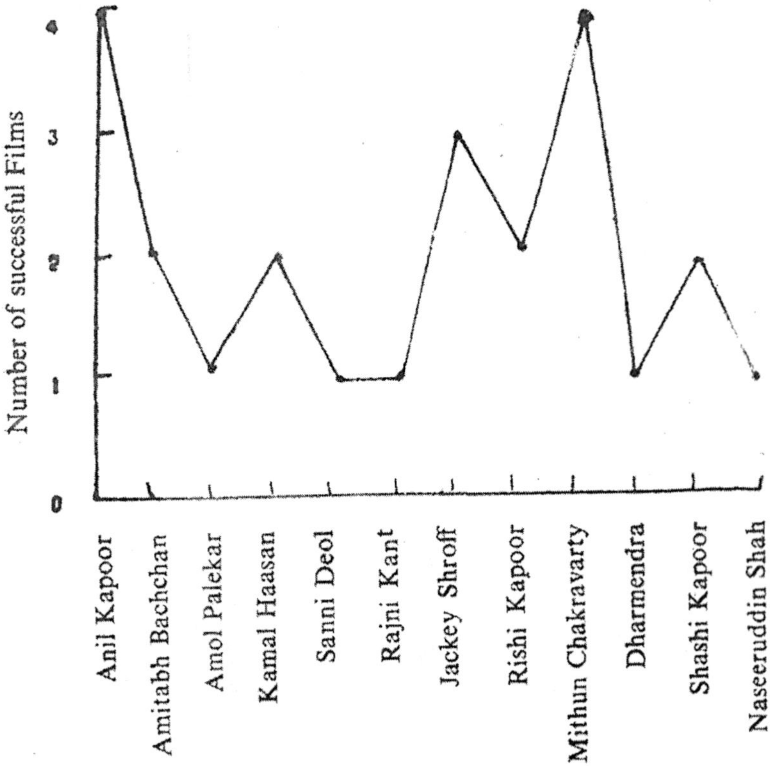

Main Actresses of Modern Hindi Films

TABLE 3.14

Main One Hundred Actresses of Modern Hindi Films

S.No.	*Name of Actress*	*S.No.*	*Name of Actress*
	1		*2*
1.	Anita Raj	2.	Aruna Irani
3.	Aasha Parekh	4.	Bindu
5.	Bina	6.	Bindya Goswami
7.	Daljit Kaur	8.	Deva Shree
9.	Dimple Kapadia	10.	Dipti Naval
11.	Farida Jalal	12.	Hema Malini
13.	Helan	14.	Hina Kausar
15.	Jai Shree T.	16.	Jaya Prada
17.	Komal Mahuvakar	18.	Komila Virq
19.	Leena Dass	20.	Mala Sinha
21.	Madhu Malini	22.	Madhu Kapur
23.	Meena T.	24.	Madhu Malhotra
25.	Meena Rai	26.	Mausami Chatterji
27.	Meenakshi Sheshadri	28.	Namita Chandra
29.	Neeta Mehta	30.	Nazneen
31.	Neelam Mehra	32.	Nandita Thakur
33.	Nutan	34.	Padma Khanna
35.	Parma Chauhan	36.	Puja Saxena
37.	Padmini Kapila	38.	Parvin Bobby
39.	Padmini Kolhapure	40.	Preeti Sapru
41.	Purnima Jairam	42.	Poonam Dhillon
43.	Preeti Ganguli	44.	Prema Narayan
45.	Rehana Sultan	46.	Rekha
47.	Rajni Sharma	48.	Ranjeeta

(*Contd.*)

1	2
49. Raksha Mehta	50. Rameshwari
51. Rati Agnihotri	52. Saira Bano
53. Sarika	54. Sita Bajaj
55. Sharmila Tagore	56. Sheetal
57. Shabana Aazmi	58. Seema Kapur
59. Sulakhshina Pandit	60. Smita Patil
61. Swarup Sampat	62. Tabassum
63. Teena Munim	64. Tanuja
65. Vidya Sinha	66. Vijayta Pandit
67. Waheeda Rehman	68. Yogita Bali
69. Zareena Wahab	70. Zeenat Aman
71. Raakhi	72. Shri Devi
73. Padma Chauhan	74. Sushma Verma
75. Malti Joshi	76. Rohini Hatkhande
77. Priya Tendulkar	78. Shashi Kala
79. Seema Dhet	80. Salma Aagha
81. Shoba Khote	82. Ruhi
83. Sadhna Singh	84. Rama Wiz
85. Tamanna	86. Rita Bhaduri
87. Jaya Bhaduri	88. Khushbu
89. Silk Smita	90. Swapna
91. Amrita Singh	92. Farha
93. Mandakini	94. Divya Rana
95. Parsis Khambata	96. Aaysha Dutt
97. Munmun Sen	98. Natasha Sinha
99. Radha	100. Bhakti Bawe

In the above table only those actresses have been included, who have made their position in commercial or art films.

An analysis of modern Hindi film's actresses and their socio-political contribution is following :

Rekha

Rekha (Bhanurekha Ganeshan) is a well known woman of India.[43] Born in Madras, she made her place slowly but regulary in the Hindi cinema. For her extraordinary personality she gave birth to "controversies". In "Umraon Jaan" titled film she got highest national award for best acting.

Rekha's Films and Social-Political Contribution

Rekha took her debut in Hindi films in 1970 with "Sawan Bhadon". This film was shown for twenty-five weeks and celebrated "silver jubilee". No one has expected that Rekha's first film should be so much successful.

Since the release of "Sawan Bhadon", she has worked with all prominent heroes in her many films. Although most of her films are commercial yet she progressed quantitatively in her acting performance.

---

43. A comment of *Sunday Magazine* "*Hindustan Times*" about Rekha : "Bhanurekha Ganeshan, or Reka, is one of the most intriguing women in the counting. And, perhaps, one of the most controversial and candid of celebrities.

    But there is more to her than the sex symbol whose daring dances the rage in film after film."

    Sunday Magazine, The Hindustan Times, Autobiograghical Account, Rekha, English Daily N. Delhi, September 1, 1985, p. 1.

TABLE 3.14

Main Films of Rekha and their Heroes

S.No.	*Film*	*Hero*
1	*2*	*3*
1.	Sawan Bhadon	Navin Nishchal
2.	Aalam	Vinod Mehra
3.	Haseenon Ke Devta	Sanjay Khan
4.	Do Yaar	Shatrughan Sinha
5.	Ek Bechara	Jitendra
6.	Gaon Hamara Shehar Tumhara	Rajendra Kumar
7.	Anokhi Ada	Jitendra Kumar
8.	Dharma	Navin Nishchal
9.	Double Cross	Vijay Anand
10.	Gora Kala	Rajendra Kumar
11.	Rampur Ka Lakshman	Randhir Kapoor
12.	Qeemat	Dharmendra
13.	Namak-Haram	Rajesh Khanna
14.	Barkha Bahar	Navin Nishchal
15.	Duniya Ka Mela	Sanjay Khan
16.	Kahani Qismat Ki	Dharmendra
17.	Kashmakash	Feroze Khan
18.	Mehman	Vishwajeet
19.	Pran Jaye Wachan Na Jaye	Sunil Dutt
20.	Woh Mein Nahin	Navin Nishchal
21.	Bhola Bhala	Rajesh Khanna
22.	Aakrman	Rakesh Roshan
23.	Dafa 302	Randhir Kapoor
24.	Dharmatma	Feroze Khan
25.	Kahte hain mujh ko raja	Vishwajeet

1	2	3
26.	Zameen Aasman	Sunil Dutt
27.	Aaj Ka Mahatma	Randheer Kapoor
28.	Dharam Karam	Randheer Kapoor
29.	Khaleeja	Randheer Kapoor
30.	Nagin	Sunil Dutt
31.	Santan	Jitendra
32.	Alap	Amitabh Bachchan
33.	Chakkar Pe Chakkar	Shashi Kapoor
34.	Dildar	Jitendra
35.	Imaan-Dharam	Amitabh Bachchan
36.	Ganga ki Saugandh	Amitabh Bachchan
37.	Ram Bharose	Randheer Kapoor
38.	Ahinsa	Sunil Dutt
39.	Khoon Pasina	Amitabh Bachchan
40.	Awara Raju	Randheer Kapoor
41.	Birju Sirju	Shashi Kapoor
42.	Chor-Swami	Shashi Kapoor
43.	Dushman Dost	Shatrughan Sinha
44.	Gardish	Dharmendra
45.	Jani Dushman	Sunil Dutt
46.	Kali Ghata	Shashi Kapoor
47.	Kartavyya	Dharmendra
48.	Khwahish	Jitendra
49.	Mere Pati ki Patni	Sunil Dutt
50.	Natwar Lal	Amitabh Bachchan
51.	Naya Bakra	Jitendra
52.	Niyat	Jitendra
53.	Nishan	Jitendra

(*Contd.*)

1	2	3
54.	Prem Bandhan	Rajesh Khanna
55.	Samandur	Sunil Dutt
56.	Ram Qasam	Sunil Dutt
57.	Suhag	Amitabh Bachchan
58.	Watan	Sunil Dutt
59.	Karam Yogi	Jitendra
60.	Khazana	Randheer Kapoor
61.	Paramatma	Shatrughan Sinha
62.	Rahu Ketu	Shashi Kapoor
63.	Sawan Ke Geet	Sanjeev Kumar
64.	Silsila	Amitabh Bachchan

The films shown in the above table have no film like "Umraon Jaan" which put her at the climax of acting as art film. Rekha also worked her for this film. In this respect, director Muzaffar Ali has written, "For me, "Umrao Jaan" was much more than a film, a sentiment. After partition, many Muslims migrated to Pakistan. A score of my relatives have also gone to Pakistan, they said when migrating—your civilization and culture shall be perished. Your language shall be finished. Now after viewing "Umraon Jaan", the same people told that culture exists in India today, but not in Pakistan. They have forgotten that there were such things in Avadh. Viewing "Umraon Jaan", they remember all this."

"A film titled as "Umraon Jaan" has been produced in Pakistan too. However, the appreciation which Rekha got for her acting performance in Indian titled "Umraon Jaan", I would like to say that it is real award for Rekha, for all of us."

"Rekha worked very hard for bearing the "get up" of Umraon. What kind of culture and dresses during 250-300 years ago in Avadh, she used to discuss all these matters with me. We have no photographs of that time, but paintings. We

Diagram 3.14 : Rekha's Main Films with Six Main Heroes

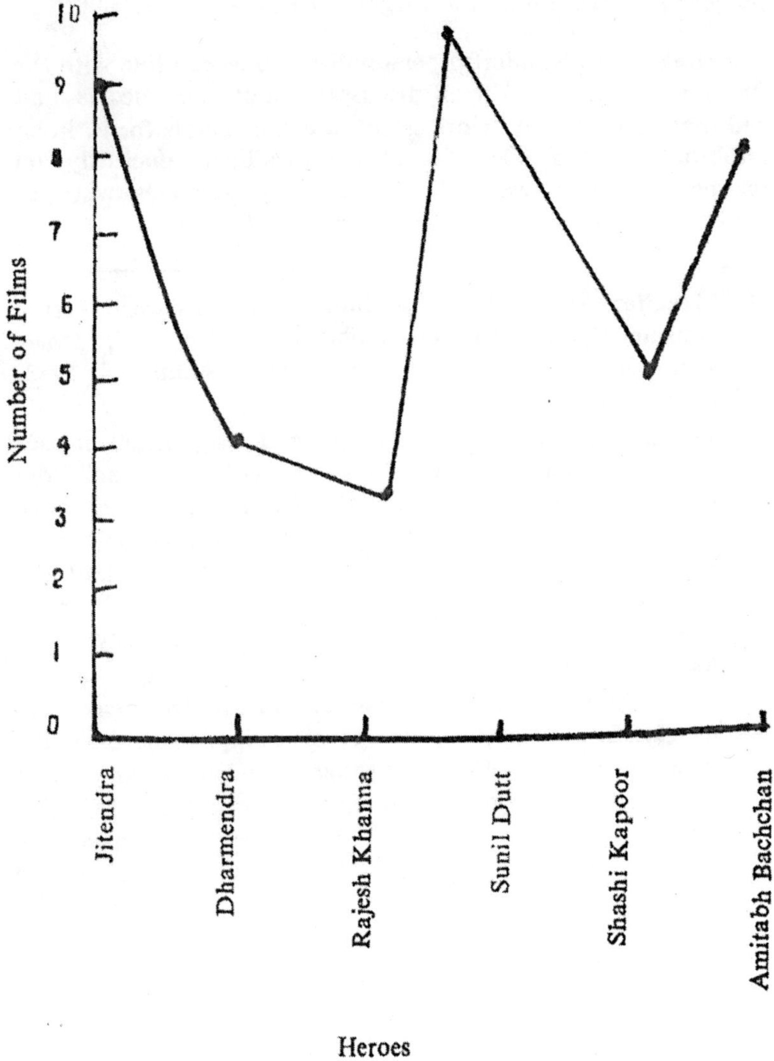

collected about one hundred and fifty paintings of ladies, prostitutes, Begums (court-ladies) and their costumes. Lucknow museum was visited and hundreds of prepared and folded betel leaves were examined. I have dowry clothes of my parents. All were looked up by Rekha. Then he took up the get up of 'Umraon' and forgot her in that character."[44]

Rekha has wonderful personality. She can live with the life of any role. She herself discussed about her success and told that "truth" and "work hard" are responsible for it, in an autobiographical article. She also throws light sufficiently on her personal courage.[45] There are few actresses who got professional as well as artistic success side by side.

---

44. Muzaffar Ali, "Ghazal se Sawari Hoi Tasweer Teri—Umraon Jaan, Jiya Hai Tujhe Rekha Ne......", *Movie Jagat*, Ibid magazine, Rekha special, August 5, 1983, p. 29.
45. Rekha writes, "At a very young age I established myself and I have made my base. Now I will go ahead from here doing many, many other things. I have been lucky and I think it is my sincerity and my truthfulness which has brought me here. I am not a hypocrite and the biggest plus point in my life is my independence. Nobody to ask and nobody to point a finger at me and say, "why have you done this "?

    I think I have the personal courage to break completely from what I have been doing. For example, suppose I decide that I no longer want to be an actress but want to do something completely different. I think I can do it. I have always had that strength inside me. I am doing something like these days. It would be stupid of me to leave—not because I cannot but because I do not want to, acting is my first love but I had to say it is a fairly big thing to do what I am doing now . . . to cut myself off like this. From doing fifty films at a time to come down to five or ten films, that's something. That takes a lot of guts. What with the flattering money that

Rekha's films are based on social and familial stories. She has no interest in politics. She did not get any opportunity to work any political film. Most of her films are social and based on family problems and are full of entertainment.

Shabana Aazmi

Shabana Aazmi is one of those actresses of Hindi films who got national awards for best acting four times. Shabana Aazmi is the daughter of well known Urdu poet Kaifi Aazmi and well known drama artist Shaukat Aazmi. She has done acting diploma from "Poona Film and Television Institute." Her mother has written in her memories:

"Shabana did not get any help for admission in the Poona Institute. She herself got application form, took photographs and sent after filling it. Thus she was selected for interview. However, when interviews were going on, the examinations were on, Shabana has written for her absence. She received a letter that they would conduct her interview at the institute after her academic examinations. After examinations, myself and Kaifi went there with her. There she answered ahead what director used to ask. She recalled dialogues within one minute. Her interview was so much rewarding that she got selection immediately.

And then Shabana won first position in every subject therein. Her teacher Tarneja liked her. And soon she was awarded scholarship. We used to send about two hundred or

---

they offer you, and the flattering roles, and the atmosphere and just being busy, and the power that goes with it. . . . Today I want to do certain other things in life. I want time for myself. I have had enough of other things. Fifteen years is a long time and I have done it all my life. I was beginning to lose touch with myself."
Rekha, "Autobiographical Account," *Sunday Magazine, Hindustan Times*, September 1, 1985, p. 4.

two hundred fifty rupees to her, now the sum was not needed."[46]

Definitely, Shabana Aazmi is an extraordinary artist. Her debut film was Shyam Benegal's titled as "Ankur".

Films and Socio-political Contribution

Shabana entered the film world through art films, but soon she worked in commercial films. Her first commercial film was "Faqira" with Shashi Kapoor. This film proved successful at Box-office and she signed several commercial films.[47] Then she was viewed films titled as "Heera Aur Patthar", "Karam", "Khel Khilari ka", "Ek Hi Raasta", and "Chor-Sipahi".

Important films of Shabana are "Ankur", "Khandhar", "Shatranj ke Khilari", "Arth", "Masoom", "Ye Nazdikiyan", "Mandi" and "Kamal" etc.

One of the secret of Shabana's success is that in all those films, in which she worked, she worked due to her choice. She did not accept any film, in which script the hero used to dominate the role of heroine.[48] Every heroine is anxious to play a role with Amitabh Bachchan but Shabana Aazmi refused to work with her. It is so because she knows that Amitabh Bachchan has his own viewers who like his "angryman" roles. Which heroine is working with him, they ignore it. Amitabh viewers have no relation with art also.

---

46. Shaukat Aazmi, "Memoirs—Shabana is not only my daughter but my friend too" (Hindi), *Saptahik Hindustan*, Weekly, May 12-18, 1985, p. 23.
47. Ashok Chopra, "Acting Pillars of Hindi Films" (Hindi), *Movie Jagat*, Weekly Hindi, Acting Special, p. 20.
48. Ajay Satia, "Shabana got best actress award" (Hindi), *Punjab Kesari*, Daily Hindi, July 20, 1984, p. 1.

Hence she is one of the top Hindi film actress.[49] Among the modern Hindi film heroines, she used to be in competition with Smita Patil and none else.

As far as is the concern of her social and political contribution, she is the daughter of a family which has been connected with left movement. Her father Kaifi Aazmi is a progressive poet and is related to communist movement, and her mother Shaukat Aazmi is linked with drama stage organisation "IPTA" having left orientations.

She worked in many art films, all related to social problems—Her films played an important role for providing respectable position to women folk in Indian society.

In the film titled as "Arth", when Shabana asks "Similarly if I would have come back living with another person, can you take back me ?" In these sentences she provides words to the developing personality of contemporary women. Generally, what kind of women we heve observed on the screen of Hindi films, the 'women' of 'Arth', is obviously different from that."

Similarly, in the film titled as "Masoom", Shabana expressed how the wife holds her right on the home, that is necessity of today. "The male has an old sentence—get out of my house, but house belongs to whom and what is its basis? The society has never given this right to ask to women. In "Masoom" Shabana draws a line for her husband saying my home, my children, then it clears that the home is due to her, who is a woman."[50]

---

49. Mr. Ali writes on Shabana—Among the actresses Shabana Aazmi continued to stay at the peak. She was declared the best actress by most authorities on cinema, by cineastes, and cinegoers alike—all on merit alone."
—Ali, "Farewell or wells 1984", *Screen*, Weekly, Dec. 28, 1984, p. 6.
50. Ajay Satia, Ibid, p. 1.

As a matter of fact, Shabana's contribution for improving the condition of Indian women is highly appreciable.

Late Smita Patil

In modern Hindi films, Smita Patil occupied an immemorable place. As an actress in the films, her contribution for the country and society was so much significant and important that she was awarded "Padam Shree".

Smita Patil was born on October 17, 1955 at Poona. In 1971, her family migrated to Bombay. She was a college student and she also joined news-reader post at the Television Centre, Bombay.

Films and Socio-political Contribution

First of all Shyam Benegal offered her a role in children film titled as "Charandas Chor". Again he offered her an important role in the film titled as "Nishant". In his next film "Manthan", Benegal selected her as heroine. After it Benegal again provided her the role of heroine in the film titled as "Bhumika". Smita got highest national award for acting for her job performance in this film.[51] She again got best heroine award for "Chakra". For this film she was also chosen for "Filmfare award". For the success in these films, her director, Shyam Benegal also worked hard, as he has viewed her talents and used it. In this respect one author opines, "During the decades of fifties and sixties, there were a number of good heroines in Hindi cinema, but then there were not such directors and films who can construct roles looking up the talents of actresses. Waheeda Rehman and Nutan performed highest types of roles in their limits. But in the decade of seventies, the Hindi cinema actresses got opportunities to play in the roles which can do justice with the changing image of

51. Ashok Chopra, Ibid article, p. 29.

women and these have place for acting too. In this decade actresses like Shabana Aazmi and Smita Patil got opportunities for progress and the decade of eighties bears the condition that these actresses have started to 'dictate' their roles and scripts."[52]

Initially, Smita Patil worked hard and communicated the real beauty of her face to the viewers. Then she worked in several commercial films. Before presenting a common dance in rain with Amitabh Bachchan in the film titled as "Namak Halal", she has performed her best roles in "Bhumika" and "Ubardha", (which released in Hindi as Subah).

To work in films and to keep herself away in any controversy in Bombay is not an easy task. Smita told that she was not given roles in many short-budget films because she has no "market value". For it, she started to work in commercial films.

Smita Patil's film life was just for ten years. Reading news at Television Centre to the film titled as "Subah" has an interesting and struggling journey. The film titled as "Nishant" and "Manthan" provided Smita an identity. But in the film titled as "Bhumika" she played the role of Marathi actress Hansa Barkar, which was a challenge, and it proved that she was a great actress.

Some other important films of Smita Patil were "Bazar" and "Mandi". Famous French director Costa Gauvaras has arranged "Re-observation Exhibition Festival" at Paris.[53]

In each of her film, a social problem is discussed. In the film titled as "Chakra", there is description of the helplessness of the women of slums. From political point of view, she was

---

52. Vinod Bhardwaj, "One face of Smita Patil" (Hindi), *Navbharat Times*, Hindi Daily, August 11, 1984, p. 5.
53. Ibid

one of the daughter of a former minister of Maharashtra government. At international level, she increased the respect of India and thus Smita Patil did notable service of the country.

An Analysis of Hindi Heroines' Films during the years of 1984 and 1985

During the years of 1984 and 1985, a score of Hindi films of different heroines have been released. The films of some new actresses got success, however, some old actresses' films proved "flop".

Commercial Success of main Film Heroines in 1984

During the year of 1894, Hindi film heroines have gone through ups and downs at commercial level.[54]

It was but natural that with the entrance of new film actresses the market value of old ones came down. As a matter of fact, it is unfortunate for Hindi cinema, that though the male artists used to play their roles as hero upto old age, however, the female artists do not get heroine roles more than ten or fifteen years. The viewers also give priority to her beauty, not to her art.

TABLE 3.16

Commercial Success of Actresses during 1984

S.No.	*Heroine*	*Number of released Films*	*Successful Films*	*Names of successful Films*
1	*2*	*3*	*4*	*5*
1.	Jaya Prada	10	4	Tohfa, Maqsad, Sharabi, Papi Pet ka Sawal Hai
2.	Shridevi	7	2	Tohfa, Maqsad
3.	Rati Agnihotri	7	1	Papi Pet ka Sawal

54. Mohan Siroya, "1984 : Trends in Hindi Cinema", *Screen*, Weekly, February 15, 2985, p. 12.

1	*2*	*3*	*4*	*5*
4.	Shabana Aazmi	8	1	Sparsh
5.	Smita Patil	7	1	Aaj ki Aawaz
6.	Hema Malini	5	1	Qaidi
7.	Mausami Chatterji	4	1	Ghar Ek Mandir
8.	Rohini Hathangari	3	1	Saransh
9.	Rekha	6	—	—
10.	Zeenat Aman	5	—	—
11.	Tina Munim	5	—	—
12.	Rina Rai	5	—	—
13.	Padmini Kolhapure	4	—	—
14.	Poonam Dhillon	4	—	—
15.	Anita Raj	4	—	—
16.	Dipti Naval	4	—	—
17.	Ranjita	4	—	—
18.	Dimple Kapadia	2	—	—
19.	Rameshwari	2	—	—
20	Surinder Kaur	2	—	—
21.	Amrita Singh	2	—	—
22.	Aaysha Dutt	1	—	—
23.	Radha	1	—	—
24.	Munmun Sen	1	—	—
25.	Divya Rana	1	—	—
26.	Meenakshi Sheshadri	1	—	—
27.	Kimi	1	—	—
28.	Swapna	1	—	—
29.	Natasha Sinha	1	—	—
30.	Bhakti Bhave	1	—	—
31.	Neelam	1	—	—

Diagram 3.15 : Main Twelve Heroines and Number of their Released Films in 1984

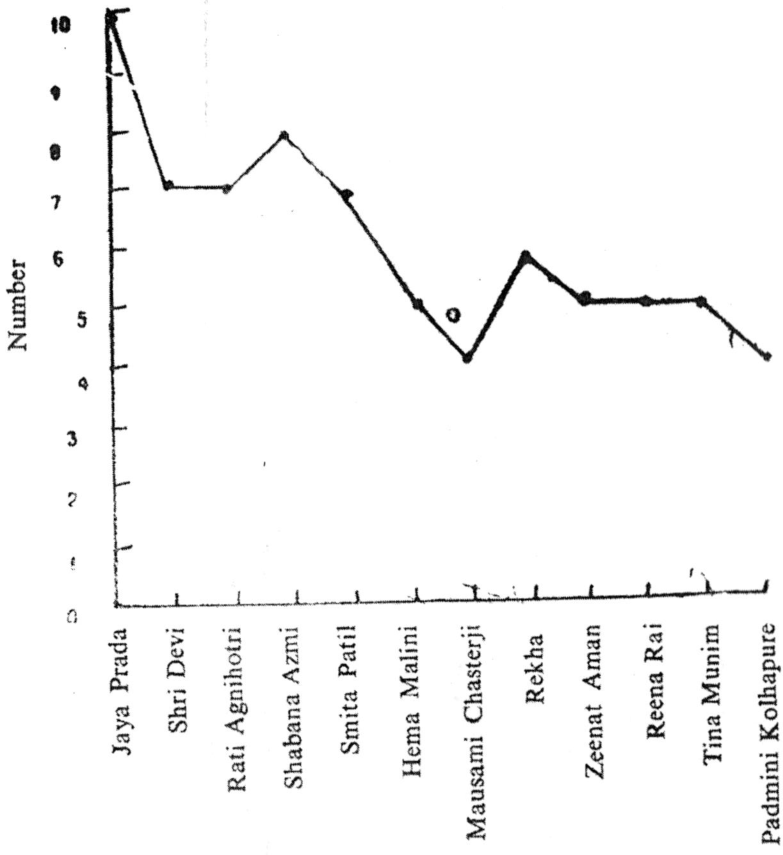

Diagram 3.16: Main Eight Actresses and their successful Films in 1984

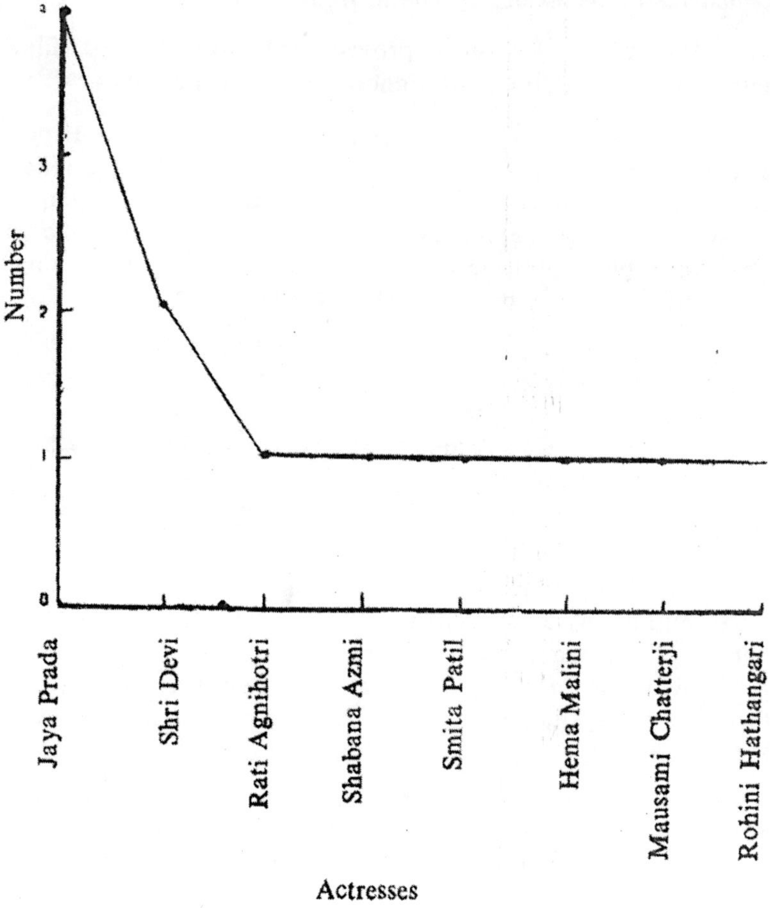

The analysis of the above table shows that during the year of 1984, the successful heroines of Hindi films were Jaya Prada and Shri Devi. However, out of thirty-one heroines, in twenty-three heroines' films, not even one film got commercial success.

Commercial Success of Main Film Actresses in the year of 1985

The year 1985 also proved revolutionary for film actresses. Amrita Singh got highest success during this year.[55]

There seem to be some qualitative changes in the Hindi cinema. The cinegoers have given priority to clean familial films in place of films full of fighting scenes. Such situation is favourable for the actresses, because in family based social films they got more opportunities to represent their acting skills, otherwise they become just "Showpieces".

The study of Table 3.17 tells us that in the year of 1985, no actresses other than Amrita Singh got cent per cent success at commercial level. The highest number of released films i.e. twelve belongs to Rati Agnihotri, however only one of her film got commercial success.

Conclusion

The analytical study of modern Hindi cinema and its actors and actresses explicits that Hindi film artists are slowly but steadily becoming conscious of their social responsibility. As far as is the concern of social and political contribution through acting, the heroines contributed more and valuable than the heroes.

Here it is notable that if the scripts of Hindi films are according to the social and political demands then the actors and actresses may provide more social and political contribution to the society.

---

55. Mohan Siroya, "1985—A Survey, A year of Revival and Consolidation for Hindi Cinema," *Screen*, Weekly, January 3, 1986, p. 20.

TABLE 3.17

Commercial Success of Actresses during 1985

S.No.	Actress	Number of Released Films	Successful Films		
			Number	Film	Percentage
1	2	3	4	5	6
1.	Amrita Singh	2	2	Sahib, Mard	100
2.	Dimple Kapadia	5	3	Arjun, Patal Bherawi, Sagar	60
3.	Hema Malini	7	4	Yudh, Durga, Aandhi Toofan, Ramkali	57
4.	Raakhi	2	1	Sahib	50
5.	Mandakini	2	1	Ram Teri Ganga Meli	50
6.	Divya Rana	2	1	Ram Teri Ganga Meli	50
7,	Tina Munim	4	2	Yudh, Aakhir Kyon	50
8.	Poonam Dhillon	10	4	Shiva ka Insaf, Tawaif, Teri Mehrbanian, Giraftar	40

(*Contd.*)

1	*2*	*3*	*4*	*5*	*6*
9.	Smita Patil	5	2	Ghulami, Aakhir Kyon	40
10.	Reena Rai	3	1	Ghulami	33
11.	Padmini Kolhapure	6	2	Pyar Jhukta Nahin, Pyari Behna	33
12.	Vijayta Pandit	3	1	Mohabbat	33
13.	Rekha	4	1	Utsav	25
14.	Meenakshi Sheshadri	11	2	Meri Jang, Aandhi Toofan	18
15.	Anita Raj	6	1	Ghulami	16
16.	Jaya Prada	7	1	Patal Bherwi	14.2
17.	Deepti Naval	7	1	Ankahi	14.2
18.	Rati Agnihotri	12	1	Tawaif	8.33
19.	Shridevi	3	—	—	—

20.	Shabana Aazmi	3	—	—	—
21.	Zeenat Aman	3	—	—	—
22.	Sadhna Singh	3	—	—	—
23.	Khushbu	2	—	—	—
24.	Farah	2	—	—	—
25.	Salma Aagha	2	—	—	—
26.	Munmun Sen	1	—	—	—
27.	Priya Tendulkar	1	—	—	—
28.	Parveen Bobby	1	—	—	—

Diagram 3.17 : Commercial success of twelve main actresses and their released films in 1985

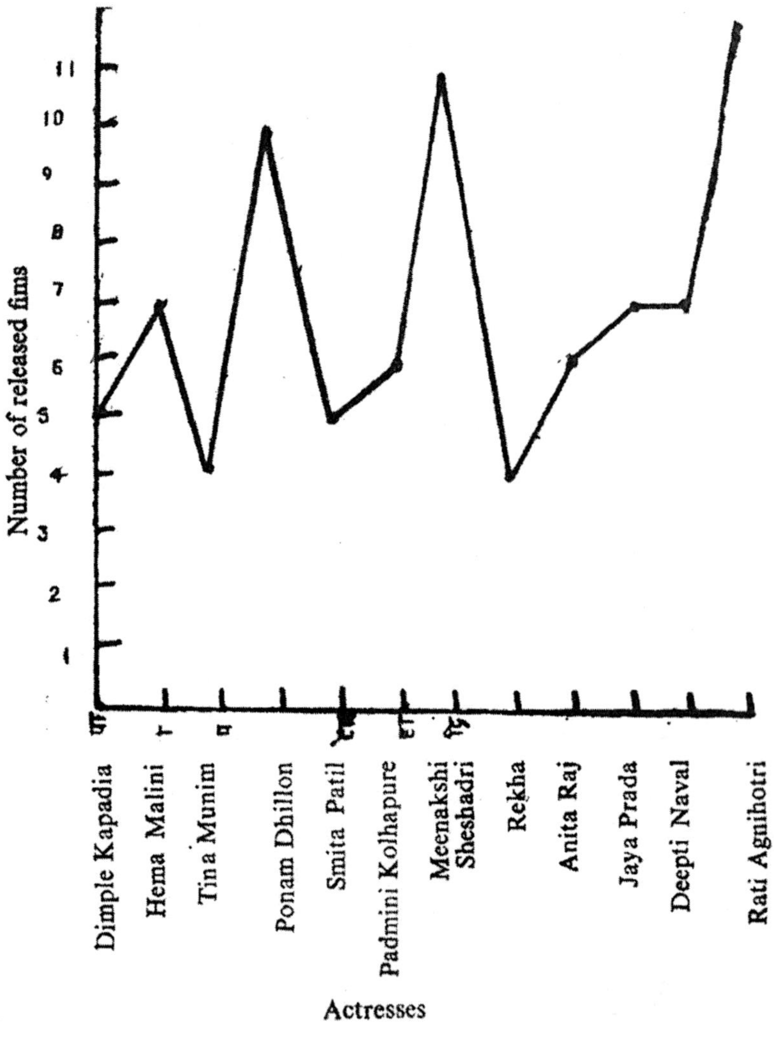

Diagram 3.18 : Commercial success of actresses whose more than one film got success in 1985

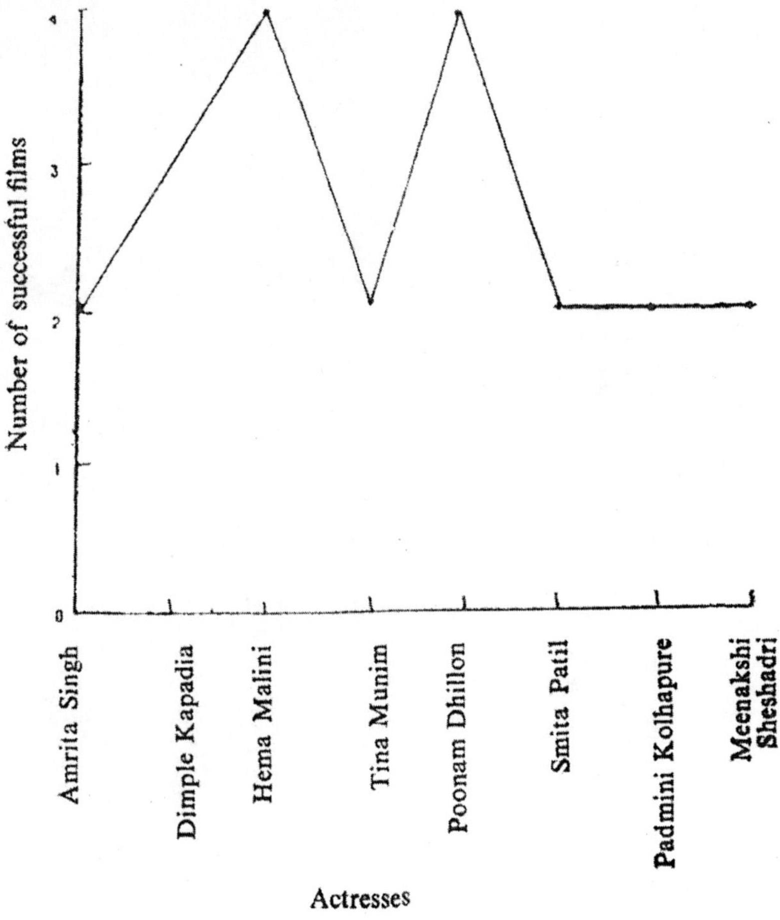

PART III

4

The Role of Hindi Cinema Institutions

The modern Hindi films and their production have no relationship with administrative institutions and their policies, how it can be possible. Indian government and state governments established such institutions which influenced modern Hindi cinema positively. Similarly, the censor policy and other policies influenced modern Hindi films. Here is a presentation of analytical study of these institutions and government policies.

(A) Film City, Bombay

The centre for production of Hindi films is Bombay. Although there are many studios in Bombay, yet for many years the cinema artists wish that there should be a "film city" in Bombay, where all kinds of facilities for shooting must be provided.

Hence "Maharashtra Film, Stage and Cultural Development" was selectcd for implementing the Film City Plan.[1] Spread over on the four hundred acre i.e. one hundred and sixty hectare area, only two floors have been constructed so far for shooting, but both of these are provided with all kinds of up to date facilities for shooting. Whole of this area is adjoining to R. Milk Colony and is rich of beautiful environmental sights. In the future planning too, the natural environment shall be kept intact. Both of these floors consist of a gallery at a higher level for light solars. So far, in the studios, old methods were used. According to that the lightmen walk on the logs hanging on cords. These hanging logs were dangerous for lightmen as well as for people working on the floor. A score of accidents have taken place due to this system. The new system of galleries is highly secure.

There are twelve make-up rooms with these galleries. Excluding make-up rooms, there are two such things, which are not found in any studio so far. Firstly there are few halls, where if producer wishes, can run his office there or he can call meetings before or after shooting. Secondly there are about one dozen such rooms to which producer, director, actors, or technicians can stay overnight if need arises. Film shooting takes place, sometimes in the day and sometimes in the night. In the night for how much time the people working in the film, have has to stay, no body knows. In such circumstances, to work without anxiety for returning home, is a facility and a need which has been overcome here.

Main Features of Film City[2]

1. *Artistic Development*

At the place of water tank, grass and garden have been particularly developed. A beauty place has been formed on

---

1. Vinod Tiwari, "Nainabhiram Chitranagri", *Maharashtra Manas*, Hindi Fortnightly, Bombay, October 25, 1978, p. 16.
2. Ibid, pp. 12-16.

three thousand square metres with trees and grass. The film industry has utilised this place for outdoor shooting at big scale. Special kind of trees have been planted on both sides of road with consultation of Forest-scientists. These trees will increase the beauty of campus. The greenery also been planted inside the studio-buildings.

2. *Pre-Examination Halls*

The size of pre-examination halls and recording rooms is 30.30×11.70 metres, in which stage for screening, sound-analysis room, houses and galleries are included. In the adjoining building, at the zero floor, there are four production rooms and on the first floor, there are administrative office, rest room, and a make-up room.

3. *Artificial Lake*

A small lake has been constructed artificially in the Film City. For it, a dam has been built of fifty five metres length. The water level is thirteen metres high and its area is thirteen thousand square metres. The capacity of this lake is twenty eight thousand cubic metres. This lake is situated within a beautiful valley, and around it are high hills, which are highly suitable for shooting.

4. *Available Apparatus*

Light : 10 K.V., 5 K.V., Multi Twenty, Multi Ten, Sun Guns and Miri Bruts.

Camera Department : Michels as per import rules, Ariflex X.R. 35 and Steady Cam. 70 mm. Sinemascope with Jhum Lenses.

Recording Department: Studio having magnetic recording apparatus and highly modern portable recorder.

5. *Studio Campus*

The whole area of studio campus is 5320 square metres, in which there is a big studio of 42.59×24.40 metres size and also a small studio of 30×18.30 metres size. There are spans of 24.50 metres and 18.50 metres for big and small studios respectively.

For both studios, there is mustic floor and walls and ceiling are sound proof. For these arrangements one lakh seventy thousand rupees were spent on big studio and ninety six thousand rupees were spent on small studio. The doors of the studio are specialy built and carrier truck can pass. Each of these doors cost one lakh rupees.

Both of these studios are sound proof. A particular kind of sound analysis system has been installed therein. The walls of the studio are double and there exists a distance of fifty millimetres between the walls for sound proof and keeping air conditioned. Such studios are just rare in foreign countries too.

There is make up department between these two studios. There are four rooms including big dressing rooms. There are several rooms for other jobs. For the benefit of producers there are rooms and verandahs at first floor.

For the artists, eleven residential flats have been constructed at first and second floor, where a canteen and a hotel are also managed. For general use, a small office is provided at zero floor. There is lift facility also.

At the first phase of this "Film City", the expenditures are assumed as 2.5 crore rupees.[3] The inaugration of "Film City" took place by the Late Deputy Prime Minister Yashwant Rao Chavan on November 16, 1977.

---

3. Ibid, p. 16.

Opinion about Significance and Importance of "Film City"

In the words of P.R.S. Pille[4]—"We wish to develop film studios area in Kerala and our Project Engineer has learnt a lot from Film City. We feel encouraged and motivated. Indian film industry can proud on the performance of "Film City".

As per Dr. Lerai M. Dearing and M.M. Dearing,[5] "India can proud on this Film City and the advanced production facilities shall be utilised. It is a fulfilment of wonderful dream.

The contribution of V. Shantaram for the construction of "Film City" is also very important. "He is the foundation pillar of the basic dream of Film City. How much intimacy he has with Rajkamal Studio, the same has with Film City".[6]

Definitely, Film City is a particular place for Hindi film makers. Maharashtra government intends to make it a significant place like universal Studio of Hollywood.[7] A lot of improvement has been taking place in the techniques of modern Hindi films. Thus these films can be compared with high level foreign films. To some extent, Film City, shall be helpful for attainment of this goal.

(B) Film and Television Institute of India (F.T.I.I.), Poona

Film and Television Institute of India, Poona, has contributed significantly in the development of Hindi films. The Institute has provided reveral good artists and technicians to the films. Shatrughan Sinha, Shabana Azami, and Rehana

---

4. President, Kerala State Film Development Corporation, Trivandram.
5. Astak Studio City, C.A. 19.604 U.S.A.
6. Noor Jehan Qazi, "Chitra Nagri—Fulfilment of V. Shantaram's dream", Ibid fortnightly, p. 23.
7. "Film City : Will it become dream city ?" (Hindi), *Dainik Jagran*, Meerut, March 24, 1985, Weekly Appendix, p. 4.

Sultan etc. got training here. However, the acting course has been postponed nowadays. Only direction, photography, and editing diploma courses are available for the trainees.

Unique in Asia

Film and Television Institute of India is a unique institute throughout Asia.[8] Many foreign students are getting education here. In the 1983-84 academic year there were 108 students, out of them fourteen were foreign based.

TABLE 4.1

Description of Foreign[9] Students

S.No.	*Country*	*Number of Students*
1.	Iran	3
2.	Nepal	2
3.	Ghana	1
4.	Lebnan	1
5.	Bengla Desh	1
6.	Nigeria	1
7.	Malaysia	1
8.	Bhutan	1
9.	Indonesia	1
10.	Philippines	1
11.	Mauritius	1
	Total Number	14

8. In the words of B.K. Karanjia, editor of *Screen*, "While there are hundreds of Institutions in this country to provide higher training in medicine, engineering and other trades and professions, the F.T.I.I. is the only institute of its kind to provide training in cinema in the entire Asian region". B.K. Karanjia, "National Disgrace", Editorial, *Screen*, Weekly, Bombay, March 7, 1986, p. 1.
9. "F.T.I.I. Appex. 149.49, Students for 1983-84", *Screen*, Ibid fortnightly, April 19, 1985, p. 6.

The above table expresses that a score of African students are also studying here.

Problems and Suggestions for Reform of the Institute

Due to different programmes at different times, many problems used to arise. The government also institute "valuation committee" to look after and evaluate its performance. In the academic year of 1983-84, a lot of changes took place in the curriculum of this institute.[10] As per the new developments in film-techniques, changes in technical courses are useful and necessary.

Generally, the students are dissatisfied due to facilities and education of the institute. Hence they have gone for

---

10. The Report for 1983-84 Academic Year :

"The second batch of the post-diploma course in film direction started from July 1984. Nine students have been admitted to this course. A series of lectures delivered by renowned film critic and historian Professor Jerzy Tooplitz was brought out by the institute. The text of the lectures was transcribed and arraaged by Miss N.S. Shahane, Film Research Officer and edited by N.V.K Murthy.

The institute and the national film archive of India jointly organised the 10th Film Appreciation Course from June 18 to July 21, 1984. Seventy participants comprising teachers, journalists, writers, media officers etc. attended it."

The report said that "the film wing offers courses leading to a Diploma in cinema with specialisation in one of the following four areas—Direction, Cinematography, Lighting and sound recording and sound engineering (SRSE). The television wing has the following five departments—television production, television films, technical operations, design and graphics and photo type research and experimental production." "F.T.I.I. : Spees, 149-49, Lacks for 1983-84" *Screen*, Ibid, Weekly, April 19, 1985, p. 6.

Diagram 4. 1: The number of foreign students at "Film and Television Institute of India", Poona in the Academic Year 1983-84

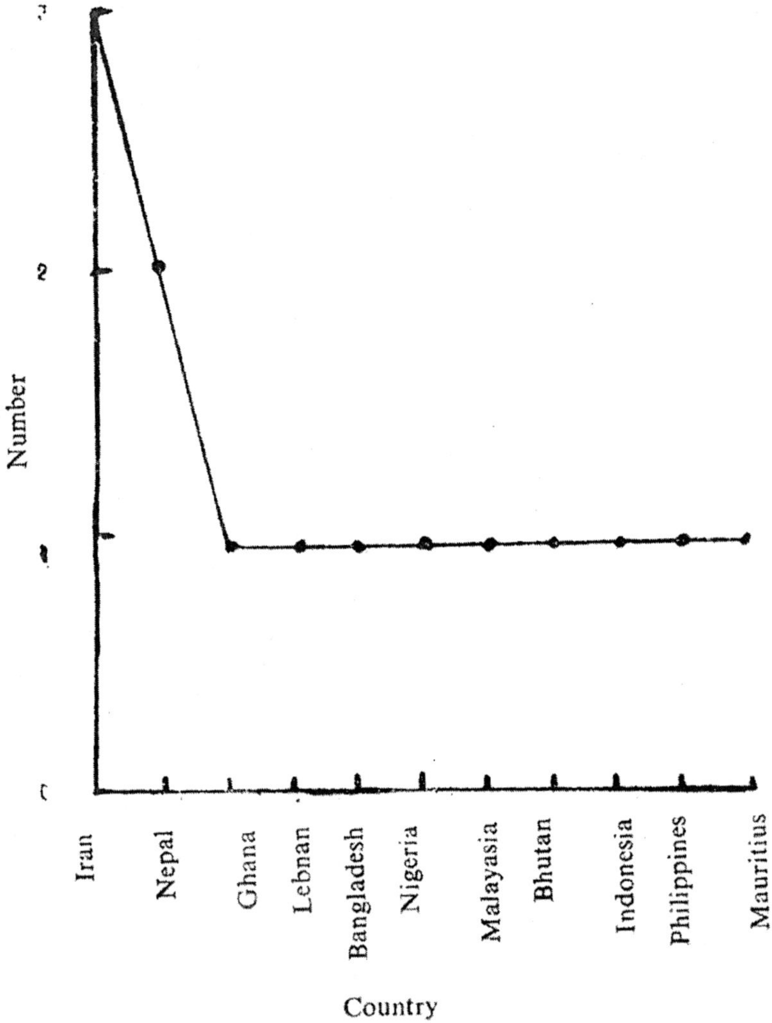

strikes at a number of times. Thus a strike took place in the second half of 1984. The performance level of the institute has come down due to it.[11] The govenment has provided sufficient autonomy to the institute for better work. We hope that this institute shall provide good technicians for production and development of Hindi films.

(C) National Film Development Corporation (N.F.D.C.)

National Film Development Corporation is an Institute of Indian government. It encourages the production of good films. If the Corporation likes any script, it can provide the sum of fifteen lakh rupees (or more if necessary) to the producer and director of the film as a loan.

An easy method to get a loan from the Corporation is that script must be based on the novel of any reputed Hindi author. The Corporation so far has sanctioned loans to the producers and directors who prepared their scripts on the basis of novels of the authors like Mohan Rakesh, Rajendra Yadav, Mannu Bhandari, Kamleshwar, Ramesh Vakshi and Nirmal Verma.

The address of the Corporation—
National Film Development Corporation
13-16 Regent Chambers,
Nariman Point,
Bombay-400021.

During the year of 1984, the Corporation provided loan for the production of seven feature films. Two films got hundred per cent loan. These both films were produced in

---

11. J.S. Srivastav, Assistant Professor at Production Establishment Department of F.T.I.I., writes,

    "Without reform in the capability of work, the Institute cannot fulfil the aspired hopes for the future."

    J.S. Srivastav, "F.T.I.I. Students Strikes, Calls and Cure", *Screen*; Weekly; December 28, 1984, p. 9.

Hindi, the first was Ketan Mehta's directed "Garam Masala" and the second was "Dev Shishu" directed by Utplander Chakravarty.[12]

The Corporation earn a lot of money through film production and other activities. It earned a profit of Rs. 62.87 lakhs in the year of 1983-84, which was particularly due to "Gandhi" films.[13] The Corporation also imports the films and distributes throughout the country.

The Corporation imported 8 films during 1980-85 period.

TABLE 4.2

Number of Films imported by Corporation

S.No.	*Year*	*Number of Films*
1.	1980-81	45
2.	1981-82	54
3.	1982-83	26
4.	1983-84	27
5.	1984-85	29
Total		181

12. "N.F.D.C. Loan for Seven Films", *Screen*, Ibid Weekly, October 12, 1984, p. 13.
13. In this respect V.N. Gadgil, Union Minister for Information and Broadcasting presented an annual report on July 29, 1985.

    "The National Film Development Corporation has sanctioned sixteen application forms in the year 1983-84 for providing loans of Rs. 119.35 lakhs. In the year 1983-84, the corporation earned Rs. 432.29 lakhs as income. The net profit in the year of 1983-84 were Rs. 62.87 lakhs while for 1982-83, the net profits were Rs. 61.68 lakhs". "N.F.D.C. Asked to Intensity Operations", *Screen*, Weekly, p. 1 and p. 16.

Diagram 4.2 : The number of imported films by N.F.D.C. during 1980-85 in each financial year

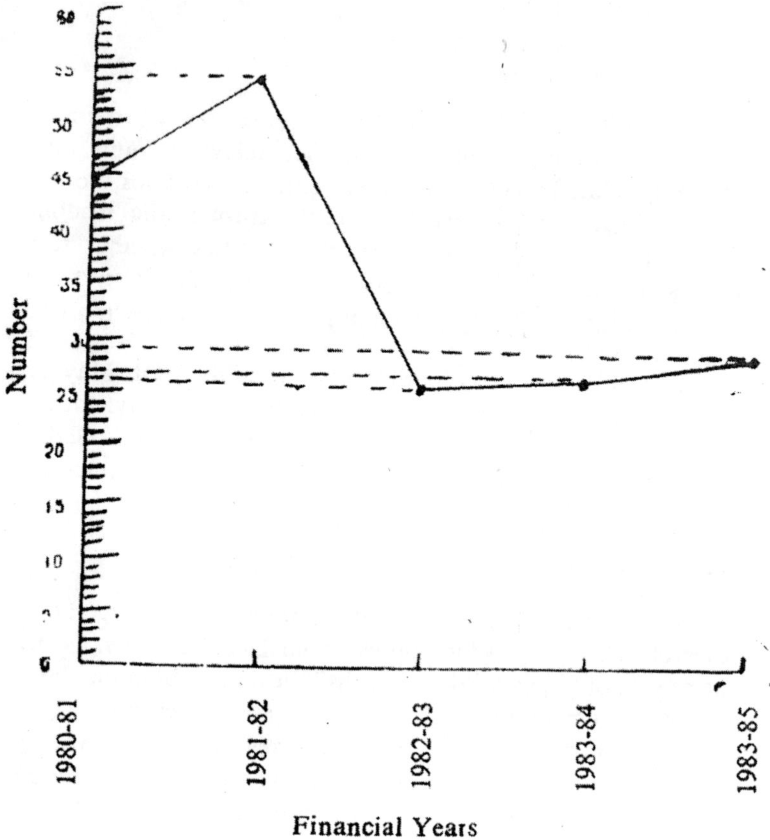

The above data explicits that the Corporation has adopted a hard attitude for the import of films in the later years, so that foreign exchange may be saved.

The National Film Development Corporation is regularly trying to improve the level of Hindi films. The Corporation always encouraged the film makers for the production of artistic Hindi films.

(D) Television

In India, the television has become one of the most influential medium of mass media. The television and films are deeply related. The television centre shows films too and particularly artistic films reach to masses through the medium of television. It may be a matter of debate that whether televisioins an obstruction in the spread of Hindi films or not, but no one can ignore the increasing popular use of television.

The television has popularised speedily. On May 25, 1985, inaugurating a television transmitter near Trivandrum, the information and broadcasting minister V.N. Gadgil informed that seventy per cent of country has been covered by the radius of television network.[14]

Imact of Television

According to a suvey of conducted by 'Operation Research Group", in the houses which have T.V. sets, 54 per cent of school going children watchs Television about one hour overy day. On sunday, about 64 per cent children watch T.V. for four hours.[15] The same survey also reveals, after surveying 1400 children of 12-14 years spread over to villages, that 60 per cent children watches children programmes regularly.[16]

---

14. *Dainik Jagaran*, Meerut, May 25, 1985, p. 6.
15. *Jan Satta*, Hindi Daily, New Delhi, February 23, 1986, p. 83.
16. *Punjab Kesari*, Hindi Daily, Delhi, February 23, 1986, p. 7.

The survey explicits that 82 per cent children watch programmes based on current affairs and social topics. Out of these, 84 per cent children seldom read newspapers.

The children like advertisement very much. About 90 per cent children told that before any programme, advertisements look them good. During the survey, 56 per cent children complained that for many reasons, the parents forbid them against T.V. watching. However, the survey tells that the parents of south India are much liberal in this respect.

The survey also points out that among all age groups people, the television news and social programmes are more popular than the newspapers.

However, whether the popularity of television has not influenced the urban culture too much, yet it had crumbled the rural culture. Never such kind of aggression took place against the heart, feelings, sentiments, body, norms and values of the rural people, what had happened after the arrival of television in the rural areas. Their culture has been uprooted, satisfaction has finished, and home-economy has become bankrupt. Yet, only ten per cent sets work there. Just after arrival of television sets, due to mechanical fault, it became useless and they feel as if cheated. To rural people, the life without television is meaningless as well as the life with television seems suspicious.[17]

With the expansion of television network and growth in the number of televisions, there is a need for the training of mechanics for repairing. The rural areas lack such facilities. If any villager purchases a set of four thousand rupees and it got some faults, but there is no arrangement for repairs.

---

17. Damodar Agarwal, "Since T.V. arrived in villages" (Hindi), *Navbharat Times*, Hindi Daily, January 15, 1985, p. 4.

Consequently, a score of T.V. sets used to be useless for many months.[18]

Since September 15, 1959 Television has been introduced in India. As per one survey, about fifty lakh sets are in the houses of Indians, and fifty million people watch different programmes on the screen of T.V. every day. However only twelve million people view films on cinema houses.[19]

Regular Dramas on Television

In India, the most popular programmes seen on television are "regular dramas". The actors, who play any role in these dramas have become popular like cinema artists.

Birh of Soap Opera

The first television serial "Soap Opera" started in America. Here after radio broadcasting, a problem came before the radi-company, that when there are no men in the house, the children are in the school, then what kind of programme must be broadcast from the Radio Station? This occurred in 1930. At the same time, an advertisement company "Procter and Gable" prepared a soap making company for broadcasting a regular familial drama (serial). The soap making company thought it profitable that at noon the house-women listening the serial dramas as well as praise of particular soap, might have used the soap too. Hence, the serial was called "Soap Opera."[20]

When the television came up, the radio programmes were converted into T.V. programmes. First it was presented

---

18. Kamal, "Will sponsor programmes finish T.V. ?" (Hindi), *Dainik Jagran*, Hindi, Meerut, September 8, 1985, p. 1.
19. Ibid.
20. Aalok Mehta, "Ham Log and Soap Opera on T.V." (Hindi), *Navbharat Times*, Ibid daily, July 29, 1984, City Edition, p. 4.

on Television during the day time. But after several independent channels introduction, there was a tough competition between T.V. serials and T.V. films.

Looking after the popularity of such programmes, the Cancer Society also used "Soap Opera" for providing information about the deadly diseases like cancer.[21] Influenced by such experiments, the other countries also serialised "Soap Opera" on their Television channels for bringing consciousness among their peoples. The United Nations Organisation appreciated such programmes prepared by Mexico Television and encouraged other countries for the same.

After the success of such experiments, the Mexico government planned "Soap Opera" for bringing consciousness among the people about family planning. The programmes presented by Television in 180 parts each of half an hour, influenced overwhelmingly to the viewers.

Influenced by this success the United Nations Oranisation counselled India, which faces population problem, to get inspiration from Mexico. Consequently in 1983, Information and Broadcasting Ministry organised a workshop in relation to "Soap Opera" and invited experts from Mexico. Thus "Soap Opera" introduced in India too.

Popular Serial "Ham Log"

"Ham Log" was the first serial presented at Indian television. "Ham Log Project" was the brain-product of former secretary of Information and Broadcasting Ministry, Mr. S.S. Gill. He has been awarded by "Padam Bhushan" for it. Mr.Gill has decided for serials on T.V. during Mexico Journey. This two hundred parts serial got sufficient popularity.[22]

---

21. Ibid.
22. Umesh Mathur, "Too much Serials on Television" (Hindi), *Dharmyug* Weekly, Bombay, March 31, 1985, pp. 9-10.

Rajni and other Serials

The serial titled as "Rajni" got so much popularity shown at the Indian television that even the Prime Minister, Mr. Rajiv Gandhi praised the heroine "Rajni" (Priya Tendulkar). Manglesh Dabral states,

"Perhaps no programme but the "Rajni" became highly popular as well as controversial. Its heroine "Priya Tendulkar" is also in discussions. The people of newspapers have also experienced her angry behaviour. The middle class women have expected such behaviour like "Rajni" in their personal life.

But the real question is that what kind of values have been taking birth with struggle against social misbehaviour? Is this jehad for a good humanistic society?

The people have many questions concerning "Rajni" in their minds, whose unveiling shall be fruitful for the society."[23]

This serial revealed all the evils present in the middle class society. Hence, it influenced the people in the direction of social change. However there are a number of irregularities in its script.

In all parts of"Rajni", it has been forgotten that the people who are responsible for evils and look as 'villains', it may be possible that they themselves are the victims of any fundamental and broad irregularity or they may be a small part of a big unjust machine. There is also no indication, that in the background of a lazy clerk, a corrupt system may be there, which left him "lazy." Such partial, half baked

---

23. Manglesh Dabral, "What are the issues behind this struggle ? (Hindi), *Jansatta*, N. Delhi, Hindi daily, Sunday Appendix, October 27, 1985, p. 1.

understanding of society, takes birth not due to gentleness, but with shrewdness, thus small evils have been exaggerated and big evils have been sided away and thus curtains are put on. In the words of German dramatist Bertiles Brecht, "We have been provided with small justices so that a big injustice may keep on".

The producer of "Rajni" Basu Chatterji, heroine Priya Tendulkar and authoress Mannu Bhandari present their logic, saying that a woman has to face such problems and irregularities in her daily life, it means that we must move forward thinking there, as the problems of all society and to go into its reason she has neither need nor time. It is her truth. To enter into politico-economic reasons is out of her affairs for it, there is no need for any remedy.

In the words of Manglesh Dabral, "No doubt, an urban middle class woman has to face such things, however, the men are also not untouched by such problems. Yet, in this logic, it had been assumed that women world-view cannot be separated from it, though sometimes it is necessary for them. It is a gentle image of an urban middle class woman, which does not reflect in real life. Why a woman should not know, understand and fight against that which has been making the society as hollow and the system as unexisted. Why does she not know the reasons of hunger, unjustice and other kind of exploitations ? Otherwise she will fight with half knowledge. It must be called an insult towards women. If men know the real causes of unjustice why women do not have the same rights ? Why the bad news should not communicate to them ?[24]

As a matter of fact, the "Rajni" serial does not present a deep solution but deals superficially, which cannot be helpful in the solution of any social problem. Any film or Television

---

24. Ibid.

serial, related to social problems, must present objective solution of the problems, hence it may get socio-political value.

The other T.V. serials which got a lot of popularity were "Khandan", "Nukkad", "Karamchand", "Ye Jo hai Zindagi" and "Vikram Betal". However"Ramayana" serial was a record as a popular serial. Majority of these serials belong to entertaining serials. For the usefulness of the serials it is necessary that their script and presentation must be as per Indian social, cultural and political environment, not a copy of foreign countries. In this respect Yugank Dheer writes, "Some producers, for speedy production of serials, are just copying foreign serials. It is an unhealthy tradition, because such serials shall be not only unnatural in our land but our culture may move towards wrong direction".[25]

There is a need that serials must be original. Hence these may be useful for our society. A score of modern Hindi film directors have shown their interest towards serials, looking up their popularity. It is a good sign.

Modern Hindi Films on Television

The Indian Television centre presents several films in Hindi and regional languages, every week. Through television millions of people watch films sitting in their homes. For the art films, which do not get success at Box-offices, television is the only medium, that millions of viewers may watch it.

At television, there should be always shown purposeful and good films, it is the demand of the people. A symposium was organised by "Delhi Film Journalist Forum" on "Films on Television". Participating in it, the then Union Minister for Information and Broadcasting Mr. H.K.L. Bhagat

---

25. Yugank Dheer, "The Coming Serials" (Hindi), *Dharmyug*, Ibid Weekly, March 31, 1985, p. 13.

said, "Purposeful and good films must be presented on television. The television can exhibit small, entertaining and socially useful films".[26] Presiding over this symposium, the editor of *Hindustan* (Hindi) daily, Mr. Vinod Kumar Mishra, said that "television is highly influential and powerful medium of entertainment".[27]

Indian television presented Hindi art films like "Paar", "Damul", "Ardh Satya" etc. However the controversial film "New Delhi Times" did not show even after getting sanction.[28] In this respect *Navbharat Times* (Hindi Daily of N. Delhi) has written an editorial as follows—

"New Delhi Times" is a realistic film related to newspapers and politics. Some unknown eyes looked up it and found objectionable. It is a matter of strangeness that the television crew members have also made up a film based on interview with the director, which would have to be shown before the film. Even then the film was found objectionable. It is obvious that two systems are on work. One is that which selects such films, finds fit for broadcasting and announces it. The second is that coverwearing system which lives behind the curtain and at the last moment hold up and push down the "explosive" materials. The joke is that this "New Delhi Times" was censored twice by the television authorities for broadcasting. However, there is no such need after obtaining censor certificate. Compelled for rupees eight lakhs, the director and producer, both have permitted not to show some parts of the film, which take six minutes time. But there is a super-censor anywhere, which is above all these censors and omnipo-

26. *Hindustan*, Hindi Daily, New Delhi, September 11, 1984, p. 3.
27. Ibid.
28. *Navbharat Times* (Hindi Daily), New Delhi, March 4, 1986, City edition, p. 1.

tent. "New Delhi Times", which was appreciated for its realism and sharpness, could not escape with his eyes".[29]

For the loose policies of Indian Television, there is criticism like above mentioned. The authorities must fix their policies for broadcasting of good Hindi films on television. A committee for selection of films may be constituted, having impartial members, who can select Hindi films with significant socio-political background, for broadcasting on Indian television.

Conclusion

Film Institute, National Film Development Corporation and Indian Television may prove how much useful for modern Hindi films, it depends upon the officials of these institutions and film-producers awakening and friendly relations with each other.

The utility of the television media éxplicits day after day. The unexpected popularity of "Ramayana" serial on Indian Television proved that television may play its due role for the protection of Hindu culture. India is one from "Kashmir to Kanyakumari", through tele-film we may increase such feelings. It is also necessary thal for the building of future generations, there must be good serials and tele-films to be shown on the television to the children. It is regrettable that sufficient steps have not been taken up in this direction. Also, there must be qualitative improvement in the educational programmes to be presented on the television. Thus it can prove its utility in the expansion of knowledge.

29. Editorial, *Navbharat Times* (Hindi), Ibid daily, March 4, 1986, City edition, p. 4.

5

Film Censor Policy

Every film used to be certified by Censor Board before its release. The Censor Board does not permit the exhibition of objectionable parts of the film. It also decides that films must be awarded "U", "A", "UA" or "S"—any one of these four categories of certificate.

Meaning of Censor

For understanding the meaning of word "Censor", we must look back towards Roman history. In ancient Rome, two officials who preside "Census" were called censor. It was started in 443 B.C.[1] Some of the jobs of "censor" were quite different from today. The jobs conferred to "Censor" in ancient Rome were following—

1. To keep schedules of tribes and election department.
2. To fix taxation with consultation of citizens.

---

1. Arjun Mehto, "Censor, Kahan Se Chala Kahan Pahuncha" (Hindi), *Madhuri*, Fortnightly, Bombay, December 24, 1982, p. 22.

3. To keep away from participation in general festivals on moral basis which was called "Regimen Mauram".
4. To deduct the names of those who could not provide taxes to census, in their lists.
5. To make arrangements for senate-election.
6. To make arrangements for tax collection and repair general public buildings.[2]

(The last two jobs were not entitled in initial period.)

Briefly, the main functions of "census" were to count the population and to keep a watch on the moral behaviour of general public. For these jobs the two English words came into being—(1) census and (2) censor.[3]

According to "The American Encyclopaedia", in modern times, censorship means control.[4] The use of this word relates to opine about behaviour and morals of others. In England those persons who survey about the non-hostel students of Oxford and Cambridge, are called "censors". The officials who issue licenses at Royal College of Physicians are called "censors".[5]

---

2. "Censorship, in its modern meaning may be defined as the control, suppression, or elimination of some or all modes of expression or behaviour, in position to established standards of belief and conduct of either public or private organisations whose prestige, power and universality enable them to act as guardians of what deemed socially right." *The American Encyclopaedia*, Vol. VI, p. 193.
3. P. Ramareddy, *Cinematography Code*, Cinematography Law Research Institute, Hyderabad, 1968-69, p. 31.
4. Arjun Mehto, Ibid article, p. 22.
5. Ibid.

Laws about Film Censorship in India

The first Hindi film "Raja Harish Chandra" was released on May 3, 1913 in Bombay.[6] Since then the production of film initiated and the government felt need for making laws about it. The first Act was promulgated in 1918 and called "Indian Cinematography Act".[7] Its provisions gave birth to censorship in India. Through this Act, "provincial censorship system" was implemented.[8] Under it, the different provinces were provided powers for censorship on films. This Act further amended in 1919 and 1920.[9] According to it, Film Censor Boards were established in Bombay, Calcutta and Madras. At that time Burma was also a part of British India, hence an office of censor board instituted at Rangoon.[10] During the decade of twenties, the film industry also took roots in Lahore, thus a separate censor board was needed for Punjab. Hence a censor board was constituted for Punjab in the year of 1927.[11]

In the censor board constituted in 1920, there were six members, out of whom three were non-governmental, representing Hindu, Muslim and Christian communities. The Bombay's Inspector General was nominated as president and two other observer members were three government members.[12] In June 1920, there were nineteen members to be appointed for the Madras censor board and twelve members for the Punjab censor board to be appointed as per Act.[13]

---

6. B. V. Dharap, *Indian Films, 1977 and 1978*, Motion Pictures Enterprise, Alka Talkies, Poona, 1979, p. 19.
7. Karuna Shankar, *Bhartiya Filmon Ka Itihas 1896-1964*, Rangbhoomi Book Depot, Delhi-110006, 1964, p. 147.
8. Captain A.K. Shinde, *Shinde's Dictionary of Cine Art and Film Crafts*, Popular Prakashan, Bombay, 1962, p. 89.
9. P. Ramareddy, Ibid book, p. 32.
10. Arjun Mehto, Ibid article, p. 22.
11. P. Ramareddy, Ibid book, p. 32.
12. Captain M.K. Shinde, Ibid book, p. 19.
13. Ibid.

To review, evaluate and study out the problems of Indian Films and Censor Act 1918, a committee[14] was set up in 1927 which was called "Indian Cinematography Committee". Its president was Diwan Bahadur T. Rangachari and hence it was stated as "Rangachari Committee".[15] "The Rangachari Committee" suggested in his report for establishment of "a central censor board", so that separate provincial censor board may be formulated. However these suggestions could not materialise till independence.

In 1949, "the Cinematography Act 1918" was amended and censorship was centralised. There were only two categories of film certificates i.e. A and U.[16] On January 15, 1951, "Central Film Censor Board" was established,[17] its central office was in Bombay and regional offices were in Madras and Calcutta.[18] The Indian government founded a committee "Film Inquiry Committee" under the presidentship of S.K. Patil.[19] It reported for a change in censor system. At last the Indian parliament passed "Cinematography Act, 1952".[20] In this Act amendments took place in 1953, 1957, 1959 and 1960.[21]

---

14. B.V. Dharap, Ibid book, p. 11.
15. Diwan Bahadur T. Rangachari (1865-1945) was a well-known lawyer of Madras. He was a Professor of Law at Madras College since 1898 to 1900. In 1908, he got selection for Madras Corporation. For 1916-1919, he was a member of Madras Legislative Assembly. He also worked as member of many other committees. "Indian Bar Committee," "Mercantile Marine Committee," and "Isher Committee" were prominent of them. He travelled many countries and represented India in many International Conferences.
16. Arjun Mehto, Ibid article, p. 22.
17. Ibid.
18. Captain M.K. Shinde, Ibid book, p. 10.
19. B.V. Dharap, Ibid book, p. 12.
20. P. Ramareddy, Ibid book, p. 17.
21. Ibid.

The objectives and reasons of "Cinematography Act 1952" were published in the gazette of Indian government.[22] The Act was welcomed everywhere and it contributed in the development of industry.

Nowadays, Central Film Censor Board has been named as "Central Board of Film Certification." Further, now two new censor certificates also institutionalised. These are "UA" and "S". "UA" certificate provided to such films to whom people above twelve years may watch. Such films are general as well as for adults too. "S" certificate is awarded to such films which may be looked upon by special kind of people.

---

22. "The Cinematography Act 1952, as it stands is of a mixed context dealing with two separate matters, namely: (a) examination and certification of films as suitable for public exhibition and (b) regulation of cinemas including their licensing. In the seventh schedule of the constitution "Sanctioning of cinematography films for exhibitions" has been included in entry 60 of the Union list and Cinema subject to the provisions of entry 60 of list I, in entry 33 of the state list. Some of the sections of the Cinematography Act, therefore, concern the central government, and some of the state governments and others both central and state governments. Some sections of the Act were amended in 1949, but only for the introduction of "A" and "U" certificates and centralisation of clear demarcation of the respective provisions of the Act with which the central and state governments are concerned, various difficulties are arising in the administration of the Act. The purpose of the present Bill is to resolve the confusion by re-enacting the provisions of the Act of 1918 as amended in 1949 separating the provisions relating to the sanctioning of films for exhibition of a Union subject from the provisions relating to licensing and regulation of cinema (a state subject)". *Gazette of India*, 1952, Part-II, Section 2, p. 220.

As per Cinematography Act, 1952" on all films either produced in the country or imported, the censorship period extends legally for initial ten years.[23] Some film producers have objections against it and they wanted to extend this period upto twenty five years in place of ten years.[24] The government of India thought about it and on September 25, 1984, joint secretary of Ministry of Information and Broadcasting issued an ordinance which was under article nine of "Cinematography Act 1952", stated that once a film has been passed by censor, needs never to be re-examined.[25] Recently, the video films have acquired too much popularity. Against illegal production of video-cassettes, the Cinematography Act was amended and this amended Act was promulgated since August 27, 1984, all over the country. In this new Act, for illegal films exhibition, there are provisions for imprisonment as well as fines more hard than before.[26] Through this amended Act, the tendency for production of illegal film cassettes may be stopped before it certified by censor.

In India, thus, film censor related Acts have been made useful and as per the requirements of the time, through amendments and changes in it.

Functions and Methods of Film Censorship

Presently, "Censor Board of Film Certification" has its central office at Bombay and excluding Madras and Calcutta, it has regional offices at Bangalore and Trivandrum. There

---

23. *Navbharat Times*, Hindi Daily, New Delhi, City Edition, October 11, 1984, p. 1.
24. *Screen*, English Weekly, Bombay, October 12, 1984, pp. 1-2.
25. Ibid and *Navbharat Times* (Hindi) daily, New Delhi, City Edition, October 11, 1984, p. 1.
26. *Punjab Kesari*, Hindi Daily, New Delhi, January 7, 1985, p. 6.

are nine members in the "Censor Board" including the president.[27] Its "Bombay Regional Consultation Committee" consists of sixty members who decide whole activities of censor. These members are used to be expert in their fields and Indian government nominates them.[28]

Any film, which reaches Censor Board for examining it, a panel of four members used to be constituted. In Bombay, there are six officers and one of their secretary. One officer watches the film with four members. For a short film, an officer and one member of panel are sufficient. The panel used to be constituted for a week out of all members. These panels watch film for the whole week. After examined by the panel, it reports to the president. Generally two films are watched in a single day. As soon as a film arrives, it is watched as early as possible. The foreign films got priority. Some members used to be nominated by Information and Broadcasting Ministry. These include journalists, professors, house-wives and businessmen. These people have no pay. One member got fifty rupees for watching one film as honorarium.[29] Before providing certificate, the film gets selection for one of the four categories—'U' (general), A (adults), UA (general but for above twelve years old people) and 'S' (special).

After deciding about a film on its category, the film producer has following options—

(A) He can forward an application for reconsidering about their decision and can express his view through an interview.

If the director did not satisfy with the decision of "Revising Committee", then he can put his fact before the

---

27. Ibid.
28. Ibid.
29. Ibid.

Ministry of Information and Broadcasting in New Delhi, which will decide after watching the film. If the producer (and director) are not satisfied with it too, they can go the court.

(B) The film goes to "Revising Committee". There are at least five and at maximum ten members watch it under the supervision of the President. There used to be no member of the previous panel. After viewing the film the committee decides. If differences are there, the majority opinion gets prevalence.[30]

If some scenes of any film are against the provisions of the censor laws, the censor prohibits them from the film before sanction. The following scenes are forbidden[31] and unfit for exhibition and the censor's scissors can run against it:

(1) Any scene, after watching that the viewers' moral standard can come down it means that there are such criminal, and anti-social scenes, viewing them the people may copy up.

(2) Such scenes, in which the activities of the criminals are shown in place of crimes.

(3) Such scenes, in which the activities of the criminals have been highlighted and the adventures of such role get exaggeration and importance.

(4) Immoral, cruel and terrorising scenes.

Excluding these, such scenes and dialogues, in which the sovereignty and integrity of the country get suspicion, contempt of the court, the security of the country may be affected and adverse impact with nations friendly to the country are forbidden to show in the films[32] and the censor

---

30. Ibid.
31. Karuna Shankar, Ibid book, pp. 149-151.
32. Kiran Pandey, Ibid Article, p. 15.

can stop their exhibition. The film censor board keeps different criterias in its mind before prohibiting any scene from the film. Some parts of the film may be excluded from one film, however the same scenes may get sanction in any other film.

In several films, the double meaning dialogues and lyrics have got sanction from censor, though these were highly objectionable. The first film of Dada Kondke was full of double-meaning dialogues,[33] however it got certificate from censor board. Similarly, one of the song of "Vidhata" film is highly immoral and double meaning, but the censor's scissors did not run against it. The then executive president of Censor Board Shrimati Aparna Mohite endorsed that 'the song' has double meaning, but she presented the logic that it was a folk song; hence it got permission.[34] The viewers criticised censor board for this song.

However, it does not mean that censor board permits every kind of scene in all films. "Chhori Gaon Ki", "Ham Se Barhkar Kaun", "Sannata", "Veliyatam" (Malyalam), "Vakil Babu", "Dasi", "Aaghi Rawa" (Telugu), "Panch Qaidi", "Dil Hi Dil Mein", "Maan Gaye Ustad", "Nari", "Nanad Bhawaj" (Marathi), "Vedurida Chitragulu" (Kannada), "Kachche Heere", "Maha Trichandu" (Kannada), "Dard", "Qasam Bhawani", "Hotel", "Khoon Ka Rishta", "Jai Bajrangbali" (Kannada), "Ghungru ki Awaz", "Sarana", "Gehra Zakham", "Fifty", "Raksha", "Shaka", "Sangdil", "Gopichand Jasus", "Jiyo to Aise Jiyo", "Kahani Ek Chor Ki", "Daulat", "Kaliya" and "Ustadi Ustad Se" are such films produced during last few years, many of the scenes and dialogues of these films were not allowed by censor.[35] Many

---

33. Prakash, "Immoral and Double Meaning Dialogues and Lyrics", *Punjab Kesari*, Delhi, July 20, 1984, p. 1.
34. Ibid.
35. Manguram Mishra, "Such are scenes which prohibit censor with cruelty" (Hindi), *Madhuri*, Fortnightly, Bombay, December 24, 1982, pp. 16-17.

times, in place of prohibiting any scene, the censor provides "A" (for adults) certificate.

There is a controversial debate over the "Kiss" scenes in the films. There are "Kiss" scenes even in the films produced forty or fifty years ago. There were forty two "Kisses" in the film titled as "Zarina."[36] "Karam" was first Indian English movie which have a score of "Kisses" casted by Devika Rani and Himanshu Rai.[37] The former union minister for information and broadcasting Mr. V.P. Sathe was not against "Kiss" scenes in the films.[38]

The censor board provides permission to the foreign films with easiness. It assumes, "the film should be examined as per the people and contemporary social levels, to which it relates".[39] Here, in Indian films too, the censor board permits "Kisses" if the story demands so. Some of the recent films like "Betaab", "Tohfa" and "All Rounder" have "Kisses" scenes, which shows the liberal attitude of censor board.[40] In fact, this changed attitude of censor board towards "Kisses" is appropriate.

Sometimes, the censor board prohibits films because it contains some controversial scenes. For example, in 1984, the censor board did not approve Hindi film titled as "Jago". This film was produced by the Congress (I) Member of Parliament Shri Jambuvant Rao Dhote and he played the

---

36. *Madhuri*, Ibid Magazine, May 2, 1980, p. 51.
37. Ibid.
38. *Madhuri*, Ibid Magazine, April 4, 1980, p. 45.
39. Vinod Tewari, "The problem of censor, just a matter of understanding" (Hindi), Ibid Magazine, December 24, 1982, p. 13.
40. Rajiv Ranjan Nag and Uma Arpita, "The attraction of censor towards kisses" (Hindi), *Punjab Kesari*, Delhi, September 15, 1984.

role of a reformist. Three ministers of Maharashtra Government also acted in it. This film was examined by Examination Committee of Central Board for film certificate. The committee placed object particularly about the emergency situation. According to one member of the committee, Mr. Dhote praised emergency at every place in the country. Advocating emergency, he suggested for reimposing it. The film titled as "The Naxalites" produced by famous film producer director Khwaja Ahmad Abbas, did not get censor certificate at the initial stage. The censor board questioned the political script of the film. But it got permission for release after four months.[41] It was provided "A" certificate.

In this respect, Mr. Abbas stated that it is very difficult to produce films on political subjects, because censor officers put too much obstructions against such films.[42] Well known film producer Satyajit Ray also claims that in India, the situation for political films is not appropriate due to censor policies.[43] Sometimes it also happened that the censor permitted for public exhibition to any film, however, the exhibition had to be suspended because of the anger of the people. For example, a ban was imposed in Jallandhar against the exhibition of Hindi film "Guru Ravidas Ki Amar Kahani". The same ban was imposed at Ludhiana district.[44] This ban was imposed because a particular community expressed angrily that the 'film' depicts the life of Guru Ravidas wrongly.[45] It is notable that the film was released after censorship.

The film titled "Nikah" based on the Muslim social background, which got extreme success at Box-offices, yet

---

41. *Radhika*, Hindi Film Monthly, New Delhi, February 1981, p. 34.
42. Ibid.
43. Bharat, "A World of Satyajit Ray" (Hindi), *Amar Ujala*, Hindi Daily, Agra, October 14, 1983, p. 7.
44. *Navbharat Times*, Hindi Daily, N. Delhi, October 27, 1984, p. 5.
45. Ibid.

a case was filed for defamation against the producer and actors. Mr. Hamdad Shakeel of Srinagar filed a case in the court of Chief Metropolitan Magistrate of Delhi for defaming Muslim life and culture and basically Islamic judicial process.[46] Similarly, a case was filed at Ghaziabad by an advocate Thakur Jitendra Chauhan, against Raj Kapoor's titled as "Prem Rog". At the court of Ghaziabad Munsif Magistrate, he filed a writ petition charging that "Prem Rog" is offensive on Thakurs[47] defaming among the general masses. The Munsif Magistrate, on its complaint, issued summons for presentation in the court on October 10, 1982. Raj Kapoor filed an application for revision against this order in the court of special judge, Ghaziabad, which was rejected. Later on, he filed an application in Allahabad High Court against it, which was after consideration, accepted and the case was postponed.[48] Thus a film based on the script of a particular communitarian background and culture, used to be a problem for the censor. The censor board members are fully conscious of the fact that no film must be against the sentiments of any community. Yet, "Guru Ravidas Ki Amar Kahani", "Nikah" and "Prem Rog" are such films whose story, script or dialogues or presentation angered the related people of that community.

The film producers are puzzled due to the problems of the censor board. In 1983, "Indian Academy of Motion Pictures and Sciences" organised a seminar[49] to discuss the problems of censor, in which the then Information and Broadcasting Minister Mr. H.K.L. Bhagat, the President of "Censorship examination committee" Justice J.D. Khosla, Shri Ram Bohra, many film producers and officers of censor board participated. The film actor Amol Palekar complains

---

46. *Dainik Jagran*, Hindi Daily, Meerut, January 20, 1985, p. 9.
47. *Punjab Kesari*, Hindi Daily, Delhi, City Edition, July 8, 1984.
48. Ibid.
49. *Madhuri*, Hindi Fortnightly, Bombay, July 8, 1983, p. 28.

that the censor has no unified policy. Due to censorship, many good films deviate from the purposes. Hence it is needed to be liberal.[50]

As far as is the concern about cenorship, the film actor Shashi Kapoor expressed that "to criticise censor has become fashion, nowadays."[51] A cine-critic views that "our censor board has been fulfilling its responsibilities."[52] On criticism of censor the views of Shri Vinod Tiwari, editor of *Madhuri* are notable as follows:

The highest point of censor criticism took place in such things, where contradiction looks obvious. If we think seriously about the prohibited scenes of the films by censor, we come to know that sometimes there are objections, where it looks quite unnecessary and somewhere such things have been permitted which angers the people continuously. Criticising censor, on this point, we must keep in our mind two things. Firstly, the members of the censor board belong to different viewpoints of the society. They have developed ideologically as per their education, family environment, post, and social status. Hence, there are sufficient probabilities that there might have been a gap between the common men and board member's point of views. Where this difference becomes too much, there is full scope for criticism.

Secondly, the countries where important decisions like to discontinue censorship, can be taken and implemented without opposition, are very little, in respect of the size of our country. In countries like India, where there are differences based on language, religion, traditions are too much, it is not

---

50. *Punjab Kesari*, Hindi Daily, Delhi, January 15, 1985, p. 5.
51. *Mayapuri*, Hindi cinema weekly, N. Delhi, July 27, 1980, p. 6.
52. Karan Arora, "Our censor board has been fulfilling its responsibilities" (Hindi), *Dainik Jagran*, Hindi, Meerut, Weekly Appendix, February 10, 1985, p. 4.

easy to set a simple general point of view for whole of the country. Here, at some places the women wander without hesitation having uncovered their breasts. At other places, the women covered from face to feet, looked up disgraceful, to come out of their homes. Although, somewhere, the girls wear shirts without sleeves and garments revealing upper parts of back, are common as modern dresses, yet at other places these are the symbols of nudity. In such a situation, if two kinds of censorship prevails, it does not mean but corruption. In fact the environment of the film needs it and hence the censor permitted it. However, it would have been happened, that they themselves, at any time, would have raised questions.[53]

The job of censor is such that how much it may be liberal and impartial, it must be criticised. However, the censor board has become too much liberal to provide "U" certificates to the films. In 1982, the censor board provided 'A' certificate to 27 films out of 507 Indian films. However, in 1981, 202 films got 'A' (for adults only) certificate out of 737 Indian films. Hence, the percentage to provide 'A' certificate was 29.4 per cent in 1981 and it came down to 5.3 per cent in 1982.[54] Similarly in the year 1982, out of 174 foreign films, 68 films got 'A' certificate.[55]

In the year of 1984, the censor board certified 833 films.[56] Of these, the Madras regional office certified 515 and Bangalore, Trivandrum and Calcutta based regional offices certified 24, 16 and 61 films respectively.[57] However in 1983, the total of the certified films was 740.

---

53. Vinod Tiwari, "Shesh Phir (Editorial Hindi)", *Madhuri*, Dec. 24, 1982, p. 5.
54. *Punjab Kesari*, Hindi Daily, Delhi city edition, June 8, 1983, p. 5.
55. Ibid.
56. *Screen*, English Cine Weekly, Bombay, January 18, 1985, p. 11.
57. *Navbharat Times*, Hindi Daily, N. Delhi, January 27, 1985, Sunday special, p. 3.

TABLE 5.1

The Number of Different Films Certified by Censor in 1983-84

S.No.	*Language*	*1983*	*1984*
1.	Telugu	134	170
2.	Hindi	132	165
3.	Tamil	128	148
4.	Malyalam	112	121
5.	Kannada	72	81
6.	Bangla	49	35
7.	Gujrati	27	30
8.	Marathi	20	25
9.	Oriya	12	14
10.	Punjabi	19	10
11.	Bhojpuri	11	9
12.	Assamese	4	5
13.	Haryanvi	1	4
14.	Nepali	2	4
15.	Rajasthani	4	2
16.	Manipuri	3	2
17.	English	1	2
18.	Urdu	4	1
19.	Brij Bhasha	—	1
20.	Khasi	1	1
21.	Garhwali	1	1
22.	Tulu	1	1
23.	Sindhi	—	1
24.	Sanskrit	1	—
25.	Kashmiri	1	—
	Total	740	833

Recently, the "Film Certification Board" adopted a liberal attitude for sanctioning "Kiss" scenes due to the needs of script. Consequently, it is abused in "Sagar" and "Ram Teri Ganga Meli." In some particular circumstances, only in adult films, if it is natural, nobody shall object against it but the film producers exploited this liberal attitude. Hence there are a score of "Kiss" scenes in such films which used to be viewed by all family members. It is harmful for the society.

Conclusion

The film censorship contributed highly for the development of film industry. The problems raised due to censorship must not create bitter environment and censor's criticism must be always constructive and purposefully, not with vested interests. It is in the interest of all.

Since the video casettes and Video Casette Recorders have become common, the responsibility of censor board intensified too much. Now millions of people look film in their homes, they can watch any day any time. In such a situation, the immoral, violent and double meaning dialogues and scenes must not be allowed in any film, so that the television media may not become polluted.

6

Main Indian Film Exporters

Indian film industry stands up at the first place all over the world. India occupies not only good place in producing films, but also in exports. In the year 1980-81, a total of 1712 films were exported, of these 1275 were Hindi films.[1] Similarly, in the year 1983-84, out of the 1170 films exported, 800 and in the year 1984-85, out of 861 films 514 were Hindi films.[2] In the Britain, United States of America, Arab countries, Latin and African countries, a huge number of Indians non-resident as well as resident live. Among these Indians, the majority have deep interest in Hindi films. Excluding it, a score of foreign peoples also like Indian films for its sweet music. Hence, foreign exchange of crores of rupees used to earn through the export of Indian films.

---

1 Indian films are source of foreign ,exchange earnings. Recently the "National Film Development Corporation" has adopted the policy to encourage export film industry. Consequently, in spite of video expansion, the film export increased rapidly. With it, the rights for selling video casettes in foreign countries, a policy has been formulated. Thus the harm done by video-smuggling may be stopped. The N.F.D.C. keeps contact with the distributors and exporters of Indian films.

2. *Screen*, English Weekly, Bombay, June 28, 1985, p. 15.

TABLE 6.1

The Number of Films produced and exported of different Indian Languages in the years 1980-81, 1983-84 and 1984-85 and their Value

S. No.	Language	1980-81		1983-84		1984-85	
		Number of Films	Value in Rupees Lakhs	Number of Films	Value in Rupees Lakhs	Number of Films	Value in Rupees Lakhs
1.	Hindi	1275	1262.11	800	742.15	514	489.43
2.	Tamil	251	141.98	226	108.19	174	75.07
3.	Malyalam	112	81.26	88	89.33	74	64.29
4.	Punjabi	12	5.07	15	6.48	5	2.18
5.	Telugu	22	5.09	20	8.02	54	18.96
6.	Bengali	25	3.49	16	12.30	27	25.12
7.	Gujrati	10	4.97	2	0.47	3	0.92
8.	Kannada	3	3.11	3	3.23	2	5.46
9.	English	—	—	3	1.75	6	11.92
10.	Marathi	1	0.09	2	0.45	2	0.41

11.	Rajasthani	—	—	—	—	—	—
12.	Konkani	—	—	—	—	—	—
13.	Urdu	—	—	1	0.30	—	—
14.	Bhojpuri	1	0.26	—	—	—	—
Total		1712	1507.43	1176	967.67	861	693.76
The export of rights of video films in foreign countries and their value		—	—	217	185.07	163	155.76
Grand Total		1712	1507.43	1393	1152.74	1024	849.52

The Table explicits that in the year of 1980-81 was more export than the year of 1983-84 and 1984-85. Also the income was too more in 1980-81. The export of Hindi films is more than other language films.

TABLE 6.2

The situation of income (Rupees in lakhs) by export of Indian films to different countries

S. No.		1980-81		1983-84		1984-85		
	Country/ Area	Number of Films	Income	Number of Films	Income	Number of Films	Income	Comparison with previous year
1	2	3	4	5	6	7	8	9
1.	Afghanistan	2	1.45	11	5.56	8	4.44	— 1.12
2.	Midle East							
	1. Iran	1	0.27	24	10.46	6	1.17	
	2. Iraq	35	25.36	13	6.84	2	1.18	
	3. Israel	52	13.71	—	—	—	—	
	4. Jordan	53	18.07	33	14.30	18	8.51	
	5. Lebnan	22	7.05	6	2.89	7	3.00	
	6. Syria	5	1.34	16	8.58	7	1.57	

7. Turkey	—	—	2	0.66	—	—	
8. Egypt	20	11.90	15	12.01	8	3.39	
9. Greece	1	0.13	4	1.42	—	—	
10. Cyprus	1	0.25	—	—	—	—	
Total	190	79.32	113	57.16	18	18.72	—38 44
3. Arab Gulf	299	537.77	281	385.64	269	304.91	—80 73
4. Far East							
1. Singapore	93	63.66	82	30.07	78	38.62	
2. Malaysia	102	40.54	30	9.24	15	2.64	
3. Hong Kong	5	1.40	1	0.06	7	3.59	
4. Thailand	10	2.76	—	—	—	—	
5. Indonesia	38	38.56	36	58.96	25	50.03	
6. Brunie	—	—	—	—	—	—	
7. Taiwan	—	—	—	—	1	0.35	
Total	248	146.92	149	98.33	126	95.23	— 3.10

(*Contd.*)

1	2	3	4	5	6	7	8	9
5.	Japan	1	0.55	8	2.35	1	1.02	— 1.33
6.	Philippines	2	0.46	—	—	—	—	—
7.	Bangladesh	1	0.04	—	—	—	—	—
8.	Sri Lanka	38	43.99	55	41.03	36	15.19	—25.84
9.	Maldives	7	0.97	26	9.60	4	1.10	— 8.50
10.	East Europe							
	1. Vugoslavia	2	1.21	1	1.47	1	0.65	
	2. Bulgaria	1	0.61	6	6.48	11	10.05	
	3. Rumania	4	1.28	—	—	1	1.56	
	4. Hungary	—	—	3	1.16	1	0.62	
	5. Chzecho-slavakia	2	0.74	—	—	1	3.20	
	6. East Germany	—	—	—	—	1	5.20	
	Total	9	3.84	10	9.11	16	21.28	+12.17

11. Western Europe (Excluding U.K.)							
1. Portugal	9	3.02	—	—	1	0.86	
2. Switzerland	—	—	1	2.50	1	0.55	
3. France	8	2.36	7	7.49	4	8.17	
4. West Germany	5	1.64	2	1.55	—	—	
5. Holland	6	2.26	1	0.23	1	1.15	
6. Belgium	2	0.74	—	—	—	—	
7. Spain	1	1.15	—	—	1	0.75	
8. Scandinavia	1	0.35	8	0.89	7	3.71	
Total	32	-11.52	19	12.74	15	15.19	+ 2.45
12. United Kingdom	111	257.07	40	50.05	38	27.64	—22.41
13. U.S.A. and Canada	96	85.79	50	9.41	19	2.82	— 6.59

(Contd.)

1	2	3	4	5	6	7	8	9
14.	Latin America	2	0.59	10	4 73	14	5.27	+ 0.54
15.	West Indies	92	44.83	19	13.38	10	5.39	— 7.99
16.	Fizi Icelands	82	60.59	67	51.44	48	32.20	—19.24
17.	Sudan	27	5.33	34	12.01	5	2.19	— 9.82
18.	East Africa							
	1. Kenya	35	10.65	1	0.35	—	—	
	2. Tanzania	52	17.89	19	15.73	10	6.79	
	3. Malawi	29	8.72	—	—	—	—	
	4. Ethiopia	—	—	—	—	—	—	
	5. Swaziland	1	0.45	—	—	—	—	
	6. Zimbabwe	—	—	—	—	1	0.33	
	7. Botswana	6	2.28	—	—	—	—	
	8. Lesotho	3	1.30	—	—	—	—	
	9. Zanjibar	—	—	1	0.20	—	—	

10. Angola	—	—	—	—	5	3.55	
Total	126	41.29	21	16.28	16	10.67	— 5.61
19. West Africa							
1. Nigeria	40	19.17	14	11.46	3	1.03	
2. Ghana	—	—	1	0.31	—	—	
3. Gambia	28	12.12	30	17.28	18	7.14	
4. Sierre Leon	7	1.54	—	—	3	0.80	
5. Liberia	21	5.87	9	3.46	2	1.40	
Total	96	38.70	54	32.51	26	10.37	—22.14
20. North Africa							
1. Morocco	96	49.63	59	32.68	29	16.38	
2. Algeria	—	—	2	0.70	2	0.67	
3. Libya	4	0.99	14	5.31	5	1.74	
4. Cameron	—	—	—	—	—	—	
5. Senegal	4	1.34	—	—	—	—	
6. Gibralter	25	8.87	11	5.08	27	11.41	

(Contd.)

1	2	3	4	5	6	7	8	9
	7. Tunisia	—	—	1	0.43	—	—	
	8. Togo	—	—	—	—	—	—	
	9. Ivory Coost	1	1.35	—	—	—	—	
	Total	130	61.18	87	44.20	63	30.20	—14.00
21.	Maurtius & Madagaskar	61	19.64	42	23.17	57	24.73	+ 1.56
22.	Yemen & Djiboti	59	22.09	51	25.09	13	6.58	—18.57
23.	Australia	1	0.39	4	1.65	6	3.46	+ 1.81
24.	Newzealand	—	—	—	—	1	0.22	+ 0.22
25.	China	—	—	1	0.72	3	3.27	+ 2.55
26.	Rest of the world (excluding areas of N.F.D.C.)	—	—	1	0.97	1	0.08	— 0.89
27.	Areas of N.F.D.C.							
	1. Soviet Union	8	38.25	16	54.01	12	45.92	— 8.09

2. Burma	9	5.95	7	6.53	6	5.67	— 0.86
3. Mozambique	—	—	—	—	—	—	—
Total	17	44.20	23	60.54	18	51.59	— 8.95
28. Export of video rights in Eastern Europe excluding the areas of N.F.D.C.	—	—	217	185.07	164	155.76	—29.31

Total Income (in Lakh rupees)

S. No.	*1980-81*		*1983-84*		*1984-85*		*Comparison with previous year*
	Number of Films	*Income*	*Number of Films*	*Income*	*Number of Films*	*Income*	
1	*2*	*3*	*4*	*5*	*6*	*7*	*8*
1.	2	1.45	11	5.56	8	4.44	— 1.12
2.	190	79.32	113	57.16	48	18.72	—38.44
3.	229	537.77	281	385.64	2699	304.91	—80.73
4.	248	146.92	149	98.33	126	95.23	— 3.10
5.	1	0.55	8	2.35	1	1.02	— 1.33
6.	2	0.46	—	—	—	—	—
7.	1	0.04	—	—	—	—	—

8.	38	43.90	55	41.03	36	15.19	—25.84
9:	7	0.97	26	9.60	4	1.10	— 8.50
10.	9	3.84	10	9.11	16	21.28	+12.17
11.	32	11.52	19	12.74	15	15.19	+ 2.45
12.	111	257.07	40	50.05	38	27.64	—22.41
13.	96	85.79	50	9.41	19	2.82	— 6.59
14.	2	0.59	10	4.73	14	5.27	+ 0.54
15.	92	44.83	19	13.38	10	5.39	— 7.99
16.	82	60.59	67	51.44	48	32.20	—19.24
17.	27	5.33	34	12.01	5	2,19	— 9.82
18.	126	41.29	21	16.28	16	10.67	— 5.61
19.	96	38.70	54	32.51	26	10.37	—22.41
20.	130	61.18	87	44.20	63	30.20	—14.00

(Contd.)

1	*2*	*3*	*4*	*5*	*6*	*7*	*8*
21.	61	19.64	42	32.17	57	24.73	+ 1.56
22.	59	22.09	51	25.09	13	6.58	—18.57
23.	1	0.39	4	1.65	6	3.58	+ 1.81
24.	—	—	—	—	1	0.22	+ 0.22
25.	—	—	1	0.72	3	3.27	— 2.55
26.	—	—	1	0.97	1	0.08	— 0.89
27.	17	44.20	23	60.54	18	51.59	— 8.95
28.	—	—	217	185.07	164	155.76	—29.31
Total	1729	1507.43	1393	1152.74	1025	489.52	—303.22

The above table signifies that comparatively in the year of 1984-85 with the year of 1983-84, less income took place by export of films. Hence it is needed that there must be hard and effective step to curb video-smuggling, so that the position of film export business may be restored.

Exporters

The export of indian films takes place by many private institutions excluding National Film Development Corporation. These institutions are situated, generally, in Bombay and Madras.

TABLE 6.3

The Prominent Private Exporters of Indian Films based in Bombay

S. No.	*Export Institution*	*Main Office*
1	*2*	*3*
1.	Aashirvad Films Private Limited	Giriraj, 383C, Linking Road, Khar, Bombay-52
2.	A.G. Enterprises	Lotia Palace, 373, Linking Road, Khar, Bombay-52
3.	Asia Films	315 G, New Chernaj Road, Bombay-4
4.	Asian Films Corporation	Alankar Cinema Building, Sardar Patel Road, Bombay-4
5.	Associated Films and Finance Corporation	Anand Villa, 15th Path, Khar, Bombay-54
6.	Avtar Singh & Company Private Limited	Mahesh Chambers, IInd Floor, 391, Narsinadha Street, Bombay-9
7.	Bajaj Brothers Private Limited	Rounder Building, Kalbadevi Road, Bombay-2

(*Contd.*)

1	2	3
8.	Basant Pictures	136, Chamar Bagh Road, Parel, Bombay-12
9.	Bombay United Traders	25-26, Kailash Darshan, Kennedy Bridge, Bombay-2
10.	C.A. Corporation	Hanuman Building, Picket Road, Bombay-7
11.	Chandra Brothers	22, Ouncey Court, "A" Road, Church Gate, Bombay-20
12.	Chhabia Enterprise	Grand Kenyan, Pali Hill, Bandra, Bombay-50
13.	Cosmos International	7/36, Air Conditioned Market, Tardev, Bombay-34
14.	Dand Association	Ghatkoper (West), Bombay-86
15.	Devika Chitra	L-3, Eden Hall, Dr. Annie Besant Road, Worli, Bombay-18
16.	Dand Exports	Mandvi Chambers, 184, Samuel Street, Bombay-9
17.	Doshi International	249, Sant Tukaram Road, Iron Market, Bombay-9
18.	Ellora Films	Naz Buildings, Dr. Dada Sahib Bhakamkar Marg, Bombay-4
19.	Embassy Films	Rooptara Studio, Dada Saheb Phalke Road, Dadar, Bombay-14
20.	Excellior Films Exchange	Govardhan Building, Parekh Street, Bombay-4
21.	Film India	4/4 Air Conditioned Market, Tardev Road, Bombay-34
22.	Films and Commerce Private Limited	Novelty Chambers, Grant Road, Bombay-7
23.	Gulmarg Industries Corporation	Engineer Building, 139, Priceless Road, Bombay-2

1	*2*	*3*
24.	Indian Film Combine Private Ltd.	Kala Bhawan, 3 Mathew Road, Bombay-4
25.	International Film Distributors	Felthom House, Ballard Estate, Graham Road, Bombay-38
26.	Jairam Trading Company	166, Samuel Streat, Bombay-9
27.	Jamnadas Brothers	G-4,Dhalmal Chambers New Marine Lines, Bombay-20
28.	Jolly Films	Naz Cinema Building, Lemington Road, Bombay-4
29.	Jupiter International	Air Conditioned Market, Tardev Road, Bombay-34
30.	Kalpna Traders	99, Old Prabhadevi Road, Bombay-25
31.	Kanji Morarji	Kanmoor House, Narsi Nath Road, Bombay-9
32.	Kishore Films Distributors	Air Conditioned Market, Tardev Road, Bombay-34
33.	Kamleshwar Films Private Limited	Rooptara Studio, D.S. Phalke, Dadar, Bombay-14
34.	Krishna Films	Naz Cinema Building, Dr. Dada Saheb Bhadkamker Marg, Bombay-4
35.	Liberty Export	Church Gate, Chambers, New Marine Lines, Bombay
36.	Madhu Enterprise	Willington Catholic Colony, Santacruze, Bombay-34
37.	Daulat Corporation Private Limited	Patel Chambers, Frenya Bridge, Bombay-7
38.	Mini Movies	Hanuman Building, Picket Road, Bombay-2
39.	Monarch Film International	2/29, A.C. Market, Tardev Road, Bombay-34

(*Contd.*)

1	2	3
40.	Mukund Films	Alankar Cinema Building, Patel Road, Bombay-4
41.	Movie-T.V. Enterprises	Ranjeet Studio, Dadar, Bombay-14
42.	Natraj Enterprises	Naz Building, Lemington Road, Bombay-4
43.	Net Tune Enterprises	Palamyara, 593, 21st Street, Bandra, Bombay-50
44.	Overseas Films Corporation Pvt. Limited	Bansi Lal Mansion, Bruce Street, Fort, Bombay-1
45.	Padam Enterprises	Raj Mahal, Sir M.V. Road, Andheri (East), Bombay-7
46.	Plaza Export Private Limited	Kailash Darshan, Kennedy Bridge, Bombay-7
47.	Krishna Films	Naz Buildings, Dr. Dada Saheb Bhadkamkar Marg, Bombay-4
48.	Rajshree Productions Pvt. Limited	"Bhavna", Veer Savarkar Road, Prabhadevi, Bombay-25
49.	R.M. International	4-A, Vijay Chambers, Tribhuvan Road, Bombay-4
50.	Sai Amusements	3-C, Ganesh Bhavan, Mahim Station, Bombay-16
51.	Saligya & Company	17, A.C. Market, Tardeu Road, Bombay-34
52.	Shamlal & Company	Kutni Mansions, Narsi Natha Street, Bombay-9
53.	Shyamlal Bal Krishna & Company	Prasad Chambers, Behind Roxy Cinema, Bombay-4
54.	Sindhi Films Pvt. Ltd.	3-G, Naz Building, Lemington Road, Bombay-4
55.	Soveinier Enterprise	2/202, Sukh Sagar, Hanuman Road, Bombay-7

1	*2*	*3*
56.	Thakkar C.P.	Gul Apartments, Haji Ali, Bombay-26
57.	Thakkar Damuwbhai M.	Alankar Cinema Building, Sardar V.P. Road, Bombay-4
58.	Tiger Films Pvt. Ltd.	Jolly Bhavan, 1, New Marine Lines, Bombay-20
59.	Trimurti Films Pvt. Ltd.	B-11, Commerce Centre, Tardev. Bombay-52
60.	Tone Fims International	Kinwin Building, Fourteenth Road, Khar, Bombay-52
61.	Universal Export	19/2, A.C. Market, Tardev Road, Bombay-34
62.	Vinoda Film Distributors	6/46, A.C. Market, Tardev Road, Bombay-34
63.	Young India Exports	45, Air Conditioned Market, Tardev Road, Bombay-34

Table 6.4

Main Film Exportors of South India

S.No.	*Exporter Institution*	*Main Office*
1	*2*	*3*
1.	Abhirami Combines	6, Ramchandra, Road Madras-17
2.	A.B.S. Productions	21/B Murugaisa Naicker Colony, Ranga -Ranapuram, Kodam-bavakkam, Madras-24
3.	All India Pictures	785, Mount Road, Madras-2
4.	Ambika Films	15, Cross Baswesvara Road, Chummunjhpuram, Madras-4
5.	Amnutham Pictures	Third Cross Road, C.I.T. Colony, Madras-4

(*Contd.*)

1	2	3
6.	Anupam Films	17/D Rajaram Directors Colony, Madras
7.	Aaradhna Movies	M.B.M. Colony, Virugamavakkam, Madras-92
8.	Aaraman Enterprises	1/A, Ramrao Street, T. Nagar, Madras-17
9.	A.R.S.A. Bar Villiappan	2, Shrinagar Colony, Gundi, Madras-15
10.	Aql Films	15, Naidu Street, Mailapur, Madras-4
11.	A.V.M. Productions	16, Edward Elliates Road, Madras-4
12.	Avtar Singh & Company	6/16, Second Street, North Bog Road, T. Nagar, Madras-17
13.	Bala Subramaniam Limited	16, Edward Illiots Road, Madras-4
14.	Bhawani Rajeshwari Arts	3764, Anna Nagar, Madras-40
15.	Chandra Prabha Pictures	264, Big Bazar Street, Coimbatore.
16.	Chandrods Art Films	38, Raja Badhor Street, Madras-17
17.	Chinappa Devar Film Trust	1/1, Venkatrama Ayyer Street, T. Nagar, Madras
18.	Chitra Films	7, North Mada Street, Madras-4
19.	Chitrakalpna Films	6/A H.D. Raja Street, Madras-18
20.	Chitralekha Film Co-operative Limited	Trivandrum-17
21.	CineDistributors	Panthipara, Trivandrum-25
22.	Cine-India Production	95, Mount Road, Madras-2
23.	Messers Cini Distributors	Pruthipar, Trivandrum-25

1	*2*	*3*
24.	Deepak Films	Central Lodge, Palghat, Kerala
25.	Devaprasad Film Distributors	12, Linwood Avenue, Lady Madhavan Nair Colony, Madras-34
26.	Dhundyuthapani Films	22, Nair Road, T. Nagar, Madras-17
27.	G.B.N. Traders	8-A, Athipattan Street, Mount Road, Madras-2
28.	Gita Chitra	14, Corporative Colony, Madras-18
29.	Gemini Colour Laboratory	121, Mount Road, Madras-6
30.	Gemini Pictures Circuit, Pvt. Ltd.	121, Mount Mary Road, Madras-6
31.	Giyo Movie Productions Pvt. Ltd.	4, Scheme Road, Mahalingapuram, Madras-34
32.	Gokul Movies	B.A. Athipattan Street, Mount Road, Madras
33.	Hajini Films	1, Park New Road, United India Colony, Kodambakkam, Madras-24
34.	Indian Film Combine Private Limited	11/A-3 Mount Road, Madras-2
35.	Intercontinental Film Distrbutors	111, Mount Road, Madras-6
36.	Jagpati Art Pictures	34, Habibullah Road, Madras-17
37.	Jamal and Sayani	Cinema Film Exporters, Inganbacheri, Kerala
38.	Jyoti Films (Madurai) Pvt. Ltd.	Kashuri Rang Ayenga Road, Madras-18

(*Contd.*)

1	*2*	*3*
39.	Juno Globes Export	65, C.N.K. Road, Chepak, Madras-18
40.	Kalakendra Movies	1, C.V. Raman Road, Madras-18
41.	Kanagamani Combines	10, Venkatraman Street, Madras-17
42.	Kerala Film Distributors	4, Arumuga Nikene Street, Madras-1
43.	Krishnaswamy Associates Private Limited	5, Mahatma Gandhi Road, Shastri Nagar, Madras-77
44.	Lankal Films	65, N.G.O. Colony, Rajaram Methra Nagar, Madras-17
45.	Modern Theaters Limited	Salem-7
46.	Movie Exporters	2, Main Road, Raja Anna Malaipuram, Madras-28
47.	Movie Exporters	2, Vishwanathpuram, First Street, Madras-24
48.	Mooruman Movies.	Usman Road, T. Nagar, Madras-17
49.	Movie International	7/B, Smith Road, Mount Road, Madras-2
50.	Mathu Enterprises	7, Masilatmani, Mudaliar Road, Balaji Nagar, Madras-14
51.	Narayan Company Pvt. Limited	26-A, Mount Road, Madras-2
52.	Narayana S.A.	10, Thapar Sahib Market Lane, Madras-2
53.	Naresh Films	9,F. Kalinga Colony, K.K. Nagar, Madras-78
54.	Navnitha International	5, Maren Sahib Street, Madras-2
55.	Navrang Pictures	14, Moren Sahib Street, Mount Road, Madras-2

1	*2*	*3*
56.	Oceanic Film Distributors	Rothapetah, High Road, Madras-14
57.	Peruvaram Enterprises	7, th Main Road, Raja Annamalai puram, Madras-28
58.	Prabhakaran	4, Venkteshwar Lane, Perriyar, Pathai Madras-94
59.	Prasad Productions Private Limited	2, Saranpari Street, T. Nagar, Madras-17
60.	Premalya	2, IIIrd Cross Street, C.I.T. Colony Madras-4
61.	Prosperity Pictures	13/28 Ludge Avenue, Mailapur, Madras-4
62.	Radha Krishna Combines	23, North Bogue Road, T. Nagar, Madras-17
63.	R.K. Films	172 C, Arcot Koad, Madras-26
64.	Raman Pictures	4, Bogue Road, Madras-17
65.	R.M.S. Productions	Third Cross Street, C.I.T. Colony, Madras-45
66.	Ratan Pictures	Gandhi Nagar, Bangalore-9
67.	Sarat International	Sai Baba Mandir, Vijaywara-8
68.	Sabine Hills	47, Nallanna Mudali Street, Madras-14
69.	Shaji Movies	1124, West Anna Nagar, Madras-40
70.	Shanu Enterprises	3, Linwood Avenue, Madras-34
71.	Shahnaj Films	26, West Avenue, Mula Street, Madurai-1
72.	Shiva Productions	3, Vicent Nagar, Madras-14
73.	Shiva Enterprises	Shivalya Building, Commander-in-Chief Road, Madras-8

(*Contd.*)

1	2	3
74.	S.K. Pictures	Vasan Street, T. Nagar, Madras-17
75.	Southern International Films Distributors	13-A, Chitrakulam, North Street, Madras-4
76.	S.P.T. Films	B-269, Tenth Anenue, Ashok Nagar, Madras-83
77.	Shrinivas Arts Productions	4E, Vedchala Gardens, Madras-28
78.	Shrichitra Mahal	32, Venkatnarayan Road, T. Nagar, Madras-17
79.	Shri Films	First Street, South Gopalpuram, Madras
80.	Shrigijavalli Pictures	Balmiki Street, T. Nagar, Madras-17
81.	Shri mukambika Movies	11, Theruvenkatswamy Naiker Street, Madras
82.	Shri Vinayga Pictures	4, Bogue Road, T. Nagar, Madras.17
83.	Sterling Distributors	Aneppi, Kerala
84.	Subbu Productions	Murage Gate Road, Alwarpet, Madras-18
85.	Sujata Cine-Arts	29B, Panthen Road, Madras-8
86.	Sundram P.M.	Agrahram, Ravipuram Road, Cochin, Kerala
87.	Thriumani Pictures	60,Nandnam Extension, Madras-35
88.	Umayyavigai Combines	3, Sunkuwar Agraham Street, Chintaripet, Madras-94
89.	Union Films	44-A/1 Burkit Road, Madras-17
90.	Usha Films	18, Venkateshwar Lane, Periyar Pedai, Madras-94

The Bombay based exporting institutions export Hindi films, while the Madras and other Southern Indian cities based institutions not only export the South Indian linguistic films but these also purchase the rights of Hindi films produced there. These export-oriented institutions are in good condition and these have good reputation in foreign countries.

Conclusion

We earned 97.13 lakh rupees through the export of Indian films in 1954. Since then this number increased continuously and in 1976-77 this amount reached to Rupees 602.43 lakhs. The Indian films have been liked too much in foreign countries. Britain, America, Soviet Union, Japan, Singapore, Arab, Nepal, Srilanka, Afghanistan, Thailand, Ghana, Iran, Jordan, Korea, Lebanan, Nigeria, Mauritius, Malaysia, Hong Kong, Burma, Morocco, West Germany, Indonesia, Italy, Yemen and West Indies are those countries to whom export of Indian films has been taking place since last three decades. In these countries, a huge number of viewers are keenly awaiters of our films. There are more than two dozen institutions which export Indian films, prominent of them are "International Film Distributors", "Overseas Film Corporation", "Indian Films Combine", "Bombay United Traders", and "Ellora Films".

For improving the condition of film export and increasing demand among conventional markets, Indian government established IMPEC, about twenty years ago. Indian Motion Pictures Exporting Corporation (IMPEC), just a little time after its establishment in 1970-71, exported films worth rupees 47 lakhs. The other exporting institutions exported films worth rupees 576 lakhs. However, IMPEC did not get success as per expectations, hence the government declared its extinction five years ago. The responsibility to export films was provided to National Film Development Corporation. Due to improvidence of the Corporation, the reputation of markets for Indian films has come down. Prior, the Indian films were exhibited in Middle East and East Asian countries on commercial basis. The African countries also liked Indian films, but now Indian films do not reaeh there.

During last five years, the situation has worsened more. Although in a number of countries, the Indian cinema and artists established their identity, the demand for Indian films in Venice and France have increased manifold, in other countries its popularity came down. The film producer and actor Mr. Shashi Kapoor toured foreign countries for selling his film "Utsav", returning home he stated that during last years the demand for Indian film has decreased in the foreign markets. Now good films have to be sold up at lower prices. As per Shashi Kapoor, during the times of "Janoon" and "Kalyug" there was no such situation. The reason is that the foreign distributing companies did not permit to stay the Indian films in comparison with American and European films.

Here it is notable that the demand for Indian films in Gulf countries has increased. There in most of the cinema-houses, Indian films used to be shown. Recently, one Indian film did the business of two lakh rupees within one week. It is a matter of concern that even after all kind of efforts, we earn a little money with the export of films. We may agree that the demand for Indian films has come down, but it has several reasons. However, one reason is the smuggling in the film business. We have to lose crores of rupees due to smuggling and pilfering. According to one estimation, we used to lose about eight crore rupees in foreign exchange due to pilfering. The ten per cent discount provided to the laboratories for film print is used as pilfering.

Secondly, a score of films used to send London for processing. The colour film laboratories of London are the bases of smuggling. Here, they prepare the "negative" of the films and produce new prints out of it which used to be sold over Latin America, Africa and West Asian nations. A number of middlemen perform this job. The film producer, comes to know about this theft, when anyone tells him that one of his film has been showing in a particular city.

Another reason for decreasing demand of Indian films in foreign countries has been stated as "videotheft". Today, the video theft is not only a challenge and problem for Indian cinema, but to world cinema. Every country, individually, as well as with co-operation to other countries, wish to face this problem.

The National Film Development Corporation must change its policies to face video theft. It must adopt a new policy, which may fulfil the demand of Indian films for Indian citizens settled abroad and also it can face the video film theft, spread all over the world.

However, it is a matter of fact, as one cannot stop the spread of video cassettes, so one cannot stop the film video theft, completely. Keeping it in mind the nation must make her place in the world market. The National Film Development Corporation, also must take initiatives for securing its due place in the world market, even after video theft.

For it, the Film Development Corporation, first of all search out the places, which have potential for Indian films, however Indian films so far have not reached there. Secondly, we must know the reasons, in the areas, where Indian film demand has decreased. Probably, the video theft may not be responsible for it, and some immoral films have filled the market, adversely affecting Indian films. Hence good and interesting films must be produced and exported to such countries.

PART IV

7

Regional and Local Cinema

India is a country of different languages. The different languages spoken in different parts of the country have contributed to the development of Indian culture. Tamil, Telugu, Kannada, Malyalam, Oriya, Bangla, Assamese, Punjabi, Urdu, Bhojpuri, Rajasthani, Sindhi, Haryanvi etc. languages are those in which many films were produced and these influenced the public mind too much. The Hindi cinema is deeply related with regional and less speaking linguistic cinema. In contemporary transitional period of Indian cinema, the regional and small linguistic cinema also influenced Indian culture. Therefore, it is necessary that an analytical description of these films development may contribute to understand the Hindi film point of view.

In 1984, the Telugu films occupied highest position as per numbers. In a total of 823 films produced, 170 were Telugu films.[1] In 1983, with the production of 134 Telugu films it

1. *Jansatta*, Hindi Daily, N. Delhi, February 4, 1985, p. 2.

secured first position.[2] Not only numerically, but with the viewpoint of art and technique, the regional linguistic films hold first place.

South Indian Linguistic Films

In the history of Indian films, the south Indian linguistic films occupy a proudy place. All the four languages of south India viz. Talugu, Tamil, Kannada and Malyalam, produced films since silent films period. A descriptive analysis of all these four linguistic films is as following.

Telugu Films

The history of Telugu films started in 1909 when a popular artist Shri Raghupati Vakyaya Naidu imported "cronomagaphone" instrument and exhibited some foreign films.[3] However, authentically the history of Telugu films started when Shri Raghupati Vakyaya Naidu established "Star of the East Films" institution and his son Mr. R. Prakash produced a silent film titled as "Bhishma Pratigya".[4] This film was not only the first Telugu film but was the first of all the south Indian linguistic film.[5] During 1920-30 period, R. Prakash, C. Pullamaya and V.V. Rao produced Shajendra Moksha, Nandnar, Kanyaka Parmeshwari, Vishnu Leela and other silent films.[6]

---

2. *Screen*, Weekly, Bombay, January 18, 1985, p. 2.
3. Inturi Venketshwar Rao, "Introduction to Telugu Film Industry" (Hindi). in Devdutt Shastri edited "*Prithviraj Kapoor Abhinandan Granth*, Vishal Manch, Allahabad, 1963, p. 41.
4. Bal Shourie Reddy, "History of Telugu Films", "*Hindustan Weekly* (Hindi), New Delhi, December 27, 1964, p. 25.
5. Ibid.
6. Mahendra Mittal, *Bhartiya Chalchitra*, Alankar Prakashan Delhi, 1975, p. 563.

The first speaking Telugu film titled as "Bhakta Prahlad" was released in 1931. The main artists of this film were V.V. Subbarao and Surbi Kamla Bai.[7] This film was produced by "Movieton Flms Company" of Bombay under the supervision of H.M. Reddy. He is said the founder of "talking" films in Telugu.[8] "Sagar Movieton" produced two films "Paduka Pattabhisham" and "Shakuntla". In 1933, two companies of Bombay and Calcutta produced two films titled as "Savitri" in Telugu.[9] Since then, every year two or three films were produced. At the end of 1939, the production area of Telugu films has limited to Madras only.[10]

TABLE 7.1

Description of Telugu Films produced during 1940-1950 period in Madras

S. No.	*Name of the Film*	*Production Company or producer*	*Year*
1	*2*	*3*	*4*
1.	Bhoj Kalidas	Jai Films Limited	1940
2.	Sumangali	Vahni Pictures	1940
3.	Chandika	Bhawani Pictures	1940
4.	Apwad	Kasturi Films	1941
5.	Chunamani	Janki Pictures	1941
6.	Devta	Vahni Pictures	1941
7.	Mahatma Gandhi	Feature Film	1941
8.	Parvati Kalyanam	Praful Pictures	1941

7. Karuna Shankar, *Bhartiya Filmon Ka Itihas,* Alankar Prakashan, Delhi, 1975, p. 563.
8. Mahendra Mittal, Ibid, p. 563.
9. Karuna Shankar, Ibid, p. 117.
10. Mahendra Mittal, Ibid, pp. 565-566.

1	2	3	4
9.	Thalli Prem	Raj Rajeshwari	1941
10.	Bhalla Palli	Jagannath Production	1942
11.	Jeevan Mukti	Jemini Pictures	1942
12.	Patni	Saarthi Films	1942
13.	Deenbandhu	Roopvani Pictures	1942
14.	Bhagya Lakshmi	Shri Renuka Films	1943
15.	Pantul Amma	Saarthi Films	1943
16.	Tehsildar	Jagdish Films	1944
17.	Kamalokam	Saarthi Films	1945
18.	Swarag Seema	Vahni Pictures	1945
19.	Bhakta Tulsidas	Raj Rajeshwari	1946
20.	Graha Pravesham	Saarthi	1946
21.	Varudhni	Anand Pictures	1946
22.	Brahma Ratham	Shri Vektaram	1947
23.	Palnati Yudham	Shri Sharda	1947
24.	Yogi Waman	Vahani Pictures	1947
25.	Bhakta Sariyal	Murli Pictures	1948
26.	Drohi	Swatantra Films	1948
27.	Geetanjali	Shyamal Films	1948
28.	Gun Sundri Katha	Vahani	1949
29.	Keelughurram	Shobnachal Pictures	1949
30.	Mandesham	M.R.A. Production	1949
31.	Aahuti	Navin Films	1950
32.	Beedla Patlu	Pakshiraj Studio	1950
33.	Jeevanam	A.V.M. Productions	1950
34.	Palltarupill	Shobhnachal Production	1950
35.	Lakshmi Amma	Shobhnachal Production	1950
36.	Swapan Sundri	Pratibha Production	1950
37.	Sansaram	Sadhna Pictures	1950

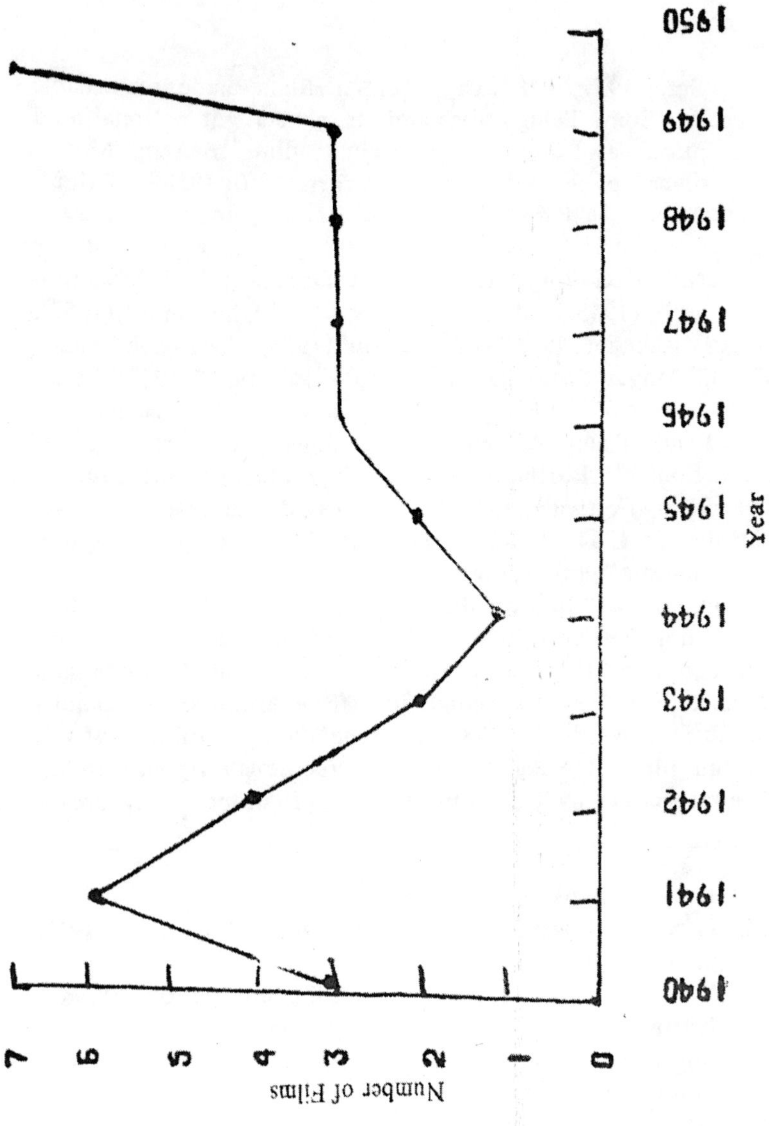
Number of Films
0
1
2
3
4
5
6
7
1940
1941
1942
1943
1944
1945
1946
1947
1948
1949
1950
Year

The study of above table expresses that during this period, mostly religious films were produced. The above diagram presents that in the year 1944, the least i.e. only one and in 1950, maximum i.e. seven Telugu films were produced respectively.

Since 1951, till today, Telugu films made remarkable process. Some Telugu films and its artists got national and internationl awards. In 1955, Telugu film "Bangru Maya" got silver prize in the state award.[11] In 1958, "Pallinti Pranamalu", in 1963, "Nammina Bantu", in 1964 "Nartan Shala" and in 1965 "Dr, Chakravarty" got silver prize of the President. Excluding these "Thondu Dongalu" (1955), "Bipra-narayana" (1955), "Ardhangi" (1956), "Adinizamu" (1957), 'Bhagya Rekha' (1957), 'Todi Kodalu' (1958), "Manglya Balam" (1952), "Mayanti Mahalakshmi(1960), "Jai Marg" (1960), "Sita-ram Kalyanam" (1961), "Shri Sampdalu" (1963), "Kulagotralu (1963) and "Ramdasu" etc. Telugu films got "certificates of distinction".[12] Furthermore, the Telugu films got international awards at Festivals and thus increased the respect of the nation. In 1964, at Jakarta Festival, the artists of Telugu film "Narthansala", Mr. Rangarao got "best actor award and its art director got "best art director prize".[13] In 1978 at Calovi Veri Film Festival, Telugu film "Oka Oriya Kaka" got prize of the jury and Film Club Prize.[14] In 1981, at Kogbasankan (France) Film Festival, Telugu film "Shankrabhramak" acquir-ed music prize.[15] In 1982, at Kualalampur Film Festival, Telugu film "Thyaggya" got "best religious scripted prize".[16] The respect got by Telugu films at international level proves

---

11. Karuna Shankar, *Ibid book*, p. 119.
12. *Filmfare*, English Weekly, Bombay, August 23, 1963, p. 30.
13. V.P. Sathe (editor), *Filmotsav 84*, Directorate of Festivals, Nariman Point, Bombay, 1984, p. 105.
14. Ibid p. 106.
15. Ibid p. 107.
16. Ibid p. 108.

the capacity for competition among them at international cinema. The Telugu films are also successful commercially too. In 1971, eleven Telugu films got topmost success at Box-Offices.[17]

TABLE 7.2

Most successful (Hit) Telugu films and their artists in 1971

S. No.	*Film*	*Artists*
1.	Bullama Bulludo	Chalam, Vijaylalita
2.	Kalyana Mandapam	Shoban Babu, Kanchan
3.	Mattilo Manikyam	Chalam, P. Bhanumati
4.	Mosagallaka Mosagdu	Krishna, Vijaynirmla
5.	Premnagar	A. Nageshwar Rao, Vanishree
6.	Pavitra Bandham	A. Nageshwar Rao, Kanchan
7.	Raitu Kutumbkam	A. Nageshwar Rao, Kanchan
8.	Ritu Bidda	N.T. Ramarao, Vanishree
9.	Sati Ansuya	Kanta Rao, Jamuna
10.	Shri Krishan Satya	N.T. Ramarao, Jaylalita
11.	Tahsidrugri Ammai	Shobhan Babu, Jamuna

An analysis of the above table presents the interesting fact that among the male artists Chalam, Shobhan Babu, Krishna, A. Nageshwar Rao, Kanta Rao and N.T. Ramarao's two, two, one, three, one and two films of each got success at Box-offices respectively. Among the actresses Vijaylalita Kanchan, P. Bhamati, Vijaynarmila, Vanishree, Jumuna and Jayalalita's one, three, one, one, two, and one of each film got success at Box-offices respectively.

17. B.V. Dharap, *Indian Films 1973*, Motion Pictures Enterprises, Alka Talkies, Poona, 1974, pp. 482-83.

Diagram 7.2 Main Telugu Films and their Artistes in 1971

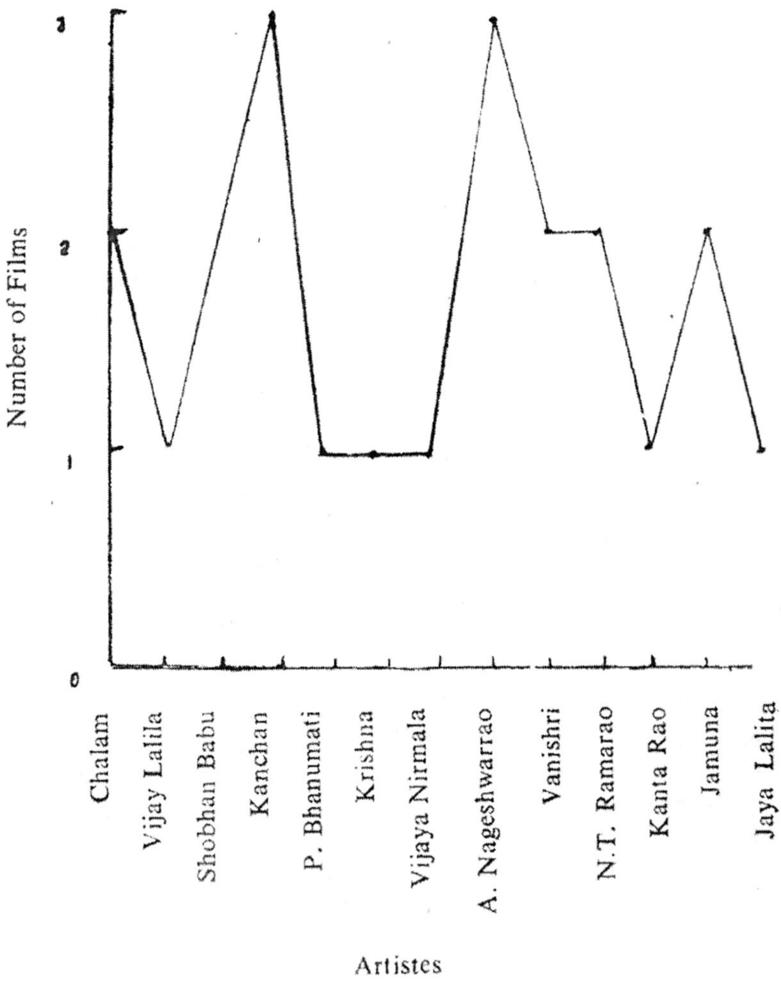

Similarly in 1972, "Badi Pantulu", "Bala Bharatam", "Bangru Babu", "Collector Tanki", "Illu Illalu", "Mannabadu Dhanavudu", "Pandati Kapooram", "Sampurna Ramayanam", "Tad Manavadu", and "Vichitra Bandham" etc got success (Hit) at Box offices.[18] In 1973 the following films[19] got success at Box-offices— "Dabbuku Lokam Dosoham", "Davudu Chasina Manushula", "Desodharakulu", "Gandhi Puttina Desam", "Jeevan Tharnagulu", "Mayadari Malligadu", "Meenarubabu", "Neeramu Shiksha" and "Sharda".

The Telugu actress "Veenashri" got Filmfare prize in three successive years[20]. In 1973 her film "Jeevan Tarangul", in 1974, "Krishnavani" and in 1975 her film "Jeevan Jyoti" won this prize.[21] She is one of the topmost actresses of Telugu cinema. Similavly, Telugu actor Shobhan Babu got Filmfare Prize three times[22]. He got this prize forhis films, 'Osita Katha' in 1974, "Jeevan Jyoti" in 1975 and "Soggadu" in 1976.[23] His film "Soggadu" established many new records of success.

Dr. Mahendra Mittal writes about qualities and disqualities of Telugu films and said, "As per qualities and disqualities of Telugu films, the aesthetic and artistie side is remarkable. A score of best Telugu films can be compared with Marathi, Bengali and Hindi films on account of diversity of subjects and to incorporate different topics. Generally, Telugu films are comedies. However films like "Sumangali",

---

18. Ibid p. 486.
19. Ibid p. 489.
20. *Madhuri*, Hindi Fortnightly, Bombay, April 4, 1980, p. 30.
21. Ibid.
22. Ibid.
23. Ibid.

a tragedy, popularised it due to the wisdom of the director and emotional acting of the artists."[24]

Although in 1984, the production of 170 films in Telugu, provided it first position in the country, yet the Telugu films have to face many problems this year.[25] Even then the number of Telugu films increased every year. Some studios have been established in Hyderabad and the producton of Telugu films has taken place with Madras simultaneously. Telugu films are the proud of Telugu people.

Tamil Films

Tamil films took debut in 1931. The first Hindi talking film "Aalam Aara" was presented by Imperial Film Company and the same company produced first Tamil film "Kalidas."[26] The dialogues of this film were in Tamil and lyrics were in

---

24. Mahendra Mittal, Ibid book, p. 570.
25. Y.V. Rao writes in *Screen* about the situation of Telugu film industry :

    "The year 1984 can be described as a bad year for the Telugu film industry. The worst drought conditions, the cyclone in Nellore and Chittor districts, the death of Mrs. Gandhi, the spurt in the distribution sector and the competition from the video parlours have caused a heavy loss to the industry.

    In 1984 the Telugu film industy increased its production to 170 films. In 1983, 136 Telugu films were released. But this increase has resulted in the failure of several films."

    Y.V. Rao, "1984—Bad Year for Telugu Industry," *Screen*, English Cine Weekly, Bombay, January 11, 1985, p. 14.
26. *Indian Talkie*, Film Federation of India, Patel Road, Bombay, 1956, p. 88.

Telugu. T.P. Rajlakshmi was its heroine.[27] In 1932, four and in 1933, seven Tamil films were produced. These films were produced by Bombay and Calcutta's Companies. The first talking Tamil film "Shriniwas Kalyanam" was produced in 1943 at Madras. This was also the first talking film of Southern India.[28] This year, fourteen Tamil films were produced.[29] During 1935, thirty eight Tamil films were produced. The scripts of most of these films were based on Hindi mythological stories, rishi-munis and widows lives.[30]

TABEE 7.3

Main Tamil Films and their Producing Companies during 1935 in Madras

S.No.	*Name of the Film*	*Production Unit*
1.	Dhruv	Pioneer Company & Angles Films
2.	Nallathangil	Pioneer Company & Angles Films
3.	Kaushalya	South Indian Films
4.	Krishna Arjun	Royal Talkie
5.	Markanday	Vale Pictures
6.	Lanka Dehan	Chellam Talkie
7.	Sati Ahlya	Chandra Bharti
8.	Gun Sundari	Shrinivas Cineton
9.	Gul Bakoli	Tamilnadu Talkie

27. Karuna Shankar, Ibid book, p. 109.
28. Mahendra Mittal, Ibid book, p. 57.
29. Ibid.
30. Ibid.

TABLE 7.4

Important Tamil Films produced during 1936-45 period and their producing units

S. No.	*year*	*Film*	*Production Unit*
1	*2*	*3*	*4*
1.	1936	Balyogini	Madras United Arts, Calcutta
2.	1936	Devdas	New Theatres, Calcutta
3.	1936	Mahabhartam	Messes Tamil Nadu, Bombay
4.	1936	Basant Sena	Tripur Talkies, Madras
5.	1936	Vishwamitra	Shrinivas Cineton, Madras
6.	1937	Ambikapathi	Shanker Company, Salem
7.	1937	Bhasmasur Mohini	Sundram, Madras
8.	1937	Chintrmani	Royal Talkies, Madras
9.	1937	Mr. Tight and Mr. Loose	Sundram Talkies, Madras
10.	1937	Kaviratna Kalidas	Genesh, Madras

11.	1937	Vipra Narayana	Madras Sound & Srinivas, Madras
12.	1937	Virat Parvam	Shrinivas, Madras
13.	1938	Seva Sadan	Chandraprabha Cineton, Madras
14.	1938	Shri Ramanuj	Yessel Films, Madras
15.	1938	Toofan Queen	Prakash Lakshmi Production, Bombay
16.	1939	Matra Bhoomi	A.L.R.M. Company, Madras
17.	1939	Trunilakantar	Tyagraj Films, Madras
18.	1939	Tyag Bhoomi	Madras United Arts, Madras
19.	1940	Child Marriage	Rukmani Pictures, Madras
20.	1940	Urvasi-Shesham	Band Pictures, Madras
21.	1940	Raja Yogam	Modern Theatres Limited, Madras
22.	1941	Ali Baba Chaleesh Chor	Ashok Films, Madras
23.	1941	Aryamala	Prithiviraj Studio, Madras
24.	1941	Ashok Kumar	Murugun Talkie, Madras
25.	1941	Maya Jyoti	Jai Laxmi, Madras
26.	1942	Kannagi	Jupiter Pictures, Madras

(Contd.)

1	2	3	4
27.	1942	Prithiviraj	Central Studio, Madras
28.	1942	Sanyasi	Jupiter Pictures, Madras
29.	1943	Mangamma	Gemini Studio, Madras
30.	1943	Harishchandra	Sarswati & Sriraj Rajeshwari Pictures, Madras
31.	1944	Jagat Laprdapan	Pakshiraj, Madras
32.	1944	Haridasas	Royal Talkie, Madras
33.	1945	Jambolingam	Premier Cineton, Madras
34.	1945	Meera	Chandraprabha Cineton, Madras

An analysis of the above table shows that during this period 85.8 per cent Tamil films were produced in Madras, 5.9 per cent in Calcutta, 5.9 per cent in Bombay and 2.9 per cent at Salem.

Diagram 7.3 : Number of Tamil Films during 1936-45 period as per year

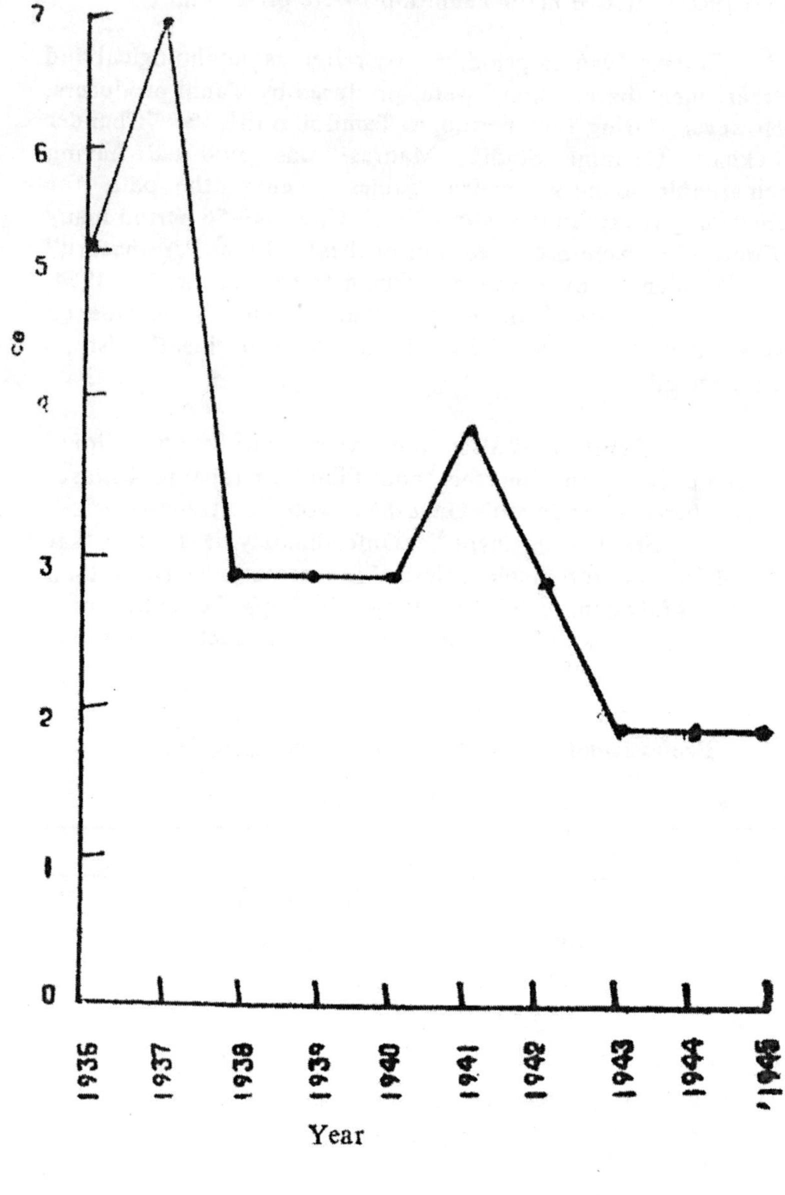

The above diagram presents that the highest nomber of Tamil films were produced in 1937 and during 1943, 1944 and 1945 only two main Tamil films were produced.

During 1946-48 priod, mostly religious, mythological and great men based films were produced by Tamil producers. However during 1948 pericd, a Tamil film titled as "Chander Lekha" (Gemini Studio, Madras) was produced having remarkable dances, sword games opened the path for imaginary royal families stories. During 1949-56 period many Tamil films were produced, out of these, "Ether Parathaturu" got President's silver award. This film was produced in 1954. Similarly, in 1956, "Mangaya Tilkam" film was President's silver award, in 1957, "Kuladevam" won President's distinction award.

The Tamil films also won awards during International Film Festivals. In 1960, the Tamil Film "Veerapadia Kattaroman" hero actor Shivaji Ganeshan won "Best Actor Prize" at Cairo Festival in Egypt.[31] Unfortunately, it is a fact that Tamil films are too much backward in international award than Bangla, Malyalam and Telugu films. Perhaps the reason for it is the passiveness of Tamil producers with respect of festivals.

TABLE 7.5

Professionally successful Tamil Films during 1971-73

S. No.	*Year*	*Film*
1	*2*	*3*
1.	1971[32]	Kulama Ghulama
2.	1971	Riksha Vakram
3.	1971	Sawale-Samali
4.	1972[33]	Gananaoli

31. V.P. Sathe (editor), *Ibid book*, p. 104.
32. B.V. Dharap, *Ibid book*, p. 482.
33. Ibid, pp. 485-486.

1	2	3
5.	1972	Kasethan Kadabulada
6.	1972	Nalla Neeram
7.	1972	Pattkada Pattanama
8.	1972	Pagunda Veeda
9.	1973	Aarang Teran
10.	1973	Bhar Thanvilas
11.	1973	Ingle Thanga Raja
12.	1973	Pantha Manam Peethu
13.	1973	Pukkari
14.	1973	Raja part Ranga durrai
15.	1973	Raja Raja Chojan
16.	1973	Surya Kanthi
17.	1973	Urgan Sutram Valibum

The study of the above table shows that during 1971, 1972 1973, three, five and nine Tamil films got professional success respectively. The Tamil people have great affection for films. Subsequently they have instituted "clubs" on the name of film artists.[34]

About the greatness of Tamil Films, one well known cinema author Dr. Mahandra Mittal writes :

"When we look upon at Tamil Films keeping artistic, emotional and aesthetical values in mind, no doubt it can be said that whatever be its position during earlier Tamil films, but nowadays the Tamil films are winning distinctive awards, so speedily, in comparison with other regional films, presents the highest points inherited, the idealistic, artistic and aesthetic senses and capacities within the Tamil Films."[35] The impact

34. Ibid, p. 489.
35. Mahendra Mittal, *Ibid book*, p. 575.

Diagram 7.4 : The number of professionally successful Tamil films during 1971-73 period, in each year

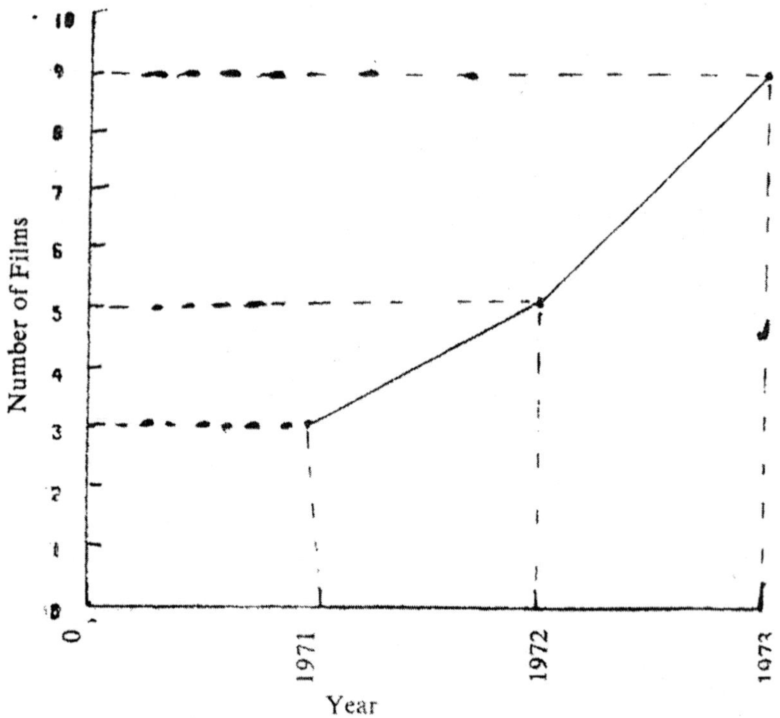

of Tamil films on Tamil people have been so vast that Tamil politics have been controlled by Tamil cinema giants. Hence the film and politics are two sides of one coin for Tamil people.

Kannada Films

Kannada language is the prominent language of Karnataka state. During silent days one film "Mrisch Kati Ka" (earthen vehicle) was produced in 1929. This film acquired popularity not only in India but also in foreign countries, particularly in Germany.[36] But the first talking film in Kannada "Dhruv Kumar" was produced in 1934, three years after the production of Aalam Aara.[37] This was produced by "Jaiwani Films, Bombay" company.[38] Its main artists were Muttu and Kanak Lakshmi.[39] The same year, "Sati Salochna" Kannada film was produced. The first Kannada film produced in South India was "Sansar Nauka" and its production unit was "Devi Films, Madras".[40] In the same year, Mr. B. Thimayya established "Mysore Sound Studio" and in 1937, produced first Kannada film titled as "Rajsu Yagya."[41]

During 1938-40 period, no Kannada film was produced. The Kannada films produced during 1941-53 period, generally related to the mythological themes.[42]

---

36. Mahendra Mittal, *Ibid*, p. 578.
37. Karuna Shankar, *Ibid*, p. 121.
38. Mahendra Mittal, *Ibid book*, p. 577.
39. Karuna Shankar, *Ibid book*, p. 121.
40. Mahendra Mittal, *Ibid book*, p. 578.
41. Ibid.
42. Ibid, pp. 578-579.

TABLE 7.6

Main Kannada Films and their production units during 1941-53 period

S.-No.	*Year*	*Film*	*Production Unit*
1.	1941	Subhadra	Birenna & Acharya, Bombay
2.	1941	Basant Sena	Pragati Pictures, Madras
3.	1942	Jeevan Natak	Gubbi C.S. Films, Madras
4.	1942	Prahlad	Kaladvani Films, Madras
5.	1943	Harish Chandra	Sarswati, Madras
6.	1943	Krishna Sudama	Kaladvani Films, Madras
7.	1943	Radha Raman	Shri Vijay Films, Madras
8.	1947	Krishna Leela	Mahatma Pictures, Madras
9.	1949	Meera	Shivananda Films, Madras
10.	1949	Dashehra	Shantiram Production, Bombay
11.	1949	Nag Kannika	Mahatma Pictures, Madras
12.	1949	Sati Tulsi	Ayangar Pandrang, Madras
13.	1951	Jagat Mohini	Mahatma Pictures, Madras
14.	1951	Tilottama	Sukhsagar Chitra, Madras
15.	1953	Jatak Palan	R.N.R. Production, Madras
16.	1953	Mangla Gauri	Modern Theatre, Madras
17.	1953	Saubhagya Laxmi	Mahatma Pictures, Madras

Diagram 7.5 : The Number of Main Kannada Films during 1941-53 Period in each year

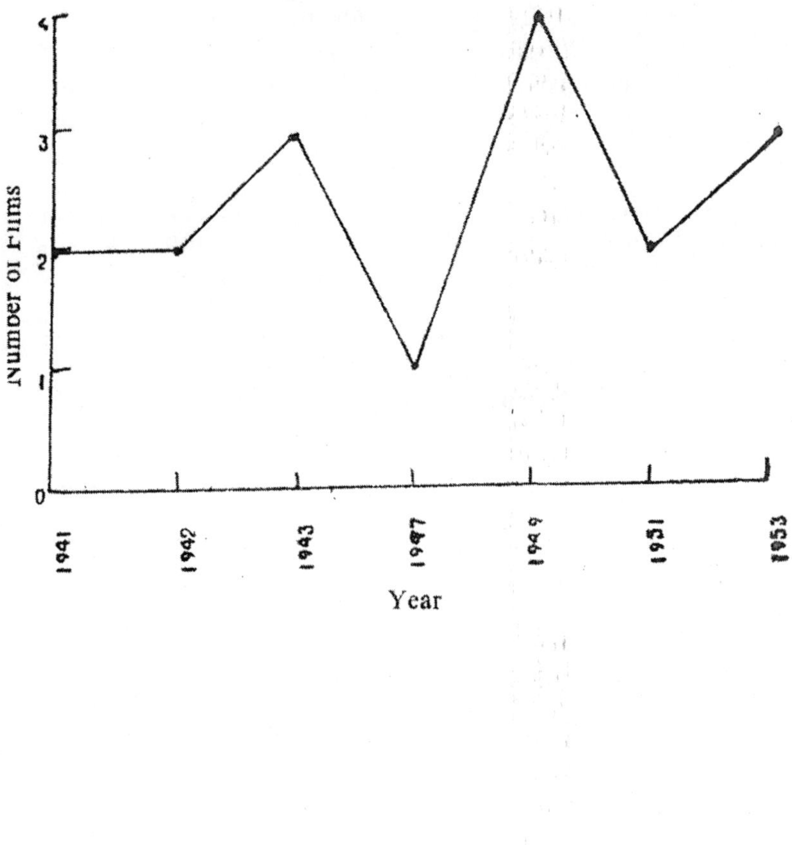

An analysis of the diagram 7.5 explicits that there were ups and down in the production of Kannada films during 1941-53 period. During Second World War, and subsequent years i.e. 1943-47 period the number decreased permanently, however after independence the situation became well.

Since 1954, after the promulgation of state awards for films, Kannada films also got encouragement. The number of Kannada films increased rapidly onwards. In 1983, seventy two and in 1984 eighty one Kannada films got censor certificates.[43]

Professionally too, the condition of Kannada films can be called satisfactory. With the point of view, 1971 proved notable for Kannada films.[44] This year many films got success at Box-offices.

In 1972, Kannada films titled as "Bangruda Manushya", "Bhole Hucha", "Hirday Sangam", "Jaga Metchide Bhaga", "Kuchla Agent 000", "Nari Munidari Mari", "Nagara Habu", and "Nanda Gokul" etc. proved successful at Box offices.[45] In 1975 Kannada films like "Eda Kull Gudada Mele", "Gandhada Gudi" and "Sampurna Ramayana" were successful at Box offices.[46]

Recently, Mr. H.M.K. Murthy contributed too much for the development of Kannada cinema. He is also elected the Presidenl of new organised "Kannada Film Producers Association."[47] As a cameraman, director and producer, his

---

43. *Screen*, English Cinema Weekly, Bombay, January 18, 1985, p. 1.
44. B.V. Dharap, *Ibid book*, pp. 483-84.
45. Ibid, p. 487.
46. Ibid, p. 490.
47. *Screen*, Weekly, Bombay, January 11, 1985, p. 14.

TABLE 7.7

The Successful Kannada Films, its artists, director and music director

S. No.	*Film*	*Main Artists*	*Director*	*Music director*
1.	Jatha Karatna Gunda Jyo aisa	Udai Kumar, Lata	B. Padmanabham	Kodandapani
2.	Kula Gaurav	Raj Kumar, Jyoti	Paketti Shivram	T.G. Lingappa
3.	Namma Sansara	Raj Kumar, Bharti	Sidhlingyah	M. Rangarao
4.	Nyaya Vedevara	Raj Kumar, Sarojadevi	Sidhlingyah	Rajan-Nagendra
5.	Pradhidvani	Raj Kumar, Aarti	B. Dorairaj S.K. Bhagwan	G.K. Venkatesh
6.	Shara Panjara	Kalpna, Gangadhara, Aswadh	S.R. Puttanna Kangal	Vijay Bhaskar
7.	Sipai Ramu	Raj Kumar, Leelavati	Y.R. Swami	Upendra Kumar
8.	Thai Devara	Raj Kumar, Bharti	Sidhlingyah	G.K. Venkatesh
9.	Vamsha Vriksha	Sarda, Venkantrao, Talgiri, Girish-Karnad	B.V. Karandh	Chandavarkar

Diagram 7.6 : Successful Kannada Films and their artistes in 1971

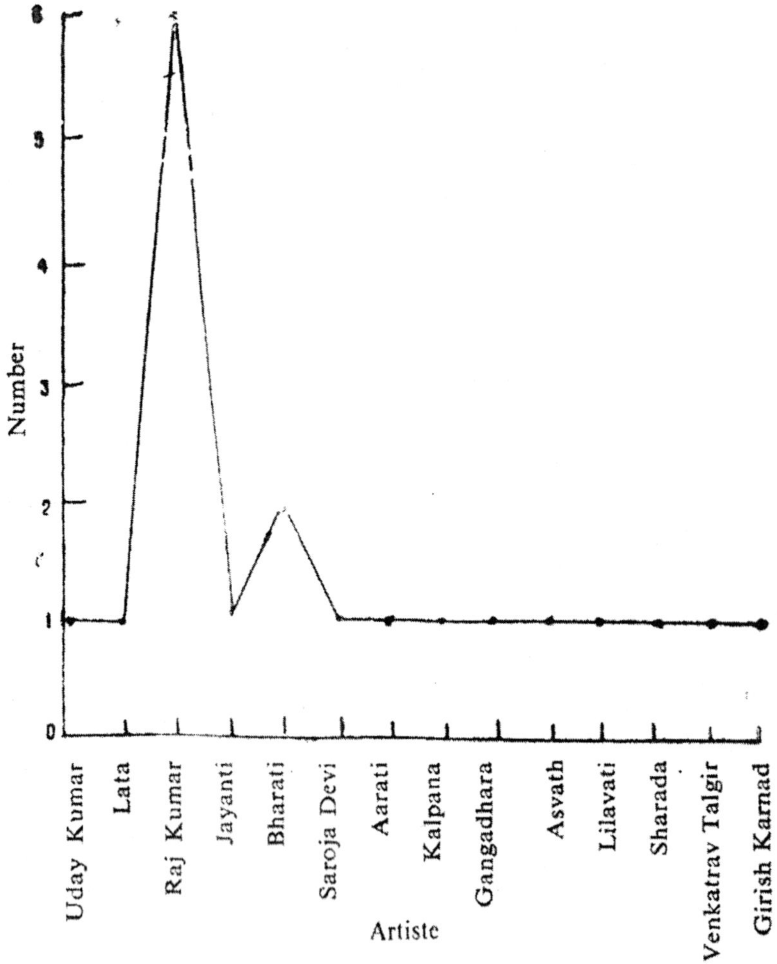

ntribution in the history of Kannada films is notable.[48] In the middle of 1984, "Central Board of film Certification" established one of his regional office at Bangalore and this office released censor certificates to 24 films.[49] The contribution of Kannada moving cinema houses is also notable for exhibiting Kannada films. As per one ordinance of the provincial government, these cinema houses have been turned as semi-permanent cinema". As per one estimation, the number of such cinema houses is 655. About ten thousand people work in these and a sum of rupees thirteen crores have been consumed in this profession. The Karnataka government earns about five crore rupees annually from such cinema houses as entertainment taxes.[50] The Kannada distributors and producers are earning a lot from these cinema houses, because the rents of permanent cinema houses are comparatively more. The future of Kannada films depends upon the factors that with professional success, how much they have artistic qualities.

---

48. G.G. Rajendra writes, " There are few people in the state of Karnataka who are concerned about the development of the local film industry. Among them, Mr. H.M.K. Murthy is the most sincere. As a cameraman, director, producer and with plans to get into distribution Murthy is definitely a very active and enthusiastic person.

    ... During the course of his third film production Murthy took active part in organising the Kannada film producers. The Kannada Film Producers Association was thus formed under his presidentship and for the first time the exhibitors in Karnataka began to take the producers seriously. The screen of Kannada films in all the theatres of Karnataka now became a reality. The production of Kannada films increased from 15 to 20 films a year to between 60 to 80 in 1983-84."

    G.G. Rajendra, "H.M.K. Murthy—The producer is the real Architect," *Screen*, English cine Weekly, January 11, 1985, p. 14.
49. *Screen*, Bombay, January 18, 1985, p. 11.
50. *Jansatta*, Hindi daily, N. Delhi, March 6, 1987, city edition, p. 5.

TABLE 7.8

Main Malyalam Films and their producing units during 1950-55

S. No.	Year	Film	Production Unit
1	2	3	4
1.	1950	Prasanna	Pakshiraj Studio, Coimbatore
2.	1950	Chandrika	Krishna Production, Madras
3.	1950	Chachi	Kailash Pictures, Madras
4.	1950	Nalla Tanka	K. & K. Productions, Madras
5.	1950	Shashidharan	Kailash Pictures, Madras
6.	1950	Istri	Kamala Films, Madras
7.	1951	Jeevit Nauka	K.K. Production, Madras
8.	1951	Nav Lokam	Popular Production, Madras
9.	1951	Ramt Bandham	Jai Bharat Pictures, Madras
10.	1951	Yachkam	Keral Production, Trivandrum & Coimbatore

11.	1952	Amma	Associated Production, Madras
12.	1952	Aatm Shanti	Citadel Films, Madras & Coimbatore
13.	1952	Desh Bhaktam	Pakshiraj Studio, Coimbatore
14.	1953	Aashadipam	Associated Production, Madras
15.	1953	Jinova	Chandra Pictures, Coimbatore
16.	1953	Lok Niti	Kailash Pictures, Madras
17.	1954	Grah Devta	Nagur Cine Production, Madras, Coimbatore
18.	1954	Neelakkumil	Chandratara Production, Madras, Trivandrum and Coimbatore
19.	1954	Sneh Seema	Associated Pictures, Madras, Coimbatore
20.	1955	C.I.D.	Neela Production, Madras, Coimbatore
21.	1955	Harish Chandra	Neela Production, Madras, Coimbatore
22.	1955	Natya Tara	Ravi Films, Madras
23.	1955	News Paper Boy	Mahatmaji Memorial Associated, Madras & Coimbatore

Malyalam Films

"Balam" was the first Malyalam film produced by "Modern Theatre", Madras in the year of 1938.[51] There are less evils in Malyalam films because its debut took place late. In the year 1940, "Gun Ambika", in the year of 1941, "Prahlad", in 1948, "Nirmala", in the year of 1949 "Valli Navshatram" titled Malyalam films were produced. About two dozen Malyalam films were produced during 1950-55 period.

There are many more Malyalam films produced during this period, excluding above mentioned. The next table 7.9 presents the total number of Malyalam films produced each year during this period.

TABLE 7.9

The total number of Malyalam films produced each year during 1950-55 period

S. No.	*Year*	*Number of Films*
1.	1950	6
2.	1951	7
3.	1952	10
4.	1953	7
5.	1954	8
6	1955	7
	Total	46

The Malyalam films progressed too much on account of numbers as well as qualities. The first three dimension film in India titled as "Hallo Mr. Dear Kutchatan" was produced in Malyalam.[52] The same film was dubbed in Hindi titled as

51. Mahendra Mittal, *Ibid book*, p. 582.
52. *Jansatta*, Hindi Daily, New Delhi, City edition, January 3, 1985, p. 2.

Diagram 7.7 : The Number of Main Malayalam Films produced each year during 1950-55 period

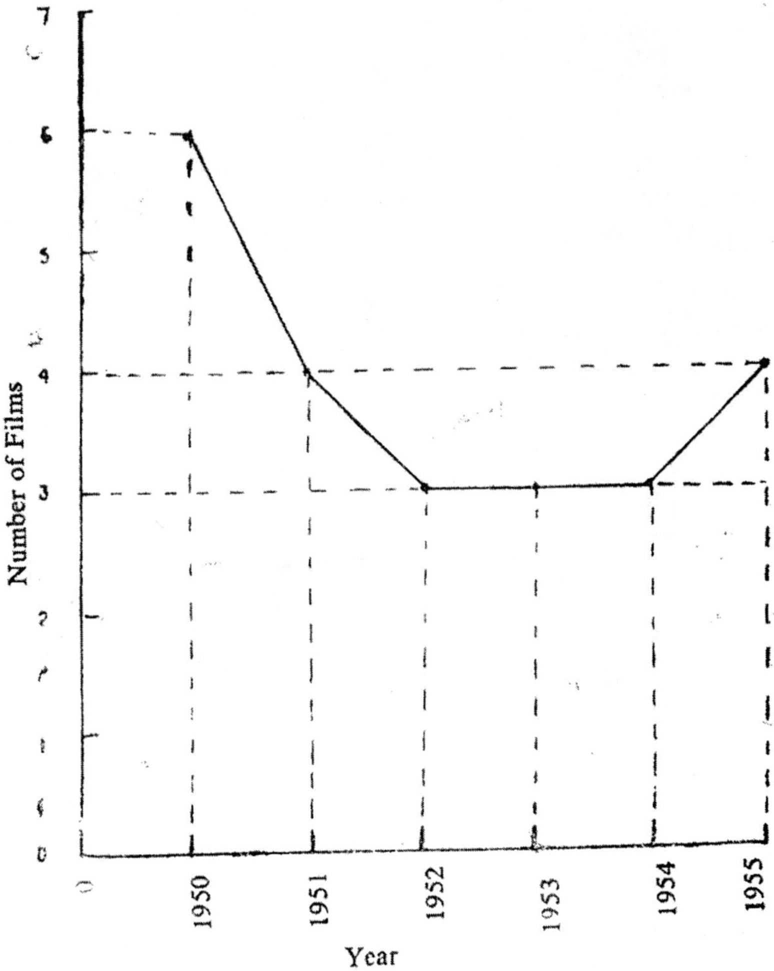

Diagram 7.8: Number of total Malyalam Films produced during 1950-55 period per year

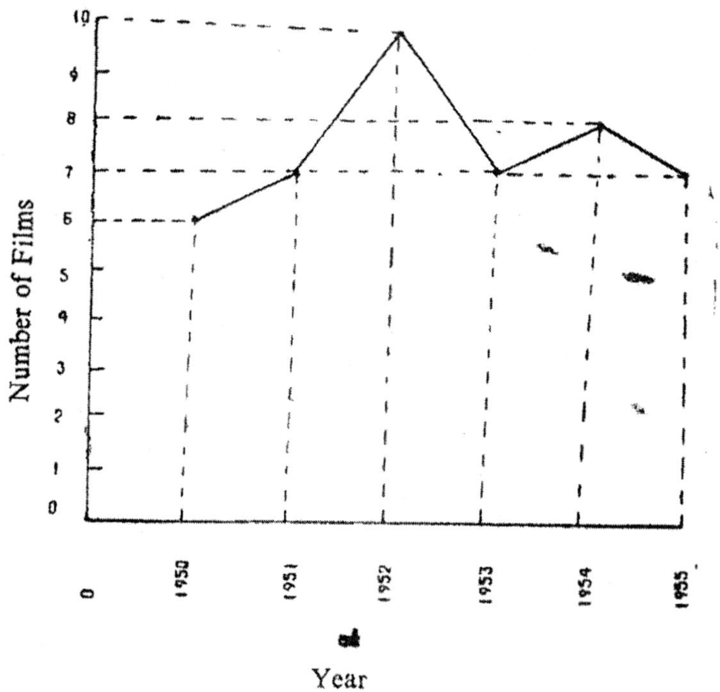

"Chhota Chetan". This film got remarkable success at Box office. In 1984, one hundred twenty one (121) and in 1983, one hundred twelve (112) Malyalam films were produced.[53] The "Central Board of Certification" also opened one of his office at Trivandrum[54] in 1984. This office issued censor certificates to sixteen films on the debut year.[55]

Malyalam films are not produced with boundation of any tradition. In this respect Dr. Mittal presented a comprehensive analyasis. He states that, "one of the significant characteristic of Malyalam films is that these are not bound with any tradition or path, as we find in Hindi and other regional linguistic films. In these films, particularly social scripts are taken and these are related to progressive ideology and expressed afterwards. Excluding it, the production of these films takes place with limited budget. Hence the industry has left mythological and highly dressed films absolutely. Thus Malyalam films, though less in number compared to Hindi and other regional films, yet it kept its originality intact. However the number of Malyalam films have been increasing rapidly during recent years.[56] Nowadays, Malyalam films are famous for sex scenes. In fact, the viewing community of Malyalam cinema is too much limited compared to others, so the producers present such things that may attract other people towards Malyalam films. Hence, due to it, there are much more sex-scenes in Malyalam films.

East Indian Linguistic Films

Like Bombay, Calcutta too, has been a prominent centre for film-making since silent-film period. The Bengali films are well known for their literary excellence and highest quality. Similarly two other languages of East India i.e. Oriya and

53. *Screen*, cine-weekly, Bombay, January 18, 1985, p. 11.
54. Ibid.
55. Ibid.
56. Mahendra Mittal, *Ibid book*, p. 585.

Assamese have many films to their credit for decades. Subsequently the description of these three linguistic films is to be presented here.

Bengali Films

It is a matter of controversy, that who could be called the "founder" of Bengali film industry.[57] However, J.F. Madan can be said the founder of Bengali film industry.[58] Mr. Madan was a Zoroastrian of Bombay and settled in Calcutta. In 1917, he started the production of Bengali films under the banner of "Madan Theatres Limited". This institution produced about one hundred films.[59] Authentically, this institution has been assumed as the foundation stone base, at which Bengali film industry was established and flourished.[60]

In 1919, the "Arora Film Company" produced first Bengali film titled as "Vish Vraksha" under the direction of Mr. Devighosh.[61] In the same year, "Madan Theatres" presented his first film titled as "Nal Damyanti". The company also produced "Bilwa Mangal", "Raja Harish Chander","Mahabharat", "Dhruv Charitra" etc. films likewise year.[62] Being silent films, the Bengali culture did not get any expression through these films. Many more such films were produced during silent-film period.

In the year 1931, after the release of "Aalam Aara", the first Bengali talking film "Jamai Shushthi" was exhibited. This film was produced by "Madan Theatres" under the direction

---

57. Ibid, p. 507.
58. Ibid, p. 509.
59. *Filmfare*, Weekly, Bombay, June 24, 1966, p. 45.
60. Devdutt Shastri, (Editor), "*Prithiviraj Kapoor Abhinandan Granth*, (Hindi), Vishal Manch, Allahabad, p. 19.
61. Mahendra Mittal, *Ibid book*, p. 509.
62. Ibid.

of Amar Chaudhary.[63] During the period of 1931-39, many popular Bengali films were produced.[64]

TABLE 7.10

Main Bengali Films produced during 1931-39 period

S. No.	*Year*	*Film*
1.	1931	Jamai Shusthi
2.	1931	Dena Pavna
3.	1932	Nater Puja
4.	1932	Chandi Das
5.	1932	Chir Kumar Sabha
6.	1932	Palli Samaj
7.	1932	Punarjanam
8.	1932	Puran Bhakta
9.	1933	Kapal Kundla
10.	1933	Mastoto Bhai
11.	1935	Bhagya Chakra
12.	1935	Roop Rekha
13.	1935	Devdas
14.	1936	Graha Daha
15.	1936	Maya
16.	1937	Mukti
17.	1938	Abhagin
18.	1938	Vidyapati
19.	1938	Desher Mati
20.	1939	Jeevan Maran
21.	1939	Rajat Jayanti

The film in the above table titled as "Nater Puja" was based on the script of Gurudev Rabindra Nath Tagore's one popular "dance drama."

63. Ibid, p. 512.
64. Ibid.

Diagram 7.9 : Main Bengali Films produced every year during 1931-39 period

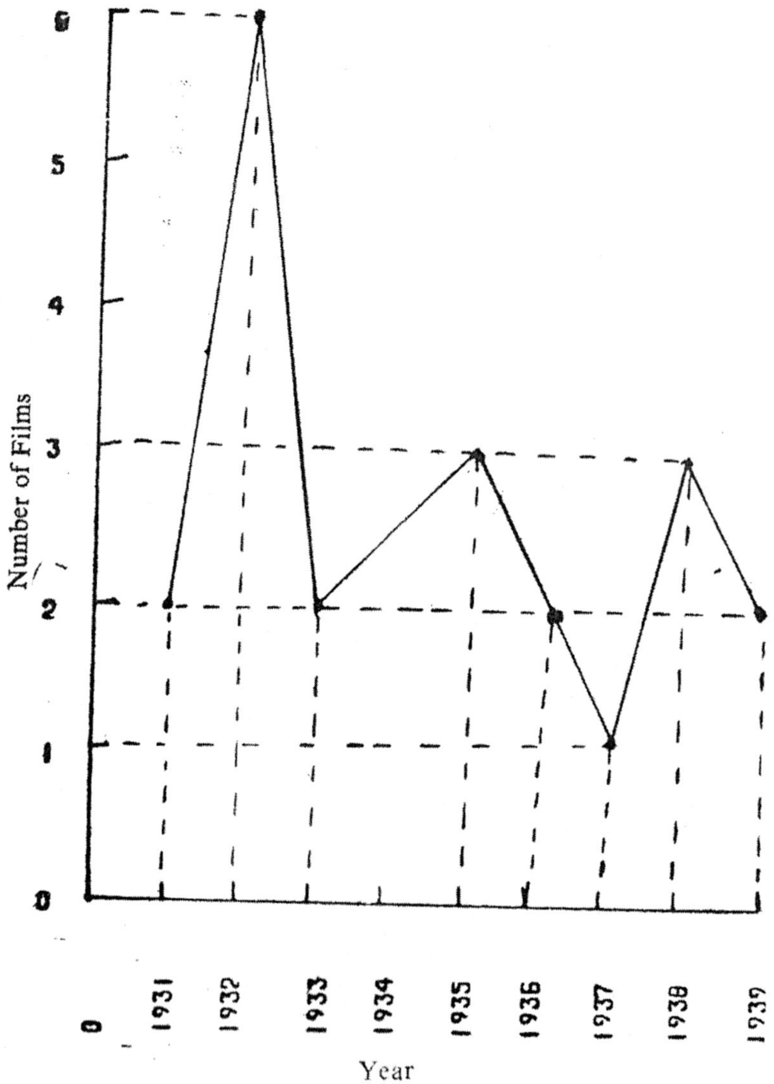

TABLE 7 11

Main Bengali Films produced during 1940-45 period

S. No.	*Year*	*Film*	*Producing Institution*
1.	1940	Alok Chhaya	Associated Production
2.	1941	Aahuti	Moti Mahal Pictures
3.	1941	Apar Opar	New Theatre
4.	1941	Parichay	New Theatre
5.	1941	Mayer Pran	M.P. Production
6.	1941	Uttar Narayan	M.P. Production
7.	1941	Nandini	K.B. Pictures
8.	1941	Pratishodh	Film Corporation of India
9.	1942	Bandi	Chitra Roop Limited
10.	1942	Parinita	P.R. Production
11.	1943	Pativrata	Arora Film Corporation
12.	1943	Wapas	New Theatres
13.	1943	Kashinath	New Theatres
14.	1943	Priya Bandhvi	New Theatres
15.	1943	Chhadam Veshi	Deluxe Pictures
16.	1943	Dewar	Indrapuri Studio
17.	1943	Mater Ghar	Bharat Laxmi
18.	1943	Shahar Thake Doore	East Talkie
19.	1944	Biraj Boe	New Theatres
20.	1944	Udmer Puthe	New Theatres
21.	1945	Kalankani	R.S. Chandanmal
22.	1945	Pather Saathi	Arora Films
23.	1945	Humrahi	New Theatres
24.	1945	Wasiatnama	New Theatres
25.	1945	Maha Prasthaner Pathe	New Theatres

All production units mentioned in the above table belonged to Calcutta. An analysis of the table shows that in 1940 one, in 1941 seven, in 1942 two, in 1943 eight, in 1944 two, and in 1945 five Bengali films were produced.

Diagram 7.10 : The Number of Bengali Films produced each year during 1940-45 period

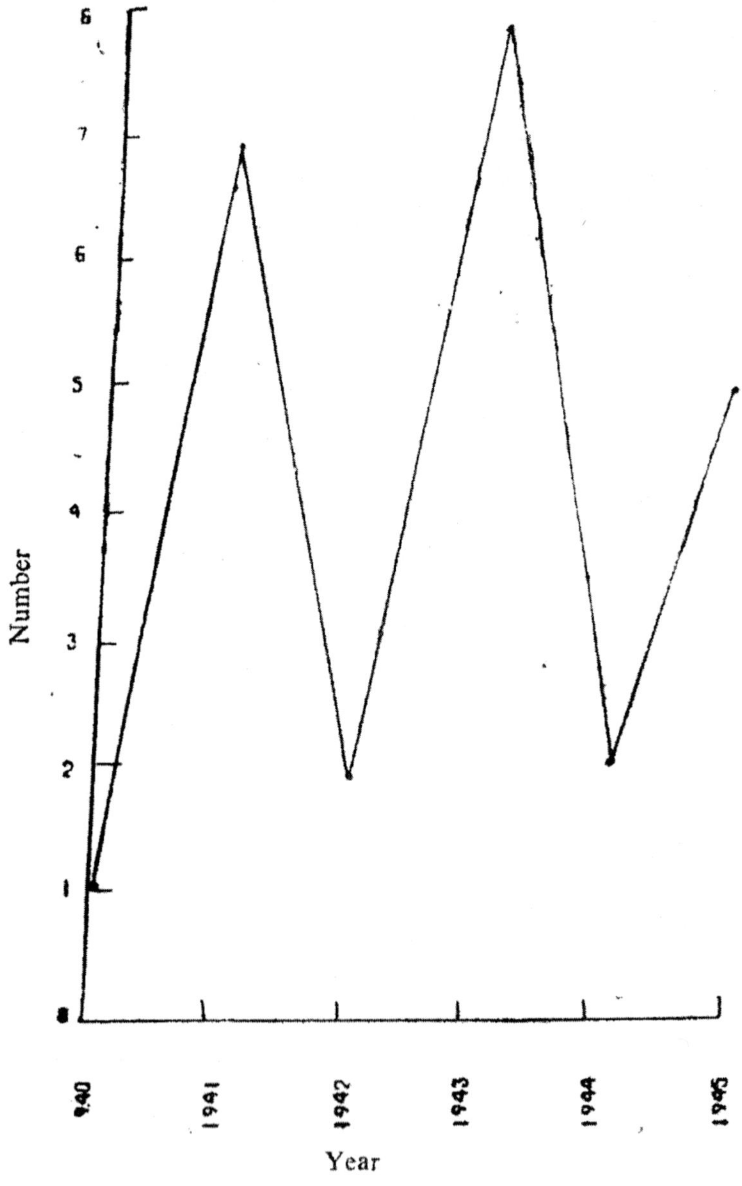

TABLE 7.12

Main Bengali Films produced in Calcutta during 1946-50 period

S. No.	*Year*	*Film*	*Production Unit*
1.	1946	Bande Matram	Chalchatika Pictures
2.	1946	Nivedita	Chitra Bharti
3.	1946	Sangram	Modern Talkies Limited
4.	1947	Abhijog	Basantika Limited
5.	1947	Chandra Shekhar	Pioneer
6.	1947	Jagran	Barua Art Production
7.	1947	Panther Davi	Associated Pictures
8.	1947	Ramer Sumti	New Theatres
9.	1947	Swayam Siddha	Indian National Talkies
10.	1948	Prativad	New Theatres
11.	1948	Mayer Dak	Cine Producers
12.	1948	Sawya Sachi	Associated Pictures
13.	1948	Tarunar Swapan	Kamini Pictures
14.	1948	Bhooli Nai	Progressive Pictures
15.	1949	Aabhijatiya	M.P. Production
16.	1949	Sankalp	M.P. Production
17.	1949	Devi Chaudhrani	Rupayan Pictures
18.	1949	Nishir Dak	Rajshree Katha Chitre
19.	1949	Parivartan	National Production
20.	1950	Apvad	Bhawani Kala Mandir
21.	1950	Arajita	Narambh Pictures
22.	1950	Vidya Sagar	M.P. Production
23.	1950	Shri Tulsidas	Kalidas Production
24.	1950	Yug Devta	Kalidas Production

Diagram 7.11 : The Number of Main Bengali Films produced every year in Calcutta during 1946-50 period

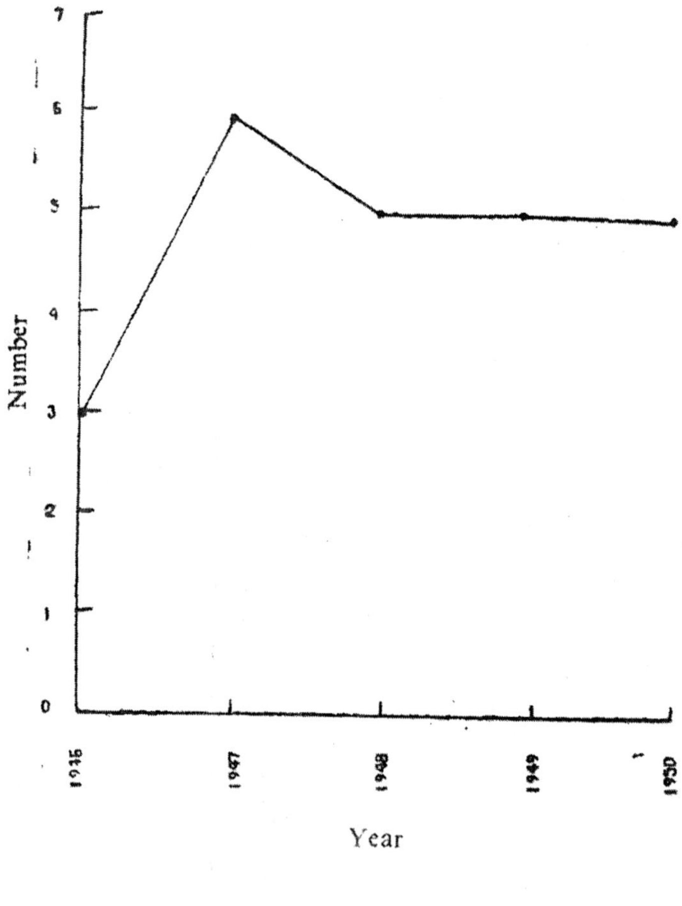

An analysis of the above table presents that in 1946 three, in 1947 six, in 1948 five, and in 1950 five main Bengali films were produced.

After independence, due to partition Bengali film industry got great setback. About forty per cent Bengali speaking people's territory separated as East Pakistan (Now Bangladesh). Due to it, the number of Bengali films viewers extremely came down, and its effects were perceived on Bengali film industry, in the subsequent years.[65]

In 1955, the great Bengali film "Pather Panchali," initiated a new period in the Bengali film history. This only film not only established the reputation of Bengali films, but also of Indian cinema, all over the world.[66] This film won so many national and international awards that its producer Satyajit Ray has become the topmost international film maker. This film is one of the best films of the world in respect of artistic and human viewpoints. This film got the "gold medal"[67] of the President in 1955.

It got "the Best Human Document" Award at Cons. Film Festival in 1956.[68] Excluding it at Manila Film Festival 1956, San Francisco Film Festival 1957, and at Vancovar (Canada) Film Festival 1958, a score of different awards were presented to this film.[69] It got "Best Feature Film" award at Straford (Canada) Film Festival in 1958.[70] The Acro-arts Theatres, New York awarded it in 1959. The "National Board

---

65. Karuna Shankar, *Ibid book*, p. 67.
66. Mahendra Mittal, *Ibid book*, p. 520.
67. Ibid.
68. B.B. Dharap (Editor), "Awards Won by Indian Films Abroad", *Filmotsav 84*, (Inaugurated by V.P. Sathe), Directorate of Film Festival, Bombay, 1984, p. 103.
69. Ibid.
70 Ibid.

of Review U.S.A." prized it in 1957.[71] After the production of "Pather Panchali," Satyajit Ray stepped up speedily at film horizon. So far he had been produced twenty five films and six small films. Different universities have awarded him "D. Litt," degree five times.[72] He had also obtained "Dada Saheb Phalke award." Recently, in the direction of Utpalendu Chakravarty, a film "Music of Satyajit Ray" has been produced on him.[73] It is a rare respect for music devotion of Mr. Satyajit Ray.

Till 1970, following films have been produced by Satyajit Ray—"Aprajito" (1956), "Apur Sansar" (1957), "Jalsadhar" (1958), Devi (1960), "Kanch Jangha" (1961), "Mahanagar" (1963), "Charulata" (1964), "Kapurush O Mahapurush" (1965), "Nayak" (1966), "Teen Kanya," "Abhiman" and "Gopi Kayen Badha Bayen" (1969). The "Charulata" is based on Rabindra Nath Tagore's story "Nashtneed."[74]

TABLE 7.13

Notable Bengali Films produced during 1951-70 Period

S. N.	*Film*	*S. N.*	*Film*
1.	Anand Math	2.	Darpchurna
3.	Durgesh Nadanni	4.	Kheldhar
5.	Karpai	6.	Shubhda
7.	Palli Samaj	8.	Mahaprasthaner Pathe
9.	Parinita	10.	Bhor Hayo Alo
11.	Bhagwan Shri Krishna Chatanya	12.	Pathik

71. Ibid.
72. *Madhuri*, March 7, 1980, p. 48.
73. *Jansatta*, Hindi daily, December 7, 1984, p. 5.
74. Mahendra Mittal, *Ibid book*, pp. 520-521.

1	2	1	2
13.	Anupma	14.	Pather Panchali
15.	Loh Kapat	16.	Aprajito
17.	Apoor Sansar	18.	Jalsar
19.	Sagar Sangame	20.	Chudit Pasham
21.	Dak Harkara	22.	Ajantrik
23.	Ganga	24.	Neele Aakasher Niche
25.	Vicharak	26.	Chalachal
27.	Devi	28.	Saptvadi
29.	Sat Pake Bandha	30.	Kanchan Jangha
31.	Mahanagar	32.	Neshtneer
33.	Charulata	34.	Kapurush O Mahapurush
35.	Nayak	36.	Swaran Rekha
37.	Tero Nardir Pare	38.	Dada Thakur
39.	Jatu Griha	40.	Aarohi
41.	Atithi	42.	Bhranti Vilash
43.	Uttar Phalguni	44.	Besho Shravan
45.	Pritinidhi	46.	Punasch
47.	Grah Dah	48.	Nirjan Sakete
49.	Aakash Kusum	50.	Anpusht Chhand
51.	Platak	52.	Hare Bazare
53.	Sageena Mehto		

Since 1970 till today, Bengali film industry has passed a long journey. In 1983, 49 Bengali films were given censor certificates. In 1984, Bengali film actresses Munmun Sen and Deva Sri Ray got opportunity to work in some Bangladeshi films. According to Mr. M.A. Sayeed, a Bangladeshi producer, who provided opportunities to the just mentioned two actresses, thought that the West Bengal (India) and Bangladesh must do joint efforts for film production. Mr. Asim Chakravarty has written in 'Jansatta' about Bengali film industry that "For last several years the Bengali films passed through a critical economic period, however in such circumstances the films in

1984 drew sufficient crowds at ticket-windows. In such films "Lal Golap" has certainly established new records of success and left behind all upto date Bengali films. Excluding this film "Dada Muni," "Padavat Priya," "Mohnar Dike," "Teen Murti," "Pujarini," "Grah Yadh," and "Shatru" also proved successful at Box-Office. But the number of exhibited film, this year, came down. Only thirty one films have been released. These are "Suryasakshi," "Dujane," "Samarpita," "Jai Prajai," "Deepar Prem," "Dada Muni," "Amar Geet," "Grah Yadh," "Vish Vraksha," "Rajeshwar," "Sagar Balaka," "Shilalipi," "Seemantram," "Lal Golap," "Paravat Priya," "Pohnar Dike," "Agni Shudhi," "Prarthna," "Aankle," "Abhishek," "Rashiphal," "Teen Murti," "Shorgul," "Poojarini," "Nagdipara,", "Diya Lalita," "Dakhal," "Pragatihasik Maan" and "Shatru." There are twenty coloured films out of these 31 films. In the Bengali film world, never such huge number of coloured films were produced.[75]

Impaet of Sex and Violence on Bengali Cinema

Well known for its higher and objective usefulness of Bengali cinema, now faces a bad impact of sex and violence on it gradually. In this respect one famous film director says that

"Previously, the highly impressive part of Bengali cinema was its emotional subject. Now this thing has absolutely finished. If we just take about "Pratikar," we find that the director gave importance only to the factor that how the hero of the film Bictor Banerji takes revenge of the oppression done against his family ? Or in some other films the formula of "lost and find" presented in more and more dramatic manner."[76] An another Bengali film producer also expressed

---

75. Prasim Chakravarty, "Success in Bengali films-1984", *Jansatta*, Feb. 15, 1985.
76. *Jansatta*, "Abundance of Sex and Violence in Bengali Cinema" (Hindi), Calcutta Correspondent, N. Delhi, Hindi daily, July 31, 1987.

same opinion. He states that "Prior, we used to work hard on any famous author's story, and prepare script. But now it seems that the new director has become story and script writers too. In such film, no attention used to be paid for the identity of artists and neither any incident of any actor touches the heart. All energies have been concentrated on romance, sex, violence, loud voiced music and eye-catching photography. For such formula film, the director feels no need of any material work."[77]

As a matter of fact, when we see overwhelming violent and sexual scenes in Bengali films, it seems that such film makers have monopolised the Bengali films industry, who have no social responsibility or sense of good cinema. The artistic Bengali film members have expressed extreme concern about this development. They have expressed their concern in public with regard to this "sex and violence" wave. Some film-makers also opined that the viewers are also interested in such extravagant films. In this situation a good film cannot get success at Box-office. Even Bengali film distributors are also showing concern about the absurd films in the name of professional cinema. A distributor said that, "It was not so as if there were no production of commercial films in Bengali. Just two decades ago, Uttam Kumar, Sachitra Sen, Savitri Chatterji and Sandhya Rai were very popular actors and artists. Now it seems, as if the actor is not an artist but an uncivilized stick beating man. In such an environment, the film-makers of serious cinema, like Gautam Ghosh, how and how much they can contribute to bring out the Bengali cinema from this present ditch. In fact the good film producers have become less day by day and absurd cinema has a flourishing time."

However this wave of "violence and sex" does not belong to Bengali cinema only, in fact it is a national problem. Indian cinema as a whole has been infected by this disease. To avoid the bad impressions and impact of "sex and

---

77. Ibid.

violence'' wave, a collective offence is necessary at the national level.

However, the future of Bengali film industry is very bright. The West Bengal government is conscious for the development of film industry. It is providing loans to the film producers and the State Government is also producing feature and children films. The future of Bengali films depends upon the co-operation with provincial government to a great extent.

Oriya Films

The main language of Orissa is Oriya. The film titled as "Sita Vivah," produced by Mr. Mohan Sunder Goswami in 1938 is assumed as the first film of Oriya.[78] After it, for a decade no important Oriya film was produced.

TABLE 7.14

Main Oriya films produced during 1950-66 Period

S. No.	*Year*	*Film*
1.	*2*	*3*
1.	1950	Shri Jaggan Nath
2.	1951	Rolls Two and Eight
3.	1951	Sapt Satya
4.	1952	Aamri Gan Jhua
5.	1954	Kedar Gauri
6.	1955	Bhai Bhai

78. *Filmfare*, Cine Weekly, Bombay, November 13, 1964, p. 28.

1	2	3
7.	1958	Shasti
8.	1958	Pritibha
9.	1959	Maan
10.	1959	Mahalaxmi Pooja
11.	1960	Shri Lok Nath
12.	1961	Nua Bou
13.	1961	Parinamo
14.	1961	Dasya Ratna Karo
15.	1961	Jaidev
16.	1962	Shri Patil Pavan
17.	1962	Manik Jyoti
18.	1962	Laxmi
19.	1962	Suryamukhi
20.	1963	Naare
21.	1963	Jeevan Saathi
22.	1964	Sadhna
23.	1966	Mateera Maneesha

The Oriya films produced during this period, amongst them, "Sadhna" in 1964 and "Mateera Maneesha" in 1966 won the President Silver Prizes respectively.[79] Since then, during these twenty years, the Oriya cinema progressed too much. In 1983 and 1984, the number of Oriya certified film was 12 and 14 respectively.[80] Oriya film industry has completed fifty years. The National Film Development Corporation has also been taking interest for the progress of Oriya films industry. In this respect a columnist in "Screen" has written, "There was a time, less than two decades ago, when the growth

79. Mahendra Mittal, *Ibid Book*, p. 542.
80. *Screen*, cine-weekly, Bombay, January 18, 1985, p. 11.

Diagram 7.12 : The Number of Main Oriya Films produced every year during 1950-66

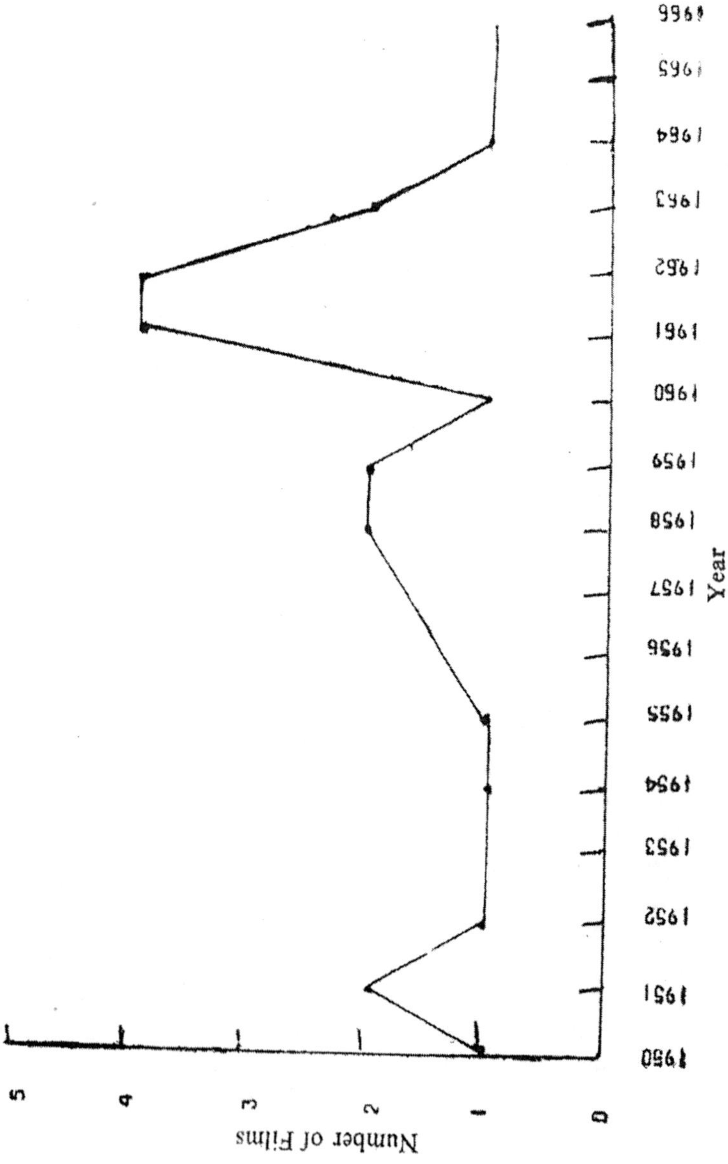

of Orissa's regional film industry was, unto most, no more than a pipe dream. A sophisticated film heretic's look at the Oriya cinema was supposed to lend him the notion that whatever the small state's other big strides in other areas, the concept of the "Oriya film" growth and expansion on lines of industrial self-sufficiency and as a contributory factor to the total image of the Indian cinema was bound to take a long period for its mature rearing, if at all it was a feasible proposition.

Not that as an industry, Oriya films have already achieved a major status. But what is truly amazing about it is the fact of the high hopes it has already engendered in the minds of the people of Orissa in course of the last few years about its rich artistic and industrial potentiality alongwith the fostering care and attention it has won on its merit from the National Film Development Corporation. The Corporation accorded to this year's golden jubilee celebrations wonderful co-operation and help that proved a great incentive to the organisers."[81] Orissa Film Development Corporation has been also encouraging the production of Oriya films in the state. One columnist of "Screen" cine weekly writes, "The OFDC was the State Government's brain child and the organisation was now engaged in its ceaseless and almost round the clock activity in the process of materialisation of the State Government's pet scheme to rear the state film industry into significance so as to take its rightful place in the sphere of Orissa's all round national, social and economic growth."[82]

A score of film producers have shown their interest for the production of Oriya films because of State Government's active co-operation. The number of theatres is less in Orissa, if the State government pays attention in this direction, the people may get more and more Oriya films to be viewed.

---

81. "Golden Jubilee of Orissa Cinema—A landmark in the eastern industry", N.K.G., *Screen*, Cine Weekly, Bombay, July 27, 1984, p. 16.
82. Ibid.

Assamese Films

Assamese film industry has a brief history. Mostly Assamese films are produced in Calcutta. "Jogmati" was the first Assamese film[83] produced in 1935. It was produced by "Chitrakala Movieton, Calcutta."[84]

TABLE 7.15

Main Assamese Films produced during 1939-62 period

S. No.	*Yeer*	*Film*
1	*2*	*3*
1.	1939	Indra Malti
2.	1941	Manomati
3.	1948	Shiraj
4.	1949	Viplavi Krishan
5.	1949	Praghat Pragya Jyotish
6.	1953	Runimi din
7.	1954	Sati Baula
8.	1955	Feol Funkash
9.	1955	Neemila Aankhen
10.	1956	Acra Bator Sur
11.	1956	Smirtir Parash
12.	1956	Lakheemi
13.	1956	Sarapat

83. *Filmfare*, Cine Weekly, Bombay, March 22, 1963, p. 35.
84. Ibid.

1	2	3
14.	1957	Ghumuh
15.	1957	Mak Aru Mauram
16.	1957	Nutan Prithivi
17.	1958	Roga Police
18.	1959	Puveran
19.	1959	Chak Nayya
20.	1962	Shakuntla

The scarcity of financial resources is even today one of the great obstruction for the production of good Assamese films. In this respect Pradeep Vishwas a columnist in *Screen* writes, "... The new crop of film-makers cannot produce good films in the absence of proper finance. No business magnate is willing to dole out money to these film makers who desire to do something good for the people of Assam. Thus, while national awards inspired the band, lack of finance has crippled them. Atul Bordoloi, Dr. Saikia, Padam Barua and Monoranjan Sur are all victims of financial scarcity. Even the Assam Financial Corporation, the expected saviour of good cinema, has failed to prop these socially aware film-makers."[85] Hence, if the state government provides grants and loans at minimum interest then the production of Assamese films may be increased. In 1984, only five Assamese films were produced.

Western Indian Linguistic Films

Maharashtra and Gujrat are two important states in Western India. Marathi and Gujrati are the main languages of Maharashtra and Gujrat respectively. Marathi and Gujrat cinema are comparatively developed with many regional cinema. In the subsequent part we present a brief description of it.

85. Pradeep Vishwas, "Assamese cinema lacks leadership", *Screen*, Weekly, Bombay, January 4, 1985, p. 14.

Marathi Films

In 1932, produced by Prabhat Film Company, Poona, "Ayodhya Ka Raja" is considered the first Marathi film.[86] Since then Marathi cinema had progressed sufficiently.

TABLE 7.16

Main Marathi Films produced during 1932-66 period

S. No.	*Year*	*Film's Name*
1	*2*	*3*
1.	1932	Ayodhya Ka Raja
2.	1932	Shyam Sunder
3.	1935	Sant Sakhu
4.	1933	Singhgarh
5.	1935	Vilasi Ishwar
6.	1936	Chhaya
7.	1937	Kanku
8.	1937	Duniya Na Mane
9.	1937	Bakt Damaji
10.	1937	Gangavtaran
11.	1938	Brahamchari
12.	1938	Gopal Krishna
13.	1939	Bhagwa Jhanda
14.	1939	Barandivi
15.	1939	Netaji Palkar
16.	1940	Ardhangini
17.	1940	Devmani
18.	1940	Sant Dhyaneshwar
19.	1941	Ghar Jamai

86. Mahendra Mittal, *Ibid book*, p. 547.

1		3
20.	1942	Basant Sena
21.	1943	Paisa Bolto Ahe
22.	1943	Ram Rajya
23.	1944	Bhakticha Mala
24.	1944	Ramshastri
25.	1946	Rukmani Swayambar
26.	1946	Jai Bhawoni
27.	1947	Ram Joshi
28.	1947	Jai Malhar
29.	1948	Balidan
30.	1948	Bhagya Rekha
31.	1948	Moruchi Maosi
32.	1948	Bande Matram
33.	1949	Braham Ghotola
34.	1949	Meet Makhar
35.	1949	Manache Paan
36.	1949	Sant Janabhai
37.	1949	Sant Namdev
38.	1950	Gokulcha Raja
39.	1950	Kalyan Khajina
40.	1950	Kranti Veer Vasudev Balvant
41.	1950	Sonyachi Lanka
42.	1950	Banshacha Diva
43.	1951	Amar Bhopali
44.	1951	Parijatak
45.	1951	Swarajyacha Shiledar
46.	1952	Pand Goanche Shahne
47.	1952	Lakhachi Goshte

(*Contd.*)

1	2	3
48.	1952	Chhatrapati Shivaji
49.	1952	Maicha Pajar
50.	1953	Vahir Nichya Bangdiya
51.	1953	Mahatma
52.	1953	Saubhagya
53.	1954	On Pouse
54.	1954	Maharani Yeshubai
55.	1954	Mahatma Phule
56.	1954	Jhanjavat
57.	1955	Ganget Ghore Nahale
58.	1955	Punvechi Raat
59.	1956	Mulga
60.	1956	Devdhar
61.	1956	Me Tulas Tujhaya Angani
62.	1957	Grah Devta
63.	1957	Devajaga Ahe
64.	1961	Kanyadan
65.	1962	Manini
66.	1962	Vyjayanta
67.	1963	Prapanch
68.	1963	Maja Hosilka
69.	1964	Rangalya Ratri Asha
70.	1965	Pathlag
71.	1965	Chhota Jawan
72.	1965	Padchhaya
73.	1965	Kai Chamatkar
74.	1965	Pahun Re Kiti Bat
75.	1965	Sukha Chi Chawli
76.	1965	Thora Tanchi Kamla
77.	1965	Vaishakh Vanva
78.	1966	Tochi Sadhu Olkhawa
79.	1966	Sheras Sawa Ser
80.	1966	Shatvaya Malusra
81.	1966	Kela Ishara Jata Jata
82.	1966	Pavan Kanthcha

Since 1962, till recent years, the period may be termed as a Development and Higher Standard period for Marathi films. The name of V. Shantaram has become immortal in history of Marathi films. He provided higher artistic standard to the Marathi films. At Box office, in recent period, Amitabh Bachchan of Marathi films "Dada Kondke" films got highest success. In 1984, twenty five Marathi films got censor certificates while in 1983 this number was twenty.[87] The Maharashtra government has decided to set up a separate film corporation for the development of Marathi films named "Kolhapur Chitranagri Mahamandal."[88] Thus Kolhapur film city shall be one of the important centre for Marathi films.

The Maharashtra government provides all kinds of facilities for the progress of Marathi films to the producers. As there is no entertainment tax on Marathi films inside Maharashtra, these films earn sufficient income. In all, the future of Marathi films seem bright.

Gujrati Films

The debut of Gujrati films took place in 1932 when Mr. Chiman Lal B. Desai Produced "Narsi Mehta."[89] Since then till 1962 a score of notable Gujrati films were produced.

Since then till recent times Gujrati film industry progressed sufficiently. The Gujrat government provides every kind of facility to producers. Well known Gujrati film producer Mr. Ram Bohra told the author in an interview held in Bombay that in Gujrat, every Gujrati first eight prints have no taxes to be paid.[90] Hence, many film producers who failed

87. *Screen*, Weekly, Bombay, January 18, 1985, p. 11.
88. Pandit Shimpi, "Separate Corporation for Kolhapur film city", *Screen*, Weekly, Bombay, Feb. 22, 1985, p. 17.
89. Mahendra Mittal, *Ibid book*, p. 555.
90. Ram Avtar Agnihotiri, "An Interview with Shri Ram Bohra, film producer and director", *Cross Examination*, Hindi Weekly, Bombay, December 1, 1978, p. 9.

TABLE 7.17

Main Gujrati Films produced during 1932-62 period

S. No.	*Film*	*S. No.*	*Film*
1.	Narsi Mehta	2.	Sati Savitri
3.	Sansar Leela	4.	Ghar Jamai
5.	Do Kharab Jan	6.	Achhut
7.	Ranank Devi	8.	Baharvatio
9.	Bhakt Ambreeb	10.	Bhakta Surdas
11.	Krishna Sudama	12.	Meerabai
13.	Sati Jasma	14.	Guna Sundri
15.	Mangel Phera	16.	Godano Bel
17.	Ajamil	18.	Bhai Bahin
19.	Gandhiji	20.	Jogidas Khuman
21.	Jeevan Palto	22.	Jai Ranchhor
23.	Jaisel Toral	24.	Karyavar
25.	Nanad Bhojai	26.	Sati Son
27.	Satyavadi Harish Chander	28.	Sawaki Maan
29.	Prithivi Vallabh	30.	Bhakt Pundlik
31.	Guniyal Gujratan	32.	Mahatma Mooldas
33.	Raja Bhrathari	34.	Satyavan Savitri
35.	Seeta Vanvas	36.	Vevishal
37.	Akhand	38.	Sharad Poonam
39.	Vana Pap	40.	Kanyadan
41.	Lagan Bandhan	42.	Mangal Sutra
43.	Maguni Masi	44.	Nag-devta
45.	Vidhata	46.	Sati Analde
47.	Menhdi Rang Layo	48.	Nandan Van

in Hindi cinema, try in Gujrat film industry. Nowadays Ahmedabad and Baroda have also film production facilities for

Gujrat films. In 1984, 30 Gujrati films were certified by the censer. However in 1984 its number was twenty seven.[91]

Other Linguistic Films

There are films produced in other languages too excluding the above languages. These are Bhojpuri, Punjabi, Haryanvi, Sindhi and Brij Bhasa films and these films are liked in the respective regions.

Bhojpuri is a branch of Hindi and spoken up in the Bihar State. Director, Shri Kundan Kumar produced first Bhojpuri film "Ganga Maiya Tohe Piyari Chadybo" in 1963.[92] Influenced by its popularity and success several Bhojpuri films are produced. The main Bhojpuri films are "Lagi Nahin Chhoote Ram," "Nehar Chhotal Jai," "Balma bara nadan," "Kob Haihe gavanva hamara," "Jekra Charanva mein lagle paranva," "Sita Maiya," "Sanya Bhaile Milanva," "Nag Panchmi," "Hamara Sansar," "Bhoji," "Loha Singh," "Solah Singar Karen Dulhaniya," "Ganga" "Videsia" and "Kab Aiyhain Sajanva Hamar."

One artist of Bhojpuri films stated about the characteristics of Bhojpuri films that, "The viewers of the Bhojpuri films must feel self-expression in the films, hence it is necessary that the environment, dress, culture, behaviour, even the houses must be similar as are found in this region." Bhojpur is a romantic region. The romance has a particular significance in its culture. In 1984, nine Bhojpuri films got certificates from the censor.

"Heer Ranjha" (1932) and "Zulm-e-Kans," "Mirza Sahiba" (1933) were the earliest films of Punjabi language.[93] Since then till now a score of Punjabi films have been pro-

---

91. *Screen*, English Weekly, Bombay, January 18, 1985, p. 11.
92. Ibid, p. 14.
93. *Filmfare*, Weekly, Bombay, March 22, 1963, p. 25.

duced. The Punjabi film "Nanak Nam Jahaj Hai" got sufficient appreciation. Most of the Punjabi films are full of entertainment.

Haryanvi language film titled as "Chandraval" established many historical records.[94] Impressed by the success of this film, many Haryanvi films were declared like "Laddo Basanti,"[95] "Chhora Jat Ka,"[96] "Ke Sapne Ka Zikar"[97] and "Chhora Haryana Da." The first film in Sindhi language was "Avana" of producer Mr. Masand.[99] Subsequently "Jhule Lal," "Ahe Na Ahe," "Ladli," "Sindhua Ke Kinare," "Hozmale" and "Antra Ta Mandiri Ahiya" films were produced.[100] However, commercially, the Sindhi films did not get success. The debut film of Brijbhasha titled as "Brij Bhumi" got popularity in Western Uttar Pradesh, Eastern Rajasthan and some parts of Haryana. Its producer and director is Shri Shiv Kumar.[101] Looking upon its success other film-makers got attraction for film production in Brij Bhasha.

---

94. Devi Shankar Prabhakar, "Laddo Basanti shall be a road stone" (Hindi), *Punjab Kesari*, Hindi Daily, Delhi, December 1, 1984, p. 1.
95. Ibid.
96. Sunder, "Ek Haryanvi Film—Chhora Jat Ka", *Punjab Kesari*, Sept. 15, 1984.
97. Vidya Sagar (critic), "Haryanvi film "Ke Sapne Ka Zikar" *Punjab Kesari*, Hindi daily, December 8, 1984, p. 1.
98. *Screen*, Weekly, Bombay, February 22, 1985, p. 19.
99. Utpal Vyas, "Sindhi Film—Manzil Abhi Door Hai" (Hindi)" *Dainik Navjyoti*", Hindi Ajmer, April 1,1984, p.7.
100. Ibid.... (After partition the Sindhis migrated to India in a limited number and settled in Bomday, Gujrat, Rajasthan, and Madhya Pradesh. Some scholars assume Kutch language as Sindhi, hence above mentioned films were popular in these regions).
101. Ishwar Singh Bais, "Brij Bhasha Ki Pehli Film—Brij Bhoomi" (Hindi), *Saptahik Hindustan*, N. Delhi, August 8, 1942, p. 32.

There are also efforts in film production in the languages of Rajasthan, Nepali, Manipuri, Kashmiri, Garhwali, Khasi, Tulu etc. These efforts are in the initial stages and after some years the trend and direction of these regional linguistic films can be ascertained.

Conclusion

In India, regional and small linguistic films are also popular like Hindi films. In fact, some regional films are ahead of Hindi films in quality. Thus Hindi film industry is not rival to regional linguistic films but both are complementary. There must be healthy competition between Hindi and regional films. It is good for the country.

The importance of regional cinema lies in view of its contribution for the security of local village culture. In the regional diversities of India, it is necessary that regional languages must get development. The regional cinema provides full opportunities for its development. The development of regional cinema also provides opportunities for the development of Hindi cinema, as Bhojpuri, Rajasthani, Haryanvi and Brij Bhasha's producers, directors and actors are also linked with Hindi cinema.

The regional and local cinema is playing a vital role in bringing socio-political consciousness among the local people. This fact cannot be denied.

8

Conclusion

The politics and culture are related deeply with each other. The politics of any country used to be influenced by many medias and culture is one of them. The culture expresses itself with the help of many media arts and we know that most powerful "audio-visual" mass communication is film art. The development of culture provided new extension to arts and thus it provided different new shapes to the culture and influenced "culture politics" too.

Technical Film Art and Cultural Politics

In this period of explosive development of culture, particularly, the related medias of constructive expressions, there are some thoughtable questions before it. Without solving them, the defence of "cultural values" is impossible. As a matter of fact, the new and continuously changed technology has changed the conditions and all perspectives in our performance of every kind of arts. The old thought, senses, traditions and constructive tastes of different arts are impossible for indefinite period. Not only a score of technical based arts have expressed demolishing their old structures, but also the related arts are changing their different shapes. Without understanding them properly and without identifying the limitations and probabilities, it should be difficult to discipline them. To look up at contemporary art world, the truth may be estimated. In the literature, at one level, the picture story, radio dramas, television drama, serials and films etc., new linguistic medias seem to challenge the old literary men. At another level, the cheap paperback editions, video cassettes, micro films and computers have changed the personal language and structure of the craft. The increasing prices of books decrease the number of readers. Among the fine arts, with the modern and most developed techniques for printing and shaping, and minuteness of matter and medium, the infiniteness of art pieces and its aesthetic values coming down, excluding it the capacity of coloured photography has multiplied and the availability of video cassettes of the same prints for the masses has become a reality.

The situation among the people of expressive arts is highly fearful. Due to remarkable changes in the recording, the relationship of the musician, on one side with his own medium i.e. voice and music, the method of presentation of the style and secondly with the audience has been changed rapidly. Now it is not much necessary that voice should be loud and breath should be lengthy. With it, extremely little difference of voice got recorded on sensitive recording machines, which have made the singer and the musicians highly precautious. They have been inspired to pay attention on the speed and expansion of voice instead of preciseness, so that during the critical recording process the deviation from particular set of singing (Aalap) may not be violated or seemed to be deviated. For audience, it is not necessary to sit before the singer. He can enjoy music in his private room according to his choice. At audience level, one more and new condition has been developed. The western music based on several music instruments liked to be listened with high sound volumes on complex and critical tape recorders and on decks, pop music and vocal music singing. However, to listen Indian classical music in such a way, is not possible. Thus it is influencing the selection of raags, method of presentation and style. Hence, the listeners non-alignment is also changing the structure of music. In classical music new "raags" have been developing as per choice of musicians and the old "raags" have been dust-shaped. The folk music, because of the facilities of recording, have been losing its regional identity, and particular aesthic sense and taste. Generally, it is very hard to distinguish that in a particular "music" (dhunn), how many and which music waves (dhunn) have been assimilated. Not only this, all kinds of popular western music and indigenous music so much mingled and due to commercial pressure, as much available as possible, the music sense of a general Indian listener has taken a new shape and colourfulness.

The condition of 'dance' is also similar. However, the video-recording did not take place too much, yet the presentation at the television has affected the style, time period and selection of different body parts for the dance. The classical dances demand for a lengthy training and practice. A dancer, who got training as per tradition, prepares himself and his body for a long period. But, at Television, for small programmes, such exercise and regular practice seems unnecessary for providing sudden preparation. The nature of Indian dances has been rooted in single exhibition. It is not easy to be presented these by pairs of men and women on any occasion. However, the, fashion of collective pair dance has been increasing among youth in the cities, due to contact with western culture and life style, increasing day by day, as well as the easy availability of vedio and music cassettes. This attitude is bound to influence the classical dance and particularly its structure.

With it, the folk dances of village and tribal people, have been losing their attraction because of different kinds of entertainment programmes available through new mass medias like film and television. The large scale government exhibitions and festivals in the foreign countries, in which the countryside and tribal people participate, are responsible for decline of natural, self-active and lifeness of folk dances. Their own regional, local and collective structure and character has been extinguishing.

In the field of stage and dramas, the Indian television's presentation of serials have created a situation of danger. Five and six decades ago, the stage dramas were pushed similarly by films, but after independence, the cultural renaissance period provided a new life and it stepped up after a long periodical interval i.e. after Sanskrit dramas and stage dramas period, identified itself quite separately. Again, recently due to explosion of serials at Indian television, its steps are trembling. The impact has been felt even in a stage drama's powerful place like Maharashtra. The well established commercial stage companies are feeling the scarcity of participants like actors, directors and drama-writers, there. In the Hindi region where there were no commercial stage artists, and viewers, a kind of vacuum has been formed. The directors and actors got training at National School of Drama, Delhi, as well as all stage-performers who belong to small towns are in queue for television serials. Obviously, all of these people cannot get job there, but when and who will face the bitter truth for great expectations, no forecast can be done in this respect now. However, the need is not for delinking expectations with artists but it needs a rationale self-analysis for new times, so that the new environment may be faced with understanding. The challenge is two fold—on one side it is necessary to utilise the possibilities borne out with the new technology contructively. And on the other side the ruling elite and commercial establishments can use it for their vested interests and hence a quick intervention is necessary to stop the directionless expansion and popularisation of commercial consumption culture. As a matter of fact, the developments in technology may enrich the human life. The picture stories can inspire the children and youth for literary works. A lot of literature may be ceased by time, but can be protected through micro-films, for many ages. The computer can provide knowledge about the world easily.

The rare music through sound recording and the best and highest kind of dances and stage dramas through video-recording may be proved valuable assets for the following generations. The television serials can provide knowledge about the country and the world history with great impact to masses and also can provide facts for the struggle for good life. However, all this can happen only when the author, artists and literary men pay attention and come forward for stoppage of abuse of television power by the vested politicians and businessmen. Otherwise, the day is not far off, when the commercial people may get hold over art medias and our cultural image may be tarnished. If the sensual artists will not pay due attention for the control over new technologies and extraordinary powerful mass-communication medias, the dangerous conditions may be raised. To avoid the challenges of new technologies is like to neglect the basic responsibility of construction.

Video—Initiator for the Period of Cultural Revolution

The invention of video brought human race in a new period of mass-media. The video has been spreading so speedily that the other mass-medias so far have not correctly measured the consequences of this media. In the developing countries, the video has entered just some years ago. In the third world countries, like India, video is an uninvited guest. In the third world countries and in India, the video took its debt when the television was in the stage of developing, however it is so weak that it could not face video's offence. The first victim of video was film industry. The feature films on the television had given a shock to the popularity of film industry. But the attack of video is more powerful. A film releases in the cinema halls, before it, the video cassettes are available in the market by illegal methods. Now the video is going into the country-side as a business. The video parlours have been opened even in small towns, where regular shows are going on. The film industry has been shattered by the video offence. The Indian film export has also been influenced by it. So far there were one hundred theatres in Britain, which used to show Indian films. Now these are in danger. The situation in U.S.A., Canada and other countries is same In many metropolitan cities, the number of viewers have decreased at cinema-halls. Many Indian film makers have appointed their spies to stop video theft of their films. The film producers are also demanding for change in the "copy right act." According to them, it is very urgent otherwise the film shall be prodaced by some one and the profit will be earned by others. They have also urged that every film must be released to only cinema owners, at least for three months, after that recognised video-companies can purchase the rights of distribution.

Until the video was competing with film industry, the government decision makers did not pay attention towards it. However, now, in India, video has entered in the less developed area of just developed television. As a mass communicatian, video can become an influential weapon. It is a double-edged sword. If it has been kept uncontrolled, it shall destroy all medias and will establish its authority. It shall be a new kind of cultural aggression. The Bombay based film industry has been under control of the government, indirectly. Yet, it is not appropriate to say anything about its social contribution. The situation with video shall be quite different. It has a capacity to cover each and every inch of earth. As well as what should be shown at it, is difficult to control with suitable provisions. Most of the people seem to be in earning 'profit' by heart with videos. For more profit, pure entertainment is only way. When there shall be no control, the climax of purity can be gained without hesitation. Thus, if the recent trend remains as usual, the government must change fundamentally in its institutions. Today, where there is the range of television, the radio viewers number has fell down. Those who have T.V. sets, they have said "good bye" to radio upto some extent. Now, the video seems to crumble television, in the same way. In metropolitan cities, many videoes shall be in the competition. In towns and villages, small workers may come up keeping videoes on their shoulders, to earn money. Video-parlours will open. Who will listen the government message of development and education at that time ? Or what shall be the number of its viewers or listeners? The impact may come down. The popularity which has been gained by the Television, will provide sufficient "profit" to video. What the television provides to the people, perhaps video may provide more than that. All over the Third World, what are the attempts of "development message" to each citizen, these shall be kept still without viewers or listeners. However, if with the expansion of the television, the video technique may also be related, then the situation may move towards a new dimension. The government think of "community television" to be installed in each village. If video-facilities are also provided and the local new actors may get inspiration, the particular programmes as per the social and cultural conditions of the area may be prepared and presented, the television will become interesting and positive. Thus the decentralised television idea may be implemented upto some extent. And one more media shall be helpful in the development of the particular area.

It is incorrect to look upon the changes in the field of media as a technical revolution. In fact it is a beginning of new cultural revolution. Its impact can be seen all over the human race and human behaviour. Even, in the field of justice, the new mass-communications are playing important role for setting up the viewpoint about the justice. This cultural revolution will influence the human civilisation unimaginatively. In fact, without exaggeration, the impact of it shall be more extensive, more deep and more farsighted than that of the industrial revolution of previous centuries. In respect of India, it is said that it is full of diversities. "Unity in diversity" is the well known slogan of our country. There are some slots in our tradition of unity, during recent past. The reason for it is the misunderstanding of "diversity". As a matter of fact, with a centralisation power over it, and with socially meaningful and acceptable balance can make the unity of nation more powerful. The problems raised in recent past have political, economic as well as cultural reasons. The bubbles raised by the mass-medias of the new cultural revolution must be kept in right perspective. These must be shaped as per national conditions. We must utilise the social structure of every community within its values and culture. If this new cultural revolution injured these structures, there may be gaps between different cultures of the country. As well as a cultural vacuum may be borne up. The foreign culture will get an occasion to enter, which may bring many deviations in our society and culture. The new cultural revolution has knocked our doors. Slowly, the air is blowing and mixing with our cultural environment. There are negative as well as positive, both kind of possibilities. Hence, regular awakening is necessary.

Impact of Mass-Communication Means on Youth

With technical development and new instruments of mass communication means, the shape of the social structure has been changing. The relation between the mass communication means and the youth have changed comparatively what was twenty years ago. Twenty years ago, the adult forwarding girl or boy used to take permission from his father, as a duty, to switch on the radio. However, today, no adult can imagine for such permission. The means of mass-communication provided him this kind of fearlessness or self-confidence. If we perform a survey, we shall find that many people's social behaviour got influence by the mass-communication which they have utilised since their childhood. A few decades ago, the grand-mother used to tell the stories of fairies and royal families at the night time to the sorrounding children. The children used to listen with attention and curiosity and developed their imagination power. A score of knowledge about the world affairs, they got from their teachers, guardians and texts-books. But, now the situation has changed too much. For the breakdown of joint families tradition, most of the children are away from their grand mothers. The Indian television, however, facilitated a serial "Dada-Dadi Ki Kahani", for the upper and middle families and thus a public data was available to such children. In the metropolitan cities, a mother either herself a servant or her social responsibilities are such that she tired up physically and mentally and cannót tell stories to her children. Further, the arrival of the television in homes, like a cinema, finished the tradition of telling and listening the folk stories. The youth of higher social and economic status, in comparison with the youth of lower economic and social status, show adulthood behaviour, very soon, because of the sufficient utilisation of means of mass-communication, as these medias brought them out of childhood earlier. In this respect, an interesting survey was done in the Rohtak city of Haryana. Thes urveyor was Davinder Kaur Uppal. On the basis of the data and personal observation, an interesting analysis was prepared. It was found that the teenagers refer to the T.V. programmes and news published in the newspapers, in their talks like adults. Today's child became anxious about his future very earlier. He looks a competitive life around himself, and when he makes an expectation in such an environment, he knows well the fact that for success in life, he must be competent at intelligence level. In such a situation, his self-estimation and valuation are highly impressed by the means of mass communication. In the above mentioned survey, the means of mass-communications which are studied, were radio, television, newspapers, books and films. An analysis of the data explicits that in spite of the television's extension, radio is such means, which has been utilised by the teenagers overwhelmingly. Even now, to know national and international news, the radio gets highest priority after newspapers. The listeners of B.B.C. (70 per cent) are more than the local stations (62 per cent). However, the song programmes of "Vividh Bharti" (90 per cent listeners) are extremely popular among the teenagers.

Like western countries, there are a lot of suspicions with regard to television and its impact on youth. The television is an audio-visual media, which has been utilised as an instrument for seeking knowledge and entertainment. The children and youth of the Rohtak also expressed its use in the same category. However, most of the persons described television, first as a means of recreation and afterwards as a media of knowledge. Hence, in India, the most popular programmes of television (Doordarshan) are Chitrahar and films. The number of viewers of these programmes lie between 77 and 80 per cent of the total. The cricket matches are also liked among the youth. The number of cricket match viewers is about fifty five per cent. Many critics of mass-communications have expressed the television as an alternative for the cinema. There is no doubt that in our country, the children as well as the elders, assume the television set at home as a means of film watching. The serials on the television have also a replica of films style. Even after sufficient influence of films on the Indian television, the youth regarded films as an independent means of mass-communication. Though every child watches film yet he dislikes to watch children films. Majority of the children like films titled as "Sholay" and likewise which are full of fighting and based on emotional social or so called historical scripts. Their lack of interest towards children are, firstly, non-availability of children films and their desire to include themselves too soon into the adult generation. Like young people they like to copy the actions and dresses of film actors. The female children are also interested for make up like heroines. A score of children remembered the dialogues of "Sholay" and they use it during their talks with some changes. The relations of college students, male and female, are also influenced by films. The children also developed their interest for news like adults. To know the news and their background, they depend on printed media. They like the political news printed at first page. After political news they are interested in games news. They also read out news related to adventures, crime particularly crimes against women. Their selection of magazines depends upon their interest in news. However, because the selection of magazines took place by adults of the family, hence they have least opportunity for their choice. Yet it has been observed that they like to read films and sports magazines. They are not interested in children books, while comics are overwhelmingly popular among the children. About 75 per cent children enjoy comics. In India, the comics art is a half baked copy of English comics. However it has gained a position in India as an independent art. While the literary aspect of comics may be controversial, but its popularity is out of controversy. These have made up a permanent place in the world of children. They also like to perform some miracles like "Mandrek Gerth", "Spider Man" and "Betal". It is notable that children are not too much inclined towards the projected children programmes at radio and television. Not only this, they do not pay attention to the "children columns" published in the newspapers. The availed mass-communication medias have borne out such situation that the children have learnt the behaviour of adults. Thus these means have stolen their childhood. Hence today's children, with the help of means of mass-communications, want to stand in the queue of adult people, as soon as possible. When a teenager watches the roundness of the body of a model at the television, next day he looks through side eyes, the same roundness inside the clothes of his female class fellows. Although India is not America or Europe, yet the means of mass communications are busy in making them likewise the western children.

Significant Impact of the Television

It is a matter of proud that India when knocking at the doors of twenty first century, the Indians have ten crores television sets of their own. Not only this, the time of television programmes shall be increased than now. In such a situation, the working people may not sit up near the television, but the young ones and the children would not be stopped. A well known American child-psychologist says that in America, the children of the 2-5 years age. entering into first class, have seen the television programmes for 5616 hours. Similarly, according to Leo Bogert, the children of the 5-15 age group used to watch television two to three hours everyday on saturday and sunday, this time extends towards five to eight hours. There is same situation in India. Robert Louise Shayon has traced the impact of adults from the television on the children and teenagers. He tried to search out the inspirations, for that the children and the teenagers watch the other television programmes. He says that, in the United States of America, the teenagers are neither included in the "children group" nor in the "adults group". Hence the frustrated teenagers satisfy themselves for linking adults through television. The hunger for participation, thirst for knowledge, desire for understanding and quest for "status", compel the teenagers and children to sit closed by the television. Robert Louise Shayon thinks that the younger children too have desire for contact with adults. As well as their aspirations for adventures used to be crushed by the discipline and rules of the elders. Consequently, there waves a sea of unfulfilment within their hearts. Such children and teenagers have respect for fantasy and violence and they got attraction in such programmes presented at the television. Here they enjoy the unknown pleasure but their extraordinary thirst did not get satisfaction. In the view of Mr. Shayon, the television is the shortest path available so far, which relates them with elders world. The television never tires of talking with the children. It can go upto any limit to draw their attention. The psychologists assume that the programmes shown at the television are prepared keeping in mind the all age-group peoples. Generally whole of the family wathes the television programmes. Externally, there seems to be no fault in these programmes. However, the impact on each one differs. Mostly, the elders problems are the focus of the television programmes. However, their presentation may be light or serious, the inter-conflict of the adults or their problems are represented. Mr. Dallas W. Smith, in his article "Analysis of Television", published in the "Scientific American" magazine, thirty five years ago, presented an analysis of the dramas televised from the New York City Television Centre. According to his analysis, ninety one per cent actors of the drama were adults and just nine per cent were children and youth. Similar survey was conducted in the Britain. The surveyors N.N. Openhiem, Pamela Wins and H.T. Himalweet, presented that the heroes of thirteen television dramas considered "life as tragic, unhappy and dissatisfied". As per the scripts of the dramas, they have no control over their lives and they never proved responsible for satisfactory solutions. The conclusion of the stories of these dramas were that the paths of the life are difficult and the adults could not find the solutions for these problems. Mr. Joseph T. Clapper in his article "Children and Television : A Review of Socially Prevalent Concerns", said that, "Majority of the psychologists agree that a limited extent of adult programmes are useful for the children. Thus the children are prepared to face the future problems of life, at mental level". However, too much viewing of adult programmes is harmful for children."

In such a situation, "pre-adultness and immature adultness" become a danger. Through the television, the child or the teenager thinks his immature identity of adult-world as reality. Consequently, he loses the desire to know the reality of different people and problems. In the opinion of the psychologists, the second danger poses by the regular presentation of the adults personal, familial, economic and social inter-conflicts Some scholars perceive that whether it is not root cause of the inspiration, however it cements the prejudices of the children and the teenagers. The regular observation of the adult programmes on the television, the image drawn on the mind of the children and the youth about the adults seems not to be of encouragement. For them, the adults are always in the problems and in most of the cases, they do not find any solution. As per psychologists, if such prejudice has become among the children, a score of undesirable qualities may be developed. For example, they may assume that conflict and inter-straggle are accepted social norms and they can indulge in them. It may be possible that the children may be afraid of being adults and whole of life they may be puzzled by the problems. The television may also bring forth normative conflict among the children. For instance, in a drama shown at the television the morals may win and the guardians may appreciate it, however they may proudly declare that method how they earned a huge sum leaving morality. Similarly in respect of untouchability, intercaste marriage, drug-abuse, dowry and other likewise matters, where the elders have grown up double standards, the children may be puzzled. The analysis of Openhiem, Win, and Himalweet is very interesting in this respect. They analysed the impact of the television on English children and teenagers from different angles. They have performed detailed investigations about anxiety to be adults, the expectations for employment and marriage, imitative characters, social class differences and race discrimination etc. The investigators, when asked from the children—the television watchers and the television non-watchers, that how much they are anxious to be adults the children more than twelve years indicated that they were anxious about home-leaving, school-leaving, and employment. More than the male children, the female children showed much anxiety about their problems. In the age group of ten to twelve years, the girls were more anxious about marriage, however the boys were more anxious about home-leaving. The children and the teenagers, to whom they would like to be ? In this respect, some interesting facts were revealed. Most of the people think that due to impact of the television, the children and teenagers like fame, fashion and goods. While, in fact, this is not. The children, particularly the teenagers show more interest in such things which they can own. For example, they want residence and car. What kind of job they would perform, in this respect, their interests do not develop. More is the time for viewing the television, the physical desire would increase in the same proportion. About the expectations of the marriage, the television viewers and the television non-viewers have not much difference. However their expectations about spouse were different. The expectations about the qualities of the spouse, the television watching girls of thirteen-fourteen years expected a "less jealous and merciful", however the non-watching group girls expected such husband, who may go for a walk with wife and must provide everything. For service and profession, the television increased the expectations. The children and the teenagers, generally, developed an intention towards such services and professions, which are called "white-collar jobs." They have been haunted by the "glamour" of journalism, spy-film-acting and modelling. As well as their knowledge about different professions also increased. The television have developed higher expectations among the viewing teenagers for service. In place of good artisans, they desire more for the administrative posts.

The lives of children and teenagers have been influenced by the television in several ways. According to Professor Karl Holzmer of West Germany, the teenagers always live in tension. This tension is due to non-developed moral adultness and pre-aged body matureness. In this situation of tension, the electronic media plays a negative role. For regularly watching the audio-visual media, their hearts have become highly passionate. For, continuous listening "stereotyped" sentences, their mental activeness used to be crushed. It also influences their physical activeness, negatively. They become habitual of sitting at home The time, which children and teenagers must pass in natural sports and games, at that time they are tied with the television and they satisfied with these things just watching at the television. To curtain the increasing mental tension among the children, it is necessary that they must be discouraged to watch horrorful, unaesthetic, violent and hateful scenes at the audio-visual medias. Too much watching of the television also harms the eyes of the children. As well as the mental and physical fatigue increases, the disease of non-sleeping may take place. Too much viewing of the television decreases general behaviour among them. To avoid such effects, a new code of discipline is necessary. This code of discipline must be observed not only by children and teenagers, but also by adults. The families must avoid to watch television for unlimited time. Similarly, the habit of viewing all programmes is not correct. There must be such efforts that the children and teenagers should be active viewers in place of inactive viewers. They must be encouraged to ask questions,their curiosities must be answered. The children must go out for games and sports. Some people think that the television is an instrument for keeping the children inside the house, this wrong perception should be finished.

Cultural Aggression and Means of Mass Communication

In India, at administrative level, a debate is going on about communication policy. Some people call it "Media Policy," however when we use the word "communication, its area is larger than that of the "media." But the question is that which "powers" are behind it ? It is not obvious. Generally, it seems that those who are debaters on "broad and national communication policy", they are mainly related to the television. In the development process, the role of the mass-communications is definite without doubt, and for any proposed policy, it can be a positive direction. However, in the countries of the third world, it has been utilised as one of the means of control. The Macbide Commission also observed telling about the purpose of the mass-communication that "through such policies, cultural give and take and dynamic flow of news must not be curbed. In contrast, its object should be, in a society and among different societies, to finish the dissimilarities and obstructions. One of the main objective of the communication policies should be to maintain equilibrium in the present news structure, so that the dialogues flow may wide the path, and to provide democratic shape to the mass-communication." In this respect, we find many non-balances between developed and developing nations, between rural and urban communities, between elite class and general masses, between majorities and minorities. The main purpose of communication is to minimise these disbalances and unequalities.

In our India, the area of mass-communication is very limited. Here the literacy rate was 16.7 per cent in 1951, which increased to 36.2 per cent in 1981. Out of it, 53 per cent literacy is available in urban areas. Consequently, according to the office of "Registrar of Newspapers" report, the total circulation of all newspapers is fifty millions in India. Out of these, the daily newspapers total circulation is about fifteen millions. Out of these fifteen millions, forty per cent circulation belong to only metropolitan cities of Calcutta, Delhi, Bombay and Madras. Another important media of mass communications is radio, which number of sets all over India is about thirty millions. Two third of these radio sets are in urban areas. The total number of the television sets is about twenty lakhs (two million), mainly there are in the urban areas. There are five lakh and seventy five thousand villages in India, yet the number of community radio and the television sets is one lakh and eight thousand respectively. These radio and the television sets are generally out of work or these are kept in the house of the Pradhan (President) of the village or any other influential individual of the village. Technically, the message of the radio and the television reach to ninety and seventy per cent of the population. Excluding these, the film and the theatre are prominently urban medias. Hence we can say that the mass media are urban monopoly oriented in India. The government keeps its control over two important medias—the radio and the television. A score of "committees" have been appointed for the study of problems and proposal about All India Radio and the Television in India. In 1980, the committee presided under G. Parthasarthi, called "Media Consultative Committee" accepted many proposals and these were called "News Policy for the All India Radio and the Television". However, from that time until today, these proposals have not been implemented fully. The government decided that at the All India Radio and the Television, the news to be broadcasted must be correct, objective and factful. The news coverage used to be balanced and these are not related to any particular individual. In our country, the All India Radio and the Television (Doordarshan) have become powerful medias for the news and these are playing a significant role for making the people conscious and educated.

The government of India tried its best that the means of mass communication should not be made up as the means of the cultural aggression. For the examination of films and foreign cuttural impact, the central government has initiated many steps. The foreign serials to be presented at the Indian television are examined fully before acceptance. It is the part of mass communication policy, that the films and broadcasting media should be controlled in such a way that the foreign powers have no occasion, for cultural aggression, on India through these medias. It is obvious that due to communication revolution, the human society has been influencing more widely and deeply than that of the industrial revolution. It is notable that after industrial revolution, the imperialism had made many countries as its colonies including India. The new communication revolution has been providing a new shape for the struggle about the control over human mind. There seems a danger of cultural imperialism over the countries of the Third World. Through the means of Computers and Satellites, a new electronic media may give birth to a new revolution in the area of mass communications. In this grand achievement of human race, there are hidden many dangers. The developing country, like India, must always be conscious towards these dangers.

Retrospect

The detailed study of Hindi cinema in the previous chapters indicates obviously that the Hindi cinema have acquired a significant place in the social, cultural, and political progress of the country. The Hindi films not only won respect and awards at national levels but also at international levels. Since the "Raja Harish Chandra" film as debut till today, the history of Hindi cinema is a history of proudful contribution of Hindi films towards national unity.

However, it does not mean that the Hindi cinema did not pass throngh hard paths. During the British period, the Indian cinema had to be faced many oppressive measures. The Hindi films have not been avoided by the hard censor policy of the British. However, it could not decrease the contribution of Hindi films in national consciousness. The producers of the Hindi films got inspirations from the Father of the Nation, Mahatma Gandhi, and Leader of the Nation, Jawaharlal Nehru. They prepared their scripts in such a way that the viewers can get inspirations for national consciousness and these films might have been avoided by the hard British censor policy. In the history of the national movement the contribution of the Hindi films shall be written in golden words.

After attainment of the freedom, several revolutionary changes took place in the Indian cinema. For the reconstruction of the nation, the Hindi einema, particularly, provided valuable contribution.

A score of new inventions are taking place in the technical aspect of the cinema. In the last one century, the cinema has made up wonderful progress. The first film was exhibited in a small theatre of Paris. That was a silent movie. After some years, talking films were made up, coloured films were made, then three dimensional films were made up in which the depth is also shown on the film screen with width and length. Then the size of the screen enlarged, at last it adopted the shape of a circle, the viewers can watch the film sitting in the middle of the circular screen, moving eyes towards all sides. It was named "circarama". Now, just after some years, the film screen will take the shape of a tomb, the viewers can watch the film not only around themselves but also from the floor towards the ceiling, such cinema hall shall be called "Coopolarama".

After it, there are some experiments for such cinema that the viewers not only listen and look but can also smell the screen things. They can also enjoy like touching. They can not only enjoy the colour and shape of the "flower" but can-smell its odour. Similarly if there shall be ice or fire on the screen, the viewers can feel the coldness or hotness of it. In the cinema of future, all senses of the human beings may be utilised and they would feel things fully. In fact they may feel things looking, listening, touching, smelling and tasting fully.

In the recent past years, some experiments have been successfully, to some extent, performed, in which the odour of the screen may be smelled by the viewers. Such cinema was called "Aaramorama". If there is flowers garden in any scens or there are dishes on the table, the likewise odour was spread up in the cinema hall. However these experiments did not get absolute success. Whenever, any kind of odour was spread over with any scene in the hall, just after change of the scene, the same odour could not go out completely. A part of it remains, which mixes with the next odour and wrong impression took place. Sometimes it so happened that any scene has no odour, thus the remaining smell of the previous scene produce puzzles. Hence "Aaromarama" cinema is at expériment level.

To feel the temperature of the screen, is the next step and for that suitable instruments have not come into existence. However, in the area of science, the speed of progress witnesses, that at the end of this century, the viewers may feel the temperature of the things while looking these.

The film, which we look today, in the next century its shape would have completely changed. Its shape has changed. In the television, the video tape is used in place of films. It is more stable and light compared to the film. While, after some years the video tape too will seem backward and a new better means may be develobed in its place.

A scientist who imagined about the twenty first century cinema, said that then the place of the film shall be taken up by a particular qualitative piece of glass. This piece of glass shall be prepared scientifically. It shall be equal to the size of horse-bean or lentil. And whole of the story would have been filled in it. According to it, a new instrument "Biyorama" shall be invented, to which everyman can keep on the table of his office or house. As soon as the man would put the particular piece of glass in it, the ceiling and the walls of the rooms seem to be disappeared and all around there shall be a scene of the cinema, and the viewer shall be surrounded by it. For example, if there shall be a scene of desert, the viewer shall find standing in it and he will feel the hotness of the hot sand. The sweat will appear on his face. Then he will feel thirst. A caravan of camels will pass nearby him and will reach at an oasis. There shall be looked upon a lake of cold water. Then he will not only feel the taste of the water but also the coolness of it.

We can just imagine about the cinema, of the future to a limited extent. No one knows, that in the coming years what kind of wonderful progress may take place in the field of cinema and it may change the shape of the present cinema in such a way that the viewer looking it may enjoy all of his senses.

Hence, the need is for that we must take steps keeping in mind the cinema techniques. So that not only numerically but qualitatively too, Indian films may get highest position in the world.

We, Indians, must provide particular attention towards political cinema. The political films are not a new phenomenon. In the Western countries, it had started too earlier. Before and after both World Wars, many films were produced against the war, atrocities, and dictatorship. These condemned the oppression against the individual freedom by the government. The films titled as "Battlecry of Place" in 1915 produced by Stuart Black Stone and "War Bite" produced by Walter Trisun in 1916 presented powerfully, the anti-war and individual liberty ideas. After 1970, many political films have been produced. Film producers like Ghadar, Bunthul and Andre Wazda made popular and appreciative films. These films based on the themes of common man who is caught in trap of the triangle—power, system and the politics, provided voice and new message with chain films. Some were exhibited, some were banned and some were awarded in other countries. There are not few such films but a lot of.

The film titled "The Black Banana," produced by Benjamil Hayyam was banned by the so called government of Israel due to its religious background. In 1977, the government of Pakistan banned "The blood of Hussain" produced by Zamir Dehlvi. The Turkish film director M. Kimmick had to leave his country for his film titled as "Swan—Will the Sun Rise?" In this film the wickedness of Turkish espionage police were shown. The Russian film director Sergai Parad Janov was imprisoned due to his film "The Colour of the Pomegranate." This film is banned even today. "Tall Shadow of the Wind" was first banned by Iran's King Raza Shah Pahalvi and later on by Imam Khomeini.

The films produced in South America, were too much victim of political high-handedness. The films produced by George Sanjins titled as "Courage of the People" and "The Blood of the Condor," presented so effectively the politics of Bolivia, that the common viewer stood up against the poverty, sadness and atrocities done by the government. The film producer Alfanso Khagron, is living in exile in Mexico, nowadays. A score of South American countries film producers and directors have left their countries and living in exile, due to related government oppressions.

In the recent years, many films are sufficiently discussed which revealed the political strategies and environment available in some countries. Costa Gobra's films "All the Presidents Men" and "Zed" showed the incidents so nicely and critically that highly patron of human rights, United States of America government, was puzzled. The government silently issued orders that for such films government buildings must not be utilised. In the film "Yole," the life-story of a prisoner was presented who was sentenced for the murder of a government servant, the prisoner run away into another country after breaking the prison cell. In this film, the Turkish police, Turkish political system and the government oppression was presented effectively.

In 1975, Lebnan passed through a Christian-Muslim civil war period. Scolin Doriff film titled as "Circle of Deceit" presented those unfortunate events, it also got sufficient fame. The film "Epoclipse Nan," produced by Francise Copola presented living and fearful scenes of Vietnam War and American intervention in it.

In Italy, a few years ago, the Priest agitated against the film "Last Dango in Paris," the matter was referred to the court and the court decided that the film must be fired. Among the Muslim counteries, the film producers avoid the production of such films in which there might have been revelations of oppressive kings or the ruling military junta. In Iraq, Egypt, Pakistan, Turkey, Morocco, Libya, and Saudi Arabia, light films are produced in large number, however the political films are seldom produced.

Some years ago, a film titled "Death of a Princess" was produced in Britain. It proved a hotly debated film. The Saudi

Arabia government expressed its anger against it and wrote down angry letters to all countries where it was exhibited. In this film, a Princess of Saudi dynasty "Masha" was shown having love affairs with a common youth. As per tradition, the lover and the beloved were sacrificed killing by the swords.

Presenting different tribes and depicting a power holding leader was filmed in the "Rise and Fall of Idi Amin." This film expressed very well to the African political environment and atrocities. A few years ago, in Senegal a film was produced titled as "Khala," also proved debatable due to its political background.

During last few years, in our country, in Tamil, Telugu and Malyalam languages, many films are produced which depict the lives of political leaders. However the Hindi film "Aandhi" produced by Gulzar became highly debatable due to its script and artistes. After the production of "Aandhi," a chain of the political films has been going on. In recent years, the Marathi film "Singhasan," Jabbar Patel's "Somna," Gobind Nihlani's "Aakrosh," Nahta's "Kissa Kursi Ka" and produced in Madras "Meri Aawaj Suno," "Inqilab," "Aaj Ka M.L.A. Ram Avtar," "Yeh Desh," "Chakra," "Garam Hawa," "Bazaar," "Albert Pinto Ko Gussa Kyon Aata Hai" and "Andha Qanoon" are highly famous political films.

The film titled as "Gandhi" became so much popular that it broke down all records. A film "Nehru" produced by Indo-Soviet co-operation, has also released during recent years. In this film Pandit Nehru's political and individual life, *i.e.* both aspects are shown. "Ardh Satya" is also one of the best and recent film based on the politics in India.

With the success of "Gandhi," a new era has been initiated for production of the political films. The most notable of these are, "Mohammad Ali Jinnah," to be produced by the Pakistan with co-operation of a British film company, and "Last Days of Lord Mountbatten." Recently "Heat and Dust" produced by James Ivory and released in India too, got commendable popularity. However this fact must be kept in mind that in India whatever films are produced or exhibited, must not perform the function of political pollution. India is an ancient nation state, which is emerging as a World Power, keeping its unity and integrity. Hence there shall be no permission to allow the production and exhibition of any political film which may disintegrate such a nation state.

At last, we can say that Indian films are contributing as much as possible for the reconstruction of the nation. As a means of mass-communication, the future of Indian films seems bright.

The extension of the Indian Television network (Dordarshan) helped the Hindi cinema to reach at every corner of the country. Today, perhaps, there is no place where people have not got introduction of Hindi films. Hence, the need is to maintain and to move upwardly in respect of the qualitatively aspects of the Hindi films, so that these may be more useful for the country.

Bibliography

Books

Bharucha, B.D., Indian Cinematograph Year Book, Motion Pictures Society of India, Bombay, 1938.

Chauhan, Mahavir Singh, Great Showman—Raj Kapoor, Star Pocket Books, New Delhi, 1982.

Chopra, Ashok, Amitabh Bachchan ki Kahani-Chitron ki Zubani, (Hindi).

Dharup, B.V., Indian Films 1973, Motion Pictures Enterprises, Alka Talkies, Poona, 1974.

Dinesh, Filmon Mein Parvesh Kaise Kaveen ? (Hindi), Rangbhoomi Prakashan, New Delhi, 1983.

Futtan, A.R. & Norman, Motion Pictures, University of Aukthome, U.S.A., 1964.

Grover, Ashok (Edited), Filmon ke Rashtriya Geet (Hindi), Ratan Pocket Books, Meerut, 1985.

Gupta Rooma, Vidrohi Abhineta-Amitabh Bachchan (Hindi).

Karuna Shankar, Bhartiya Filmon ka Itihas (Hindl), Rangbhoomi Book Depot, Darya Ganj, Delhi, 1964.

Kunha, Uma Da, Indian Cinema 1983-84, National Film Development Corporation. Mate Corporation, New Delhi, 1984.

Lisern, Anest, A Picture History of the Cinema, Bista Books, London, 1960.

Mittal, Mahendra, Bhartiya Chalchitra (Hindi), Alankar Prakashan, Delhi, 1975.

Reddy, P. Rama, Cinematograph Laws Research Institute Hyderabad, 1968-69.

Sahni, Balraj, Meri Filmi Aatam Katha (Hindi), Star Pocket Books, New Delhi, 1971.

Sathe, V.P., Filmotsav 84 (edited), Directorate of Film Festivals, Narimann Point, Bombay, 1984.

Shastri, Devdutt, Prithiviraj Kapoor Abhinandan Granth, (Edited, Hindi, Uttarayan), Vishal Manch, Allahabad, 1963.

Shinde, M.K., Shinde's Dictionary of Cine Arts and Crafts, Popular Prakashan, Tardev Road, Bomcay, 1962.

Shrivastava, Bachchan, Bhartiya Filmon ki Kahani (Hindi), Alankar Prakashan, New Delhi, 1968.

Other Reference Material

Indian Talkie 1931-56, Film Archives of India, Poona 1961.

Indian Talkie, Film Federation of India, Patel Road, Bombay, 1956.

Indian Cinema, Prakashan Vibhag, (Hindi), Information and Broadcasting Ministry, Government of India, New Delhi, 1965.

IMPA Silver Jubilee Souvemir, Indian Motion Pictures Producers Association, Bombay, 1963.

Gazette of India, 1952, Part II, Section II, Information Department, Government of India, New Delhi, 1952.

Film Division Catalogue. Information and Broadcasting Ministry, Government of India. New Delhi, 1958-81 (Seperate parts since 1958 to 1981 for every year).

List of Documentary Film, Film Division, Government of India, Bombay, 1970.

Newspapers and Magazines

Hindi Dailies

Amar Ujala, Agra, Bareilly and Meerut.
Jansatta, New Delhi.
Dainik Jagran, Kanpur and Meerut.
Dainik Navjyoti, Jaipur and Ajmer.
Niyaya, Ajmer.
Punjab Kesari, Delhi and Jallandhar.
Navbharat Times, Delhi.
Rajasthan Patrika, Jaipur
Hindustan, New Delhi.

Hindi Weeklies, Fortnightlies and Monthlies

Cross Examination, Weekly, Bombay.
Dharamyug, Weekly, Bombay.
Maharashtra Manas, Fortnightly, Bombay ;
Madhuri, Fortnightly, Bombay.
Movie Jagat, Weekly, New Delhi.
Saptahik Hindustan, Weekly, New Delhi.

English Dailies, Weeklies, Fortnightlies and Monthlies

Indian Express, Daily, New Delhi.
Times of India, Daily, New Delhi.
Filmfare, Weekly and Fortnightly, Bombay.
Hindustan Times, Daily, New Delhi.
Screen, Weekly, Bombay.
India Today, Fortnightly, New Delhi.
Film Mirror, Monthly, New Delhi.